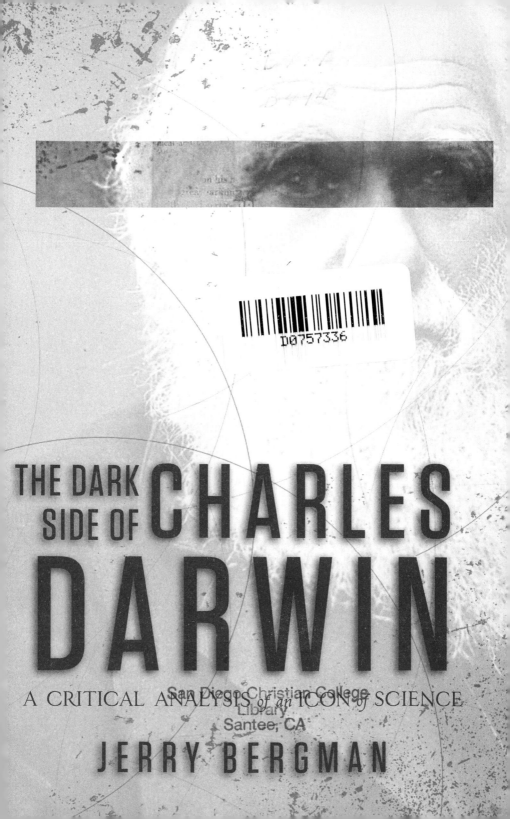

THE DARK
SIDE OF CHARLES
DARWIN

A CRITICAL ANALYSIS *of an* ICON *of* SCIENCE

JERRY BERGMAN

What others are saying . . .

Few people in the history of the modern world have had a greater negative influence on society than Charles Darwin. But few people know the real Darwin. Dr. Bergman has done a real service to both science and society by casting a bright light on the dark side of Darwin. This is a must read for all who are concerned about the erosion of our moral fiber by the hijacking of science through Darwinian evolutionism.

> Dr. Norman L. Geisler
> Professor of Apologetics, Veritas Seminary
> Expert Witness at the "Scopes Two" Trial
> (in Little Rock, Arkansas)
> Author of *The Creator in the Courts*
> www.VeritasSeminary.com
> Murrieta, CA

The Dark Side of Charles Darwin sheds much-needed light on a flawed man and his ideas. Evolution's often tragic results are built on incorrect data and anti-theistic goals. Darwin was neither objective scientist nor deserving "Saint."

> John Morris, PhD
> President of Institute for Creation Research

In his typical thoroughness, Dr. Bergman has carefully considered a wealth of literature by Darwin (both his public and private writings) and by his many sympathetic, if not admiring, biographers and commentators to reveal a more accurate picture of Darwin. Darwin was hardly an unbiased objective pursuer of truth, as his past and present devoted friends and disciples want us to believe. Rather, his writings on evolution used a mixture of scientific facts, faulty data, misinformation, plagiarized ideas, distortions of reality, and unbridled imagination to deceptively advance his anti-Christian, anti-biblical agenda, which has wreaked such social, political, theological, and moral havoc in the world. Bergman's insightful and wide-ranging study will open the eyes of readers to the depth of the spiritual battle for truth in this question of origins.

Well documented for the person who wants to dig deeper, but written in an easy-to-understand style, this book will be a great help to many. I highly recommend it.

> Terry Mortenson, PhD, speaker, writer, researcher
> Answers in Genesis

Acknowledgments

The many persons I wish to thank include Bert Thompson, PhD; Emmett Williams, PhD; Clifford Lillo, MA; John Woodmorappe, MA, MS; George Howe, PhD; Liu Yongsheng PhD; and Jody Allen, RN; for their helpful comments on earlier drafts of this manuscript. I also want to thank my wife, Dianne, and our four children, Aeron, Scott, Chris, and Misha, for their support in my work on this long project.

First printing: February 2011

Master Books®, P.O. Box 726, Green Forest, AR 72638

Master Books® is a division of New Leaf Publishing Group, Inc.

ISBN: 978-0-89051-605-8
Library of Congress Number: 2011921573

Cover by Left Coast Design

Unless otherwise noted, all Scripture is taken from the NKJV
(New King James Version, copyright © 1982 by Thomas Nelson,
Inc. Used by permission. All rights reserved).

Please consider requesting that a copy of this volume be
purchased by your local library system.

Printed in the United States of America

Please visit our website for other great titles:
www.masterbooks.net

For information regarding author interviews,
please contact the publicity department at (870) 438-5288

Master
Books®
A Division of New Leaf Publishing Group
www.masterbooks.net

Table of Contents

Foreword

Tufts University philosopher Daniel Dennett would, without question, place Charles Darwin, accompanied with his *The Origin of Species* (1859), first in the academic Hall of Fame above such intellectual luminaries as Albert Einstein or even Sir Isaac Newton. Such esteem of Britain's most notable personage would receive enthusiastic acclaim by the academic community worldwide.

The Dark Side of Charles Darwin, a very scholarly yet readable book written by Jerry Bergman, offers its readers another perspective. Dr. Bergman's examination of Darwin's beliefs and attitudes — some of which are highly undesirable and even offensive — might well be a shocking revelation to some readers. Darwinian scholars have purposely avoided such an investigation for fear that it might tarnish Darwin's hagiographic image.

Dr. Bergman's analysis correctly begins by looking at Charles Darwin's religious views. Darwin's deistic (my opinion) evolutionary worldview spawned his ideological views on racism, eugenics, and even his belief in the inferiority of women. Having read numerous books in the Darwinian field, I must confess that this is the first time that I have ever found that Darwin's attitude toward women has ever been broached. The book also features a lengthy discussion on Darwin's incessant fears that led to his struggles, both physically and mentally. Some have suggested, as cited by Dr. Bergman, that

Darwin's psychosis was directly related to his publication of *The Origin of Species*.

Personally, I believe that a significant contribution by Dr. Bergman is his questioning the legitimacy of Darwinian evolutionism or more specifically the role of natural selection. "The problem with evolution[ism] is not the survival of the fittest but the arrival of the fittest," is definitely a memorable maxim that should be pondered by all readers.

There is no doubt that this exposé will "ruffle the feathers" of some in the ivory towers of academia, namely the "new militant atheists" such as Richard Dawkins and Christopher Hitchens. It was Richard Dawkins, no doubt beaming with pride, who remarked that it was the works of Darwin that made atheism intellectually acceptable. But let me congratulate Dr. Bergman for writing *The Dark Side of Charles Darwin*. His well-documented book will provide readers with a realistic and convincing portrait of Charles Darwin—an aspect which has been long lacking within the Darwinian industry.

Dr. David Herbert, historian and author of
Charles Darwin's Religious Views (2009)

Introduction

Naturalist Charles Robert Darwin (1809–1882) is widely considered one of the greatest scientists of our age, if not the greatest scientist in the entire history of humankind. Although he did much research on a wide variety of life forms from flowers to worms, Darwin is most well known specifically for his theory of evolution. Evolution is the belief that all living organisms evolved due to purely natural forces from one or a few simple organic chemicals or life forms by natural selection. In answer to the question "who is the greatest biologist of all time?" the editor of *Science News* wrote, "There's only one answer. Any other invalidates the voter as unqualified. It's Charles Darwin."[1]

Although one of the few scientists known to most Americans and Westerners, few people know much about the dark side of Darwin, such as his support in his writings for eugenics and racism, or the reasons for developing his naturalistic evolution theory. Furthermore, Darwin's book *The Origin of Species* is widely regarded

Charles Darwin
Photo: Superstock.com

as "the most important biological book ever written."[2] Some claim that it was "one of the most influential books ever written" and possibly only the Bible and the Qur'an were more influential.[3]

Willison wrote:

> No single document in history . . . has so profoundly affected humankind's understanding of the living world. Darwin's theory of natural selection challenged all received opinion about life on earth and, in an era of intellectual, political, and scientific ferment that gave rise to the modern age, was perhaps the most revolutionary idea of all.[4]

Darwin was an icon of science during his own lifetime, and his icon status has grown enormously since then.[5] This book provides some needed balance by looking at his dark side, however briefly, and is one of a handful of new books now beginning to reevaluate Darwin's legacy. Criticism of Darwin is rare because it goes "against the grain of conformist academic praise for Charles Darwin" that is all too common in academia, the media, and our public school classrooms.[6]

It also goes against the common perception among scientists and academics that Darwin, "one of the greatest of our [science] figures should not be dissected."[7] The critical importance of Darwinism was highlighted by militant atheist Christopher Hitchens who wrote that Darwin is so important that the 21st century will be known in history as Darwin's century:

> Write the name of Charles Darwin on the one hand and the name of every theologian who ever lived on the other, and from that name [Darwin] has come more light to the world than from all of those [theologians]. His doctrine of evolution, his doctrine of the survival of the fittest, his doctrine of the origin of species, has removed in every thinking mind the last vestige of orthodox Christianity.[8]

This work does not negate Darwin's many science accomplishments, such as his study of worms, something that no one disagrees with. The fact that he had a reputation as a careful naturalist is partly why he was so successful in converting most of the scientific world to his worldview. Nor do we take issue with the common, if not exaggerated, belief that Darwin was

> one of the most likeable, congenial, self-effacing, patient men of science; a model husband and father, kind and loving, generous and humorous, magnanimous and solicitous toward his neighbors of every social rank. . . . He had too many of the natural, personal qualities of a saint, and in fact, had he not been so entirely bent on creating a godless account of evolution, he might, just might, have become one.[9]

But there is a dark side of Darwin.

Darwin's Difficulties with Others

In his autobiography, Darwin revealed another side of his personality — his rather coarse public comments about close friends. For example, he stated that William Buckland was a "vulgar and almost coarse man" who was "incited more by a craving for notoriety, which sometimes made him act like a buffoon, than by a love of science."[10]

He even claimed that Carlyle "sneered at almost everyone . . . his expression was that of a depressed, almost despondent . . . man" and "Carlyle's mind seemed to me a very narrow one; even if all branches of science, which he despised, are excluded."[11] Darwin said that one of his closest friends botanist Robert Hooker is "very impulsive and somewhat peppery in temper"; he once sent him an "almost savage letter for a cause which will appear ludicrously small to an outsider."[12] Darwin also opined much about the conflicts that scientists had with each other. For example, he stated Hooker attacked so "many scientific men" but that his attacks on Richard Owen were "well-deserved."

Darwin said Alexander von Humboldt talked too much[13] and Charles Babbage "was a disappointed and discontented man; and his expression was often generally morose." Babbage's attitude toward others was indicated in Darwin's claim that he invented a plan by which fires could be effectively stopped, but he did not want to publish it because he felt "damn them all, let all their houses be burnt."[14] These comments about his friends, while not too uncivil, are not exactly those of a "kind and loving, generous . . . magnanimous" man, as Darwin is often pictured.

Darwin once stated that when he was younger he was capable of very warm attachment, but that later he "lost the power of becoming deeply attached to anyone, not even so deeply to my good and dear friends Hooker and Huxley," a feeling that he stated gradually crept over him. He added that his chief enjoyment in life was his scientific work.[15]

Darwin's Many Achievements

Darwin's many achievements have been carefully documented in the hundreds of often highly laudatory books written about Darwin the man and Darwin the scientist, and will not be repeated here. More than 100 biographies of Darwin have been published in English alone since 1885, all of them favorable, and many very favorable.[16] To understand Darwin and his work, though, the whole story must be told, especially since many people today view him almost as a god.

This work attempts to understand Darwin the man and the impact that his work has had on society for good and evil. As we will document, "Darwin was himself in error about lots of things."[17] Actually, in "his seriously flawed book" the *Origin of Species*, he was in error about many of his central ideas, including the means of genetic inheritance and the source of phenotypic variety.[18]

It is commonly assumed that Darwin's main opposition was from clergy but, in fact, his fellow scientists were often his fiercest critics. It is a "long-disestablished myth that Darwin avoided publishing his theory for so long because he feared backlash from the religious establishment. In fact, he was much more concerned about criticism from the scientific community."[19]

Much commonly believed information about Darwin is either incorrect or misleading, and many myths exist about Darwin's life and work.[20] An example is many authors claim that his most important book, *On the Origin of Species*, was so popular that it sold out on its first day of sale. Actually, the publisher wholesaled the first printing of 1,500 copies to booksellers, a fact Quamman notes, "is the precise reality behind a loose statement sometimes made — that the first edition sold out on the first day."[21] Many minor claims such as this one are commonly part of what has become the Darwin industry. Added up, they create a myth that is far from reality.

This work is not alone in documenting a major reevaluation of Darwin and his work. One new book by a Darwin scholar and producer of a major documentary on Darwin concluded in the book's introduction that the

story that will be told in this book is light-years away from the established orthodoxy, which states that a letter from Wallace caused Darwin the rush to establish his claim to be the first to outline the theory of evolution. An increasing body of evidence contradicts the received view of Charles Darwin as a benevolent man who, alone, unaided and without precursors, was inspired to write *On the Origin of Species*. At the heart of that famous historical event lies a deliberate and iniquitous case of intellectual theft, deceit, and lies perpetrated by Charles Darwin. This book will also argue that two of the greatest Victorian scientists were willing accomplices.[22]

Davies concluded in his well-documented but controversial work that the facts he "unearthed, supplemented by new evidence discovered while researching this book," show that "there is little doubt that a compelling case can be made against Darwin that would allow any reasonable person to conclude [that] it is likely he committed one of the greatest thefts of intellectual property in the history of science."[23]

Another problem is many researchers have questioned Darwin's honesty, often in a way that attempted to absolve Darwin of wrong-doing so as not to besmirch their hero's reputation. For example, Quamman, in a very favorable biography of Darwin, wrote that Darwin tried to "assure Wallace [who also came up with a theory of evolution very similar to Darwin's theory] that 'I had absolutely nothing whatever to do in leading Lyell & Hooker to what they thought a fair course of action,' a claim that was weasely at best and arguably untrue."[24] The "course of action" was related to the fact that Wallace had sent a manuscript to Darwin outlining a theory that was so similar to Darwin's unpublished theory that Darwin was in jeopardy of losing priority, and would be accused of plagiarism if he did publish it.

Quamman adds that Darwin also misstated the "dating of his own excerpts in the Darwin-Wallace package, telling Wallace that they'd been written in 1839 now just 20 years ago! In fact, they'd been written in 1844 and 1857."[25] The date was important because Darwin was trying to claim priority for his natural selection-based theory of evolution over Wallace's very similar theory. The claim that he plagiarized the core ideas of his theory is documented in chapter 8.

Darwin and the Creation-Evolution War

Darwin is historically important for another reason: until Darwin, for most of history, science and religion were largely co-workers and partners in exploring the material world.[26] As Provenzo writes, the creation-evolution debate began with Charles Darwin and, until the "advent of Darwin, science was primarily rooted in theology. Its purpose was to demonstrate the existence of God . . . by demonstrating evidence of God's design and influence in nature."[27] The fact is,

if variations are undirected, and if natural selection calibrates only the fitness of each individual creature to survive and reproduce . . . is it possible to believe that God created humans in His image and likeness, endowing us with a spiritual dimension not shared by the best-adapted orchid or barnacle? Arguably not. There's a genuine contradiction here that can't easily be brushed away . . . what Darwin's evolutionary theory challenges . . . is the supposed godliness of Man — the conviction that we above all other life forms are spiritually elevated, divinely favored, possessed of an immaterial and immortal essence, such that we have special prospects for eternity, special status in the expectations of God, special rights, and responsibilities on Earth. That's where Darwin runs afoul of Christianity, Judaism, Islam, and probably most other religions on the planet.[28]

Since then, the orthodox science establishment as a whole has become militantly opposed even to the idea of design and purpose in nature.[29] Jones opines that Darwin himself taught that "life had no plan, but turned instead to an infinity of expedients to cope with what nature threw at it."[30] In other words, life lives only for the moment with no forethought or concern for the future, the "eat and drink and be merry for tomorrow we may die" philosophy. *The Dark Side of Darwin* discusses this side of Darwin rarely covered in books and journals. One example is the perception that humanity is one and indivisible, a view that would have been taken for granted until about the time of Darwin's birth. Christians, at least

> would have believed that everyone descended from Adam and Eve, with what biologists would refer to as a genetic "bottleneck" at the time of Noah. By the time Darwin was a student at Cambridge, though, this was being questioned. The idea that the different races had different origins (from different types of monkeys, or from different acts of divine creation, depending on the views of the proposer), began as a convenient piece of slave-traders' propaganda, intended to denigrate the humanity of Africans.[31]

As documented in chapter 11, the racism that resulted from this revolutionary view increased by many orders of magnitude after the

Darwinian revolution. Darwin's own writings gave clear and important support to this tragic historical revolution.

Also covered in chapter 12 are his eugenic views and how they influenced dictators such as Hitler and Stalin. His attitude toward women (he believed they were less evolved than men) is covered in chapter 13. Certain racial groups, such as Africans, he called savages and believed that because they were inferior humans, they would become extinct. Nothing illustrates as well the fact that at times he seemed to lack normal human compassion, even toward his family, as Darwin's obsession with killing animals (chapter 7). As Quannem wrote, "Darwin was a selfish and ruthless man in some ways, but selfless and ruthless mainly in service to his work" of proving that intelligence was not involved in the creation of the natural world, but rather time, natural law, chance, mutations, and natural selection did it all.[32] Why he was so obsessed with, in his words, murdering God is a theme hardly ever explored in the Darwin literature but central to any study of Darwin the man. This concern is explored in several chapters in this book.

Darwinism Is Now Dogma

A major problem today is Darwinism has hardened into dogma that interferes with science progress. University of Chicago biologist James Shapiro wrote:

> Neo-Darwinian advocates claim to be scientists, and we can legitimately expect of them a[n] . . . open spirit of inquiry. Instead, they assume a defensive posture of outraged orthodoxy and assert an unassailable claim to truth, which only serves to validate the Creationists' criticism that Darwinism has become more of a faith than a science.[33]

Professor Shapiro concluded that dogmas and taboos

> have no place in science. No theory or viewpoint should ever become sacrosanct because experience tells us that even

the most elegant Laws of Nature ultimately succumb to the inexorable progress of scientific thinking and technological innovation. The present debate over Darwinism will be more productive if it takes place in recognition of the fact that scientific advances are made not by canonizing our predecessors but by creating intellectual and technical opportunities for our successors.[34]

The following is one of the many examples Shapiro provides that posed major problems for Darwinism:

All cells from bacteria to man possess a truly astonishing array of repair systems which serve to remove accidental and stochastic sources of mutation. Multiple levels of proofreading mechanisms recognize and remove errors that inevitably occur during DNA replication. . . . cells protect themselves against precisely the kinds of accidental genetic change that, according to conventional theory, are the sources of evolutionary variability. By virtue of their proofreading and repair systems, living cells are not passive victims of the random forces of chemistry and physics. They devote large resources to suppressing random genetic variation and have the capacity to set the level of background localized mutability by adjusting the activity of their repair systems.[35]

In the last chapter of this work some of the major problems with Darwin's major contribution to evolution, natural selection, are briefly reviewed. In fact, as chapter 14 shows, there are "far more unresolved questions than answers about evolutionary processes, and contemporary science continues to provide us with new conceptual possibilities" for answers.[36]

Why This Book Is Important

This work is timely for many reasons, including that the 200th anniversary of Darwin's birth and the 150th anniversary of the publication of his famous book *The Origin of Species* occurred in 2009. Chapter 1 explains how Darwin successfully connived to sell his worldview to both the public and the scientists. In Darwin's own words, his goal in developing and establishing his theory was like committing a murder. Among at least the leaders of the scientific hierarchy, he destroyed the most common basis for believing in God — the argument from design, also somewhat loosely called the cosmological or teleological argument. In their mind, and that of many others, Darwin murdered God by demolishing the main basis of belief in God, at least in the minds of the orthodox science establishment.

Darwin's failed theories and ideas, including his now discredited Lamarckian views, pangenesis, and the serious problems with his scholarship (in many cases he had his facts just plain wrong), are also discussed in some detail in chapters 9 and 10. Also reviewed were the problems his conclusions pose to theism and the destruction of any ultimate purpose of human life that resulted from his theory. Last, his journey from Christian to agnostic and its effect on his well-documented severe health problems, both physical and mental, are discussed.

Endnotes

1. Tom Siegfried, "Modern Biology Owes Unplayable Debt to Darwin," *Science News* 175(3) (2009): 2.

2. R. B. Freeman, *The Works of Charles Darwin; An Annotated Bibliographical Handlist* (Hamden, CT: Archon Books, 1977).

3. David Quammen, *The Kiwi's Egg: Charles Darwin & Natural Selection* (London: Weidenfeld & Nicolson, 2007).

4. Julia Willison, "Taking a Leaf Out of Darwin's Book," *Roots Journal* 5(2) (October 2008): 2.

5. Janet Browne, "Making Darwin: Biography and the Changing Representations of Charles Darwin," *Journal of Interdisciplinary History* (2010): 358.

6. Roy Davies, *The Darwin Conspiracy. Origins of a Scientific Crime* (London: Golden Square Books, 2008), p. 20.

7. C. D. Darlington, *Darwin's Place in History* (Oxford: Blackwell, 1959), p. 57.

8. Quoted in Marvin Olasky, "The Silver Age of Freethought," *World* (November 17, 2007): 36–38.

9. Benjamin Wiker, *The Darwin Myth: The Life and Lies of Charles Darwin* (Washington, DC: Regnery Publishing, Inc., 2009), p. x.

10. Charles Darwin, edited by Nora Barlow, *The Autobiography of Charles Darwin 1809–1882* (New York: Norton, 1958), p. 102.

11. Ibid., p. 113.

12. Ibid., p. 105.

13. Ibid., p. 107.

14. Ibid., p. 108.

15. Ibid., p. 115.

16. Browne, "Making Darwin: Biography and the Changing Representations of Charles Darwin," p. 352–357 and appendix.

17. Michael Jones, edited by Jane Godsland, Ros Osmond, and Pia Pini, *Darwin's Gifts* (London: The Lancet, 2008), foreword, p. S2.

18. Quamman, *The Kiwi's Egg: Charles Darwin & Natural Selection*, p. 198.

19. Kevin Padian, "Ten Myths About Charles Darwin," *BioScience* (October 2009), 59(9): 803.

20. Frank J. Sulloway, "Darwin's Conversion: The Beagle Voyage and Its Aftermath," *Journal of the History of Biology* (1982) 15: 325–396.

21. Quamman, *The Kiwi's Egg: Charles Darwin & Natural Selection*, p. 174.

22. Davies, *The Darwin Conspiracy. Origins of a Scientific Crime*, p. xix.

23. Ibid.

24. Quamman, *The Kiwi's Egg: Charles Darwin & Natural Selection*, p. 168.

25. Ibid.

26. James Hannam, *God's Philosophers: How the Medieval World Laid the Foundations of Modern Science* (London: Icon Books, 2009).

27. Eugene F. Provenzo, *Religious Fundamentalism and American Education: The Battle for the Public Schools* (New York, NY: State University of New York Press, 1990), p. 51.

28. Quamman, *The Kiwi's Egg: Charles Darwin & Natural Selection*, p. 208–209.

29. Jerry Bergman, *Slaughter of the Dissidents: The Shocking Truth About Killing the Careers of Darwin Doubters* (Southworth, WA: Leafcutter Press, 2008),

30. Jones, *Darwin's Gifts*, p. S2.

31. "Charles Darwin: A Natural Selection," *The Economist* 390(8615) (2009): 87.

32. Quamman, *The Kiwi's Egg: Charles Darwin & Natural Selection*, p. 236.

33. James A. Shapiro, "A Third Way," *Boston Review* (February/March 1997): 6.

34. Ibid., p. 6.

35. Ibid., p. 2.

36. Ibid., p. 1.

PART ONE

Darwin and Christianity

CHAPTER 1

How Darwin Overthrew Creationism Among the Intellectual Establishment

Chapter Synopsis

It is commonly assumed that Darwin was an active naturalist who, through his research, stumbled on the theory of evolution and then convinced the scientific world of his discovery due to its over-whelming scientific evidence. In fact, Darwin never did have good evidence for the origin of species, but convinced the scientific world by propaganda and even social pressure using deception and not evidence. Furthermore, it is commonly assumed that Darwin's motives were purely scientific but, in fact, his motives were primarily religious. He knew that his theory would demolish the strongest proof of God's existence (evidence from design, called the teleological argument) and this was a major source of motivation in his efforts to convert the world to the worldview now called evolution or Darwinism.

Introduction

Until Darwin's *On the Origin of Species* (often called *The Origin of Species* or *The Origin*) book was published in 1859, the dominant orthodox scientific explanation for the origin of life was creationism.[1] Before the Darwinian revolution, special creation was almost universally accepted by both sectarian religion and science. More specifically, before Darwin's publication, "Most scientists who had opinions on the subject were special creationists."[2] In fact, "Prior to the development of evolutionary theory, almost 100 percent of relevant scientists were creationists. Now the number is far less than 1 percent."[3]

Historically, the strongest argument for the existence of God was the proof from design called the teleological argument. It is this argument that Darwin attempted to destroy. Darwinism also replaced the scientific establishment's view that the world was "nearly perfect, and harmonious" with the view that the world was "violent and amoral . . . lacking a divine purpose."[4] How and why did this revolution that affected almost every area of science and society occur?

The Darwinian Revolution

A common assumption in Western society is that the Darwinian revolution was based on the accumulation of scientific evidence that eventually convinced the academic community of the theory's scientific validity. In fact, the overthrow of creationism and its replacement by Darwinism was largely accomplished by political, and not scientific, means. Darwin himself admitted in the introduction to his *Origin of Species*:

> I am well aware that scarcely a single point is discussed in this volume on which facts cannot be adduced, often apparently leading to conclusions directly opposite to those at which I have arrived. A fair result can be obtained only by fully stating and balancing the facts and arguments on both sides of each question; and this cannot possibly be done here.[5]

Of course, as will be documented, this laudable goal was not even attempted in the thick two-volume set *Origin* because Darwin did not want to present both sides. As we will show, "To understand the scientific revolution that Darwin initiated, we must move beyond the simple assumption that his theory triumphed," because Darwin marshaled an overwhelming body of scientific evidence that substantiated it.[6]

Even Darwin expressed major doubts about his theory, although only to close friends. In December 1857, he wrote to George Bentham that he should expect to be disappointed with the *Origin of Species* book when it was published because the book would be

> grievously too hypothetical. It will very likely be of no other service than collecting some facts; though I myself think I see my way approximately on the origin of species. But, alas, how frequent, how almost universal it is in an author to persuade himself of the truth of his own dogmas.... I certainly see very many difficulties of gigantic stature [in my theory].[7]

Even after the Darwinian revolution was complete and creationism was successfully suppressed in secular academia, many scientists still "had doubts about the efficacy of natural selection as a mechanism of evolution."[8] Natural selection, the chief mechanism that Darwin popularized, was widely rejected by biologists until long after Darwin died. Furthermore, their major objections to selection theory were never overcome in Darwin's lifetime, and his followers were forced to argue around these problems rather than solve them. Open criticism of the selection theory grew in intensity during the last decades of the 19th century, and explicitly anti-Darwinian versions of evolution were accepted by many scientists.[9] As chapter 14 documents, a resurgence of doubt about the ability of natural selection to account for the enormous variety of life is occurring in our day.

In short, "The advent of Darwinism was a social event within the scientific community and must be understood in terms of changing loyalties as well as changing research programs."[10] Bowler described the Darwinian revolution as a carefully orchestrated political attempt to convert both the common people and the scientists to his view. For example, Bowler noted that Darwin realized

> he must be very careful to minimize the materialistic aspects of his theory in any public pronouncement. He knew that, whatever the growing dissatisfaction with creationism, the vast majority of naturalists and ordinary people would only be willing to tolerate a process of "creation by law" if they felt that the law somehow expressed a divine purpose. In the

1844 Essay he had even introduced the concept of natural selection by first creating the image of a quasi-divine overseeing Power, which could pick out useful variants just as the animal breeder does in a domesticated species.[11]

Desmond and Moore, in their massively detailed biography of Darwin, described him as "shrewd," explaining that years of "cajoling" his correspondents, which is "a bit like extracting money from his father — had taught him how to get what he wanted," and what he wanted — his life goal — was nothing less than to replace supernaturalism with naturalism.[12] Ironically, geologist Charles Lyell's "religious beliefs had formed the 'essential fabric' of Darwin's own ideas on species and varieties."[13]

Deception Required to Replace Supernaturalism with Naturalism

Darwin and many of his disciples knew that deception, such as inferring that a "quasi-divine Power [God]" was required to direct evolution, was needed in order to convert the world to the evolutionary naturalism worldview — the goal of many leading Darwinists, including T. H. Huxley and Ernest Haeckel.[14] Many of Darwin's leading disciples knew that using the misleading "quasi-divine Power" claim was deceptive, which was obvious from later sections of Darwin's 1844 essay.

Darwin and his disciples did not believe that a "quasi-divine overseeing Power" existed that "picked out useful variants" to sire the next generation, but rather they believed natural selection functioned without "forethought and depends solely on the day-to-day operations of the most ordinary natural laws. The metaphor of the superintending Being was merely a device that would help those with theistic beliefs to come to grips with the idea."[15] Darwin also tried to convince his readers that his idea "belonged under the aegis of traditional religion" when he knew full well that it did not.[16]

Darwin also claimed that he was "determined" to "give the arguments on *both* sides" and "view all the facts . . . to see how far they favor or are opposed to the notion that wild species are mutable or immutable." Adding that he wanted to use his "utmost power to give all arguments and facts on both sides . . . I intend . . . to show (*as far as I can*) the facts and arguments for and against the common descent of species."[17] Of course, Darwin intended to do no such thing. His claims of "balance and doubt were a public mask. Despite appearances, he knew exactly what he was doing. For fifteen years he had committed himself unequivocally to one side."[18]

In other words, Darwin used the deceptive temporary stop-gap ploy to gradually lead the populace to naturalism and atheism. Although the theistic implications of Darwin's theory do not openly appear in his *Origin of Species*:

> The very term "natural *selection*" helped to encourage the view that nature was, after all, an intelligent agent. It was in Darwin's own interest to preserve as much as possible of the traditional view that natural development represented the unfolding of a divine purpose.[19]

Darwin's theory in fact did not involve any divine purpose, but rather was a purely naturalistic mechanism involving only genetic variation caused by his now rejected theory of gemmules and natural selection.[20] Today the origin of new information is theorized to be caused by such genetic mechanisms as mutations. Furthermore, the end goal of the Darwinian movement was very clear, namely "to take control of areas of thought once regarded as the province of theologians and moralists."[21] To achieve this goal, Darwinists had to deal with the opposition that was often based on efforts to resist the atheism that Orthodox Darwinism implied and often openly advocated.

Darwin was very open about his views in his private writings, admitting that he "could not see how anyone ought to wish that Christianity be true," but he "kept up a public front of traditional belief and went to great lengths to convince readers that his views were not ungodly."[22] For example, in the second edition of *Origin of Species* Darwin favorably quoted the "leading critic of skepticism" to deceptively make it appear that his ideas could be interpreted "in the context of conventional natural theology."[23]

Darwin's work was designed to disprove theism and for this reason he realized the process of overthrowing the theistic worldview would be slow. He had to be discreet. In a letter to Charles Lyell dated March 28, 1859, Darwin debated the best approach to get his 1859 book accepted, noting that *The Origin*

> is not more *un*-orthodox, than the subject makes inevitable. That I do not discuss [the] origin of man. That I do not bring in any discussions about Genesis, &c., and only give facts, and such conclusions from them, as seem to me fair. — Or had I better say *nothing* to Murray, and assume that he cannot object to his much unorthodoxy, which in fact is not more than any Geological Treatise, which runs slap counter to Genesis.[24]

Although a clear motivation of Darwin was to completely overthrow theism, most of his disciples realized that, initially at least, the most feasible route to atheism was to convert the population to theistic evolutionism, then to atheism, because

> most of Darwin's opponents were concerned about those aspects of his theory, which "tended to undermine the old belief that nature was a divinely planned structure. They were willing to accept evolutionism but *only* if they could believe that it represented a process with a structure and a goal that was imposed on it by God."[25]

Darwin saw the usefulness of exploiting the "useful idiots" who supported the idea that no inconsistency existed between evolution and theism even though Darwin and his key disciples knew full well that there was an unbridgeable chasm between the two worldviews, as documented in chapter 2.[26] For this reason, he exploited the language of natural philosophy in order to undermine natural philosophy by using theological language and ideas to convince readers that his worldview was similar to that of theistic evolutionists.

In short, as Moore argued, Darwin used theological language to convince readers of non-theistic evolution — evolution that did not need God but was not antagonistic to God.[27] Thus, Darwin "used theological tradition for persuasive advantage rather than fighting it to affirm his own convictions" about the unnecessary role of theism in explaining the origins of variety in the living world. The core leaders of the Darwin movement, such as Huxley and Haeckel, were "unwilling to accept Darwin's totally open-ended view of the evolutionary process," but insisted on the honest view that the direction of evolutionary change was "under the control of purely material forces. In the end, the success of Darwinism rested not on a general acceptance of the selection theory but on the exploitation of evolutionism by those who were determined to establish science as a new source of authority in Western civilization."[28]

Bowler noted that many of the scientists who opposed Darwinism were not biblical creation diehards as commonly claimed, but they

> were willing to accept the general idea of evolution and adapt it to their own beliefs. But on the whole they were suspicious of the ideological agenda that lay implicit in the Darwinians' appeal to the universal efficacy of natural law. They objected to the image of haphazard development at the heart of Darwin's theory because they wished to retain the view that nature was in some senses the expression of a divine purpose and because they did not believe that progress was merely the summing up of a vast multitude of trivial everyday occurrences.[29]

Politics Critical

The clear implications of Darwinism were a key problem that Darwin had to overcome. Selling Darwinism necessitated tact and required deliberate reconstruction efforts to produce an image that would encourage people to accept Darwin's worldview. For this reason, Darwin "exploited ideas that he himself rejected, especially those involving religion" to help sell his idea to the public.[30] That politics were critical in the Darwinian revolution is also illustrated by the fact that Darwin had built up a large network of scientists, including biologists, who he prepared to receive his ideas. Darwin then worked on them, gradually converting them to his worldview. To do this, Darwin

carefully built up his contracts with those biologists whom he saw would be most likely to welcome a new initiative, including even those such as Huxley. . . . The glue that would hold the supporters together, *despite their different scientific interests, was the belief that natural developments were governed by law rather than divine predestination.* By presenting evolution as a process governed solely by the normal laws of nature they could imply that social progress was the result of individual human efforts, the centerpiece of the liberal philosophy.[31]

Actually, a central issue in Darwin's later life was the long-term goal of making converts from theism to agnosticism or even atheism. For example, Desmond and Moore wrote, "Hooker was coming around," but had not yet "embraced Darwin's new gospel. . . . the problem Hooker still faced was a common one: the origin of life itself."[32] Darwin, realizing this problem was common, "kept ultimate origins out of the picture" in order to sell his "new gospel."[33] It was well recognized that one could argue for changes in life forms, but to argue for the naturalistic origin of life was far more difficult, especially after Louis Pasteur, Francesco Redi, and others had documented that life can only come from life. Darwin also depended on his disciples

to fight his battles both in the public arena and in the "behind the scenes" activities of the scientific community in which new policies were decided. Fortunately, he had chosen followers who were particularly adept at playing the political game.[34]

Darwin also "relied heavily on a variety of rhetorical strategies to produce a persuasive argument."[35] Politics and rhetorical strategies were not only critical in overthrowing creationism, but were often more important than the science of establishing evolution itself. Even Darwin's central supporters, including Huxley, had only a limited commitment to certain aspects of Darwin's theory that were viewed as central by modern biologists.

Many scientists, such as Huxley, were willing to fight on Darwin's side of the battle to overthrow creationism even though they had major reservations about Darwin's theory itself, especially his central idea of natural selection. Nonetheless, they worked tirelessly to overthrow theism and to establish Darwinism as the only accepted origins story. When Huxley finally "began to use the idea of evolution in his paleontological work, his real inspiration was Haeckel's largely non-Darwinian" ideas.[36] Even major disagreements were dealt with by Darwin in such a way so as to ensure that his friends and critics alike stayed in his camp.

> Some biologists began to develop openly non-Darwinian theories of evolution based on Lamarckism or the idea of inherently progressive trends. Darwin's great achievement was to force the majority of his contemporaries to reconsider their attitude toward the basic idea of evolution, but he did this despite the fact that many found natural selection unconvincing.[37]

This step was taken by Darwin purely for political expediency. The fact is, the majority of committed Darwinians, even though most were not from the same scientific background and accepted Darwin's theory for different reasons, all "shared a commitment to scientific naturalism."[38] A major reason Darwin was forced to rely heavily on politics to achieve his revolution was because he had little scientific evidence to support his theory.

> In 1859, when Charles Darwin published *The Origin of Species*, he had no more evidence in support of his theory than did the Creationists, whose view of the world he was attempting to overthrow. Darwin's argument had so many

theoretical weak spots that he was forced, in large parts of the *Origin*, to argue not so much the correct theory as the least objectionable one. Far from delaying publication of his ideas, as earlier scholars have suggested, given the quality of Darwin's evidence and the nature of his theory, he was probably forced to publish his ideas too soon.[39]

In short, Darwin was trying to sell "an uncertain theory on a highly controversial subject" to the public.[40] The opposition to Darwinism was also often due to non-scientific reasons, especially social and religious. Although "many scientific arguments against evolution" existed,

underlying most of them was a desire to resist the Darwinians' assumption that evolution could be used as a model for the liberal view of progress favored by the middle classes. Some of the arguments could be well appreciated by a pseudo-Darwinian such as Huxley, since they often reflected the underlying values of the morphological tradition in biology. But the Darwinians can be distinguished from their opponents quite clearly on the question of design or purpose in the universe.[41]

Bowler concluded that even a

pseudo-Darwinian such as Huxley wanted to use evolutionism as a means of rejecting the traditional view that nature can only be explained as an expression of a higher Power whose intentions are fulfilled by the pattern of evolutionary development. The opponents *did* wish to retain this view and they were prepared to marshal an impressive battery of arguments to defend their alternative image of evolutionism.[42]

Even Darwin's classic magnum opus "the *Origin of Species* was tailored as much as possible to" sell his idea to the public more than to scientists.[43] Darwin also took a great interest in promoting his theory and kept in close touch with his key disciples, such as Hooker and Huxley, who were battling for Darwinism in the outside world.[44] This "battle" often resembled a modern political war.

Darwin as a Super Salesman

Darwin actively campaigned to win the political war, and for this reason he built up an "immense communications network that allowed him to draw information from — and to influence — an ever-increasing number of biologists."[45] Much of his vast correspondence was designed to convert others to his worldview. The political issues were also very important for many of Darwin's followers. For example:

> Huxley's decision to promote a thoroughly progressionist version of evolutionism may also have been prompted by his recognition of the growing social tensions of the 1860s. In his campaign to persuade working men that their interests lay more with reform than with revolution, the inevitability of evolutionary progress offered an excellent model on which to base his image of social development.[46]

One of many examples of Darwin's activity in propagating his evolution ideas was a letter dated April 6, 1859, sent to Alfred Russel Wallace. In the letter, Darwin noted that Asa Gray, whom he had been working on, finally "converted" to his ideas. Darwin could hardly contain himself when he declared "our best British Botanist . . . is a *full* convert, and is now going immediately to publish his confession of Faith; and I expect daily to see proof-sheets."[47] In a letter dated March 14, 1861, Darwin wrote to one correspondent who was not persuaded by his arguments. Darwin bragged, "I have been successful converting some few eminent botanists, zoologists, and geologists" and realized that conversions will be slow.[48] The extent of his efforts at converting others is documented by the fact that in a half century he exchanged more than 14,000 letters with some 1,800 correspondents, and "just managing his voluminous mail was truly an astounding feat."[49]

The evolutionism movement seized on those parts of Darwin's writings that served their purpose, often their political and religious purposes. Some scientists, including Hooker and Wallace, largely supported a pure Darwinian ideology, but many persons accepted the term "Darwinians" only "because they saw Darwin as the key figure who had initiated the great debate, not because they found his theory of natural selection particularly convincing as an explanation of how evolution worked."[50]

Darwin's own political goals and his open opposition to creationism — his major nemesis — were also a very clear focus of his work. His *Origin of Species* is often referred to as one long argument against creationism. The political movement that Darwin started soon went well beyond Darwin himself, as evidenced by the fact that "Darwinism" became much more than Darwin's own ideas: "In the outside world the concept of evolution was being used by both scientists and non-scientists alike for their own purposes."[51] The *Origin* played the complex role as a catalyst in the transition to late-19th century progressionist evolutionism movement that saw evolution as the great agent that caused the progression of simple cells to humankind. Darwin was not just a salesman, but a very

> good salesman. He knows that what he has to say will not only be troubling for a general reader to take but difficult to understand — so he works very hard not to lose his customer. The book opens not with theory but in the humblest place imaginable: the barnyard, as Darwin introduces us to the idea of species variation in a way we, or certainly his 19th-century audience, will easily grasp — the breeding of domestic animals.[52]

Darwin knew full well the consequences of his theory, namely that humans were "no longer the culmination of life but merely part of it; creation was mechanistic and purposeless.[53] In view of the lack of agreement on a mechanism for evolution, and the many disagreements among Darwin's followers about even the central aspects of the theory, Bowler concluded the "dramatic transformation" that

Darwin's book caused within the scientific community, as we will explain, could be explained *only* by social trends.

Importance of Social Trends

The social trends were a critical factor in gaining support for Darwinism. Scientists in the middle 1800s were increasingly looking for alternatives to creationism, producing a social environment that was very open to Darwin's ideas. The problem was the alternatives were often baseless, mystical, or both. One idea, promulgated by Robert Grant, taught the direct "generation" of one species into another occurred by some unknown force. In one issue of *The London Investigator*, each writer "offered a cosmic alternative to 'Creation' — an upward-sweeping progression, powered from below, underwritten by strict laws," a view that was vague and lacked rational or scientific support.[54]

Bowler even suggested that Darwin was able to begin his scientific and cultural revolution only because he linked his evolutionary ideas to general trends in Victorian intellectual life that reflected the changing views of religion and God in all of Western society. An important factor in this step was the ongoing social unrest existing in Western society in Darwin's age, and science

> was an important battleground because any challenge to the authority of scripture threatened to undermine the conceptual foundations of the establishment's claim that the existing structure of society was divinely preordained. Evolutionism . . . could be used to suggest that nature was an inherently progressive system. Social progress could be seen as a continuation of natural evolution, the inevitable replacement of outdated forms by those more advanced. . . . Darwin and the majority of his followers came from a class that saw evolution as a means of demonstrating the superiority of new ways of looking at nature and society.[55]

In 1854 Desmond and Moore reported that Darwin wrote that the "time was ripe to begin; with young reformers on the rise" to destroy "the supernatural fabric of creation [that Darwin was convinced was] in shreds" and naturalism was ready to take over.[56]

Many of Darwin's supporters were biologists, some of which "could not even appreciate the main implications of the selection theory," yet were very successful in bringing about a general transition from creationism to evolutionism. As science historian, Bowler writes, the conventional image of the debate has been focused on a few highly visible confrontations, especially the 1860 Oxford meeting

> at which Huxley is popularly supposed to have demolished the anti-evolutionary arguments of Bishop Samuel Wilberforce. Scientific rationality is supposed to have demonstrated its superiority over traditional superstition. We now know that his image is a false one created by the supporters of scientific rationalism to bolster their own interpretation of the past in which science is ever triumphant in the "war" against religion.[57]

When the meeting ended, Huxley was unable to convince the majority of people in his Oxford audience of the validity of evolutionism

> and the general conversion to evolutionism was not completed for some years. To explain what was going on, historians are now looking beyond the evidence for evolution to the social pressures that were at work within the scientific community and within Victorian culture as a whole.[58]

For a detailed discussion of the debate myth, see "The Huxley-Wilberforce Debate Myth" by Jerry Bergman.[59] Darwinian "science" was clearly governed by philosophy, such as the "morphological tradition." One example of this tradition is that Darwinists arranged both fossils and living species

> into the most plausible evolutionary "tree," but the shape of this tree would be reconstructed from abstract comparisons that paid little attention to the practical realities of adaptation or to the geographical dimension of evolution. The

morphological tradition was firmly established in pre-Darwinian biology and would survive the transition to evolutionism, but it remained a fertile soil within which both pseudo-Darwinian and non-Darwinian ideas would flourish.[60]

Evidence that philosophy dominated the set of motives behind selling evolutionism is shown by the fact that much debate existed among biologists about the *science* behind Darwinism, but far more agreement existed about the descent with modification *philosophy*. This was true in spite of the fact that many morphologists concluded that many problems existed

with natural selection and it was only a matter of emphasis, which determined whether an individual biologist would become a pseudo-Darwinist or an outright opponent of Darwinism. It was easy for a student of animal form in the abstract to imagine that some characters were not shaped by adaptive pressures at all and equally easy to imagine that the transition from one species to another might be instantaneous, that is, by saltation rather than gradual transformation.[61]

The problem of natural selection is covered in more depth in chapter 14.

Darwinism as a Major Means to Destroy Theism

Many leading Darwinists accepted Darwinism purely because they saw it as a means of achieving political change — especially toward the destruction of theism and the establishment of naturalism, first among scientists, then among the population at large. One example was Huxley (a.k.a. Darwin's Bulldog), who knew of "no plausible hypothesis on the mechanism of change," yet he joined Darwin because he was a "staunch advocate of scientific naturalism." Huxley even disagreed with Darwin over the *fundamental basis* of his theory, gradualism, and argued that evolution might sometimes function by "dramatic saltations rather than by the selection of everyday variations."[62]

In spite of "substantial reservations about the theory that Darwin was never able to overcome," Huxley was a determined Darwinism advocate, mainly because he knew that Darwinism was critical to overthrow creationism, which was Huxley's main goal. He saw clear political advantages "of adopting agnosticism as a public philosophy" and the establishment of Darwinism as the "scientific" theory of creation "was a further asset in his campaign to raise the image of naturalistic science [i.e., naturalism] and convert a creationist world to evolution."[63] Huxley also argued that change could be "directed" along fixed lines toward a predetermined goal, a theory called vitalism, and selection served to eliminate the biological changes that started to evolve in a harmful direction:

> There is nothing to suggest that Huxley ever became a Darwinist in the sense that he . . . was inspired by the detailed theory that Darwin had proposed. Huxley is, in fact, a classic example of a pseudo-Darwinian. He accepted evolution because of his enthusiasm for naturalistic explanations, not because he appreciated the real logic of the Darwinian theory.[64]

Even when the war against creation was largely won, it was a political victory, not a scientific one. Most biologists, including the co-founder of Darwinism, Alfred Russell Wallace, and many others, still did not accept the mechanism that is today considered to have the central role in evolution, natural selection and the inheritance of acquired characteristics called mutations.[65] Bowler writes:

> By the late 1860s the debate was largely over; so many scientists had converted that there was no longer any possibility of going back. . . . Evolutionism was now secure, although natural selection was still widely regarded as only a part of the overall mechanism of change.[66]

A small number of scientists resisted for decades the Darwinian revolution's goal to replace creation and supernaturalism with naturalism and, eventually, achieve the end goal of atheism. For example,

Sir Charles Lyell realized that Darwinism would result in humans losing their "'high estate,' i.e., their special status in creation. He would be reduced to gutter level. Lyell was still shoring up human dignity, protecting it from [the] radical degradation" of Darwinism.[67]

Evidence that Darwin believed his book would convert people from creationism include a letter to Baden Powell dated January 18, 1860, where he wrote that he did not know how many readers of his *Origin* book were "induced . . . to give up the doctrine of creation" as a result of reading his book, indicating that he expected that this was one result of his work.[68]

Suppression of Dissidents

Even before the political war against the creationists was largely won by Darwinists, suppression of dissidents began. For example, in the late 1800s Darwin's opponents, including Samuel Butler, "were complaining that the Darwinists had taken control of the scientific community and established a new dogmatic orthodoxy that suppressed any attempt to question its basic assumptions."[69] Bowler, in his study of this event, found that Darwinians rapidly "gained a stranglehold on the scientific community" and

> formed a tightly-knit group held together by personal loyalties and commitment to a particular ideology. It was *not* held together by a shared research program . . . [but] the commitment to a belief that nature was governed universally by the operations of natural law . . . allowing them to present a united front even when their scientific work did not mesh very well together.[70]

The fact is:

> Darwin's great triumph was that he had used his own unique approach to evolution as a catalyst that had enabled the exponents of progressionism to transform Victorian thought. Although his own vision of evolution as a haphazard process driven by the pressures of local adaptation had

little to offer those who sought to reconstruct the ascent of life on earth, the appearance of a new mechanism of change had turned the balance in the general debate over the plausibility of natural development.[71]

Even though many major disagreements existed among Darwinian scientists "they maintained a united front against the common enemy" — the creationists — and

worked tirelessly to ensure that evolutionary papers would be published and that scientists favorable to their cause would have access to research funding and academic appointments. It was by playing this game — not by fighting bishops in public — that Huxley fulfilled the expectations that Darwin must have had when he recruited him. Modern scientists may be reluctant to admit that the success of a new theory rests on the public-relations skills of its early supporters, but there can be little doubt that Darwin's initiative succeeded (where it could very easily have failed) because he had already planted the seeds of a political revolution within the scientific community.[72]

The end result was that the "orthodox" scientists became the "new source of intellectual authority, taking over from the moralists and theologians who had once dictated how human nature was to be understood."[73] The Darwinists were also determined to maintain their authority by any means, ethical or unethical, both then and now.[74]

Summary

Darwin once stated that theists believe it was impossible to conceive "that this grand and wondrous universe, with our conscious selves, arose through chance," and many conclude that this was "the chief argument for the existence of God."[75] It is clear that "Darwin's intense desire to set forth a God-free view of evolution" caused him to argue for "an account of human development in which everything about human beings, even their moral capacities, is explained entirely as the result of natural selection, that is, of the struggle for survival where the more fit eliminate the less fit."[76]

Darwin knew that to "murder" God he had to come up with a naturalistic theory of the origin of life. In this he was enormously successful, and managed to convert the larger part of the scientific community and much of the rest of the world to his naturalistic theory of origins and, as a result, "destroyed the strongest evidence left in the nineteenth century for the existence of a deity."[77] In the minds of many scientists, Darwin had murdered God. Professor William B. Provine made this very clear:

> When Darwin deduced the theory of natural selection to explain the adaptations in which he had previously seen the handiwork of God, he knew that he was committing cultural murder. He understood immediately that if natural selection explained adaptations and evolution by descent were true, then the argument from design was dead and all that went with it, namely the existence of a personal god, free will, life after death, immutable moral laws, and ultimate meaning in life. The immediate reactions to Darwin's *On the Origin of Species* exhibit, in addition to favorable and admiring responses from a relatively few scientists, an understandable fear and disgust that has never disappeared from Western culture.[78]

Darwin did this with a theory that lacked substantial scientific evidence and, in the past century and a half, has become increasingly difficult to defend scientifically, especially after the advent of the DNA molecular revolution and the enormous fossil finds uncovered in the past century that document stasis, not cell to human evolution. Furthermore, Darwin's goal was very clear: "The main purpose of Darwinism was to drive every last trace of an incredible God from biology. But the theory replaces the old God with an even more incredible deity — omnipotent chance."[79]

To achieve this goal, Darwin's disciples had to recast evolution in more acceptable terms. An example is that although evolutionism was materialistic, by emphasizing the purposefulness of nature Darwin did not openly "threaten to sweep away the whole foundation of traditional thought," at least not until later. This required that scientists, such as Darwin and Huxley, "restate the case for evolution in a way that would allow them to maintain the attack on creationism while reconstituting the theory as a basis not for revolution but for gradual progress."[80]

Endnotes

1. Robert Marshall, *Living Anatomy: Structure as the Mirror of Function* (South Victoria, Australia: Melbourne University Press, 2001).

2. Thomas Glick, *The Comparative Reception of Darwinism* (Chicago, IL: The University of Chicago Press, 1988), Science, p. 401.

3. Mark Isaak, *The Counter-Creationism Handbook* (Westport, CT: Greenwood Press, 2005), p. 12.

4. Randy Moore, "The Persuasive Mr. Darwin," *Bioscience* 47(2) (1997): 107.

5. Charles Darwin, *The Origin of Species* (London: John Murray, 1859), p. 2.

6. Peter Bowler, *Charles Darwin* (Cambridge, MA: Basil Blackwell, 1990), p. 139.

7. Charles Darwin, edited by F. Burkhardt, *The Correspondence of Charles Darwin*, Volume 6 (New York: Cambridge University Press, 1990), p. 495.

8. Bowler, *Charles Darwin*, p. 139.

9. Ibid.

10. Ibid.

11. Ibid., p. 106.

12. Adrian Desmond and James Moore, *Darwin; The Life of a Tormented Evolutionist* (New York: Time Warner, 1991), p. 406.

13. Roy Davies, *The Darwin Conspiracy: Origins of a Scientific Crime* (London: GoldenSquare Books, 2008), p. 71.

14. Barry G. Gale, *Evolution Without Evidence: Charles Darwin and The Origin of Species* (Albuquerque, NM: University of New Mexico Press, 1982).

15. Bowler, *Charles Darwin*, p. 106.

16. Moore, "The Persuasive Mr. Darwin," p. 112.

17. Charles Darwin, edited by F. Burkhardt, *The Correspondence of Charles Darwin*, Volume 5 (New York: Cambridge University Press, 1989), p. 155, 294, 379.

18. Desmond and Moore, *Darwin: The Life of a Tormented Evolutionist*, p. 415.

19. Bowler, *Charles Darwin*, p. 106.

20. Moore, "The Persuasive Mr. Darwin," p. 108.

21. Bowler, *Charles Darwin*, p. 127.

22. Moore, "The Persuasive Mr. Darwin," p. 112.

23. Ibid., p. 113.

24. Charles Darwin, edited by F. Burkhardt, *The Correspondence of Charles Darwin*, Volume 7 (New York: Cambridge University Press, 1991), p. 270.

25. Bowler, *Charles Darwin*, p. 138–140.

26. Moore, "The Persuasive Mr. Darwin."

27. Ibid., p. 112.

28. Bowler, *Charles Darwin*, p. 139–140.

29. Ibid., p. 150–151.

30. Moore, "The Persuasive Mr. Darwin," p. 107.

31. Bowler, *Charles Darwin*, p. 147, emphasis mine.

32. Desmond and Moore, *Darwin: The Life of a Tormented Evolutionist*, p. 412.

33. Ibid., p. 412.

34. Bowler, *Charles Darwin*, p. 148.

35. Moore, "The Persuasive Mr. Darwin," p. 108.

36. Bowler, *Charles Darwin*, p. 148.

37. Ibid., p. 128.

38. Ibid., p. 140.

39. Gale, *Evolution Without Evidence*, book cover.

40. Ibid., p. 143.

41. Bowler, *Charles Darwin*, p. 150–151.

42. Ibid., p. 150–151.

43. Ibid., p. 128.

44. Ibid., p. 127.

45. Ibid., p. 127.

46. Ibid., p. 148.

47. Darwin, *The Correspondence of Charles Darwin*, Volume 7, p. 279, emphasis in original.

48. Frank J. Sulloway, "Darwin's Conversion: The Beagle Voyage and its Aftermath," *Journal of the History of Biology* 15:325–396 (1982): 325.

49. David Herbert, *Charles Darwin's Religious Views; From Creationist to Evolutionist* (London, Ontario: Hersil Publishing, 1990), p, 59.

50. Bowler, *Charles Darwin*, p. 128.

51. Ibid., p. 128.

52. Malcolm Jones, "Who Was More Important: Lincoln or Darwin?" *Newsweek* (July 7–July 14, 2008): 32.

53. Ibid., p. 32.

54. Desmond and Moore, *Darwin: The Life of a Tormented Evolutionist*, p. 413.

55. Bowler, *Charles Darwin*, p. 145–146.

56. Desmond and Moore, *Darwin: The Life of a Tormented Evolutionist*, p. 415.

57. Bowler, *Charles Darwin*, p. 145.

58. Ibid., p. 145.

59. Jerry Bergman, "The Huxley-Wilberforce Debate Myth," *CRSQ* 46(3) (Winter 2010): 177–184.

60. Bowler, *Charles Darwin*, p. 140.

61. Ibid., p. 140.

62. Ibid., p. 142.

63. James Moore, "Deconstructing Darwinism: The Politics of Evolution in the 1860s," *Journal of the History of Biology* 24(3) (1991): 406.

64. Bowler, *Charles Darwin*, p. 142.

65. Fern Elsdon-Baker, "Spirited Dispute: The Secret Split Between Wallace and Romanes," *Endeavour*, 32(2) (2008): 75.

66. Bowler, *Charles Darwin*, p. 132.

67. Desmond and Moore, *Darwin: The Life of a Tormented Evolutionist*, p. 413.

68. Charles Darwin, edited by F. Burkhardt, *The Correspondence of Charles Darwin*, Volume 8 (New York: Cambridge University Press, 1993), p. 40.

69. Bowler, *Charles Darwin*, p. 139.

70. Ibid., p. 150.

71. Ibid., p. 150.

72. Ibid., p. 148–149.

73. Ibid., p. 146.

74. Jerry Bergman, *Slaughter of the Dissidents: The Shocking Truth About Killing the Careers of Darwin Doubters* (Southworth, WA: Leafcutter Press, 2008).

75. Charles Darwin, edited by Francis Darwin, *Charles Darwin, His Life Told in an Autobiographical Chapter and in a Selected Series of His Published Letters* (New York: D. Appleton and Company, 1892), p. 61.

76. Benjamin Wiker, *The Darwin Myth: The Life and Lies of Charles Darwin* (Washington, DC: Regnery Publishing, Inc., 2009), p. xii.

77. Nigel Williams, "Darwin Celebrations Begin," *Current Biology* 18(14) (2008): 579.

78. John Marks Templeton, editor, *Evidence of Purpose: Scientists Discover Creativity*, "Dare a Scientist Believe in Design," by William B. Provine (New York: Continuum, 1994), p. 30.

79. Theodore Roszak, *Unfinished Animal* (New York: Harper & Row, 1975), p. 102.

80. Bowler, *Charles Darwin*, p. 146–147.

CHAPTER 2

Why Darwinism Demands Atheism

Chapter Synopsis

This chapter documents that Darwinism, the belief that natural law alone can account for the entire living and material world, is irreconcilable with theism. This conclusion has been openly expressed in very strong unequivocal terms by many eminent atheistic and theistic scientists, a number of whom are quoted in this chapter. Scientific research has also found that the vast majority of eminent scientists see an irreconcilable chasm between Darwinism and theism.

Introduction

U.S. District Judge Jones ruled in the 2005 Dover, Pennsylvania, Intelligent Design court decision that no contradiction exists between modern Neo-Darwinism and theism. The judge ruled:

> Both Defendants [Dover Area School Board of Directors] and many of the leading proponents of ID make a bedrock assumption, which is utterly false. Their presupposition is that evolutionary theory is antithetical to a belief in the existence of a supreme being and to religion in general. Repeatedly in this trial, Plaintiffs' scientific experts testified that the theory of evolution represents good science, is overwhelmingly accepted by the scientific community, and that it in no way conflicts with, nor does it deny, the existence of a divine creator.[1]

Many, if not most, eminent biologists openly disagree with Judge Jones and have expressed this disagreement in the strongest terms possible. For example, University of Chicago professor of biology Jerry Coyne wrote that science has delivered several crippling blows to humanity's theistic worldview, and the most severe blow was

> in 1859, when Charles Darwin published *On the Origin of Species,* demolishing, in 545 pages of closely reasoned prose, the comforting notion that we are unique among all species — the supreme object of God's creation, and the only creature whose early travails could be cashed in for a comfortable afterlife . . . like all species, we are the result of a purely natural and material process.[2]

Coyne notes that the views of theologian John Haught, who testified in the Dover case about the harmony of evolution and theism, have been soundly rejected by most scientists. Specifically, Haught's view contended that, although life may have evolved,

> the process was really masterminded by God, whose ultimate goal was to evolve a species, our species, that is able to apprehend and therefore to admire its creator. This progressivist and purpose-driven view of evolution, rejected by most scientists, has been embraced by Haught and other theologians.[3]

In contrast to Haught, who also testified in the Dover trial that Darwinism and Christianity are fully compatible worldviews, the late Harvard professor Stephen Jay Gould, one of the most eminent evolutionary biologists of the last century, rejected the idea that the "improbability of our evolution indicates divine intent in our origin."[4] Rather, Gould noted, evolutionists have concluded that humans are "pitiful latecomers in the last microsecond of our planetary year."[5] Gould also wrote that no

> scientific revolution can match Darwin's discovery in degree of upset to our previous comforts and certainties. . . .

Evolution substituted a naturalistic explanation of cold comfort for our former conviction that a benevolent deity fashioned us directly in his own image, to have dominion over the entire earth and all other creatures.[6]

Gould concluded that humans are a "tiny and accidental evolutionary twig . . . a little mammalian afterthought with a curious evolutionary invention" called the human brain.[7] Gould has made it clear elsewhere that Darwinism demands atheism, adding that

> although organisms may be well designed, and ecosystems harmonious, these broader features of life arise only as consequences of the unconscious struggles of individual organisms for personal reproductive success, and not as direct results of any natural principle operating overtly for such "higher" goods . . . by taking the Darwinian "cold bath," and staring a factual reality in the face, we can finally abandon the cardinal false hope of the ages — that factual nature can specify the meaning of our life by validating our inherent superiority, or by proving that evolution exists to generate us as the summit of life's purpose.[8]

Kansas State University biology professor Scott Todd opined that a stark contrast exists between the Darwinian and theistic worldviews that Judge Jones ruled "in no way conflict" with each other, noting that the "crucial difference between what the creationists believe and what the proponents of evolutionary theory accept concerns the issue of whether the origins of life were driven by randomness or by an intelligent creator."[9]

Design by an intelligent Creator and the effects of randomness are diametrically opposed worldviews, two ends of a dichotomy that is separated by a chasm. The fact is that

> evolutionary theory weakened one of the most intuitively compelling arguments for the existence of God: the argument from design. Theists going back at least as far as Thomas

Aquinas had argued that the intricate design found in organisms was evidence of a designer, namely God . . . neither Hume nor anyone else had been able to think of a better explanation, and the design argument retained much of its force. Darwin changed all of this. His theory of natural selection provided a naturalistic account of the origin of species — an explanation for design without a designer.[10]

Professor Nigel Williams was even more blunt, writing that Darwin "destroyed the strongest evidence left in the nineteenth century for the existence of a deity."[11] Professor Francisco Ayala explained in detail why Darwinism ruled out theism, namely because it negated the need for an intelligent Creator for the reason that "Darwin's greatest contribution to science" is he led the way to prove that natural law can create all that is real, and no need exists for an intelligent Creator because "organisms could now be explained . . . as the result of natural processes, without recourse to an Intelligent Designer."[12]

The Darwinian revolution marked the end of the age of belief in the design argument among scientists. Oxford University professor of the history of science I. B. Cohen concluded:

Darwinian revolution was probably the most significant revolution that has ever occurred in the sciences, because its effects and influences were significant in many different areas of thought and belief. The consequence of this revolution was a systematic rethinking of the nature of the world, of man, and of human institutions. . . . This event, a declaration of revolution in a formal scientific publication, appears to be without parallel in the history of science.[13]

Scientists in Darwin's day knew that this revolution was upon them. Botanist and phrenologist Hewett C. Watson wrote to Darwin on November 21, 1859, informing him that Darwin was "the greatest Revolutionist in natural history of this century, if not of all centuries." Adding that only a quarter of a century ago he and Darwin were two of the very few persons who doubted special creation.[14] Ernst Mayr concluded that Darwin "caused a greater upheaval in man's thinking than any other scientific advance since the rebirth of science in the Renaissance."[15]

The Most Significant Revolution in History

In the minds of many, if not most Darwinists, the Darwinian Revolution has resulted in explaining away the task that once required a Creator and has replaced Him by blind, unintelligent, and amoral natural laws. This is because "Darwin's theory of natural selection accounts for the 'design' of organisms, and for their wondrous diversity, as the result of natural processes, the gradual accumulation of spontaneously arisen variations (mutations) sorted out by natural selection."[16] Ayala concluded:

> Mutation and selection have jointly driven the marvelous process [of evolution] that, starting from microscopic organisms, has yielded orchids, birds, and humans. The theory of evolution conveys chance and necessity, randomness and determinism . . . this was Darwin's fundamental discovery, that there is a process that is creative, although not conscious.[17]

The fact is, nowhere in Darwinism is there any mention or need for God, or even an Intelligent Creator, a fact that "raised an uncomfortable possibility: If God is not needed to explain the design in nature — which was generally considered the best evidence for a designer — maybe God does not exist at all."[18]

Darwin knew that his evolution theory not only supported atheism, but atheism was a logical result of his theory. Although Darwin personally "discouraged militant arguments against religion because they supposedly have little effect on the public, he nevertheless indirectly supported their use of his theory to propagate atheism."[19] An example is, in 1880, Darwin wrote a letter to atheist Edward Aveling saying, "it appears to me (whether rightly or wrongly) that direct arguments against christianity [sic] and theism produce hardly any effect on the public." Darwin added that instead of arguing directly against Christianity, the task of converting people to atheism

> is best promoted by the gradual illumination of men's minds, which follow from the advance of science [i.e., evolution]. It has, therefore, been always my object to avoid writing on religion [for publication, and for this reason] I have confined myself to science."[0]

Darwin once said that he was with the atheists "in thought" even though he preferred to call himself an *agnostic* as opposed to an atheist, possibly in deference to his devout wife.[21] Interesting is the fact that, as noted in a review of Richard Dawkin's book *The God Delusion,* Dawkins and other atheists usually ignore the faith-based nature of their own convictions:

> As Dawkins acknowledges and physicists have shown, the existence of conscious, rational beings is a wildly improbable outcome. To insist that we are simply the products of the workings of, ultimately, physical laws is to avoid the question of the nature and origin of those laws. To say that there is no evidence for God is merely, therefore, an interpretation, justified in one context but quite meaningless in another. Everywhere we look, there is evidence of . . . something of a startling intelligibility.[22]

University of Chicago professor Jerry Coyne wrote that there exist

> religious scientists and Darwinian churchgoers. But this does not mean that faith and science are compatible, except in the trivial sense that both attitudes can be simultaneously embraced by a single human mind. (It is like saying that marriage and adultery are compatible because some married people are adulterers.)[23]

Cornell Professor William Provine wrote that the

implications of modern science produce much squirming among scientists, who claim a high degree of rationality. Some, along with many liberal theologians, suggest that God set up the universe in the beginning and/or works through the laws of nature. This silly way of trying to have one's cake and eat it too amounts to deism. It is equivalent to the claim that science and religion are compatible if the religion is effectively indistinguishable from atheism. Show me a person who says that science and religion are compatible, and I will show you a person who (1) is an effective atheist, or (2) believes things demonstrably unscientific, or (3) asserts the existence of entities or processes for which no shred of evidence exists.[24]

One scientific study concluded that "science and religion have come into conflict repeatedly throughout history, and one simple reason for this is the two offer competing explanations for many of the same phenomena."[25] This study found from scientific research that *increasing* the value of one view of biological origins (Darwinism) *decreases* the value of the other view (theism) because the "two ideologies are inherently opposed, and that belief in one necessarily undermines belief in the other."

The researchers concluded that, just as it is impossible to believe a single proposition can be both true and false at the same time, likewise one cannot logically and simultaneously believe in two contradictory explanations of life's origins. Either God created life, thus creationism is true, or purely natural forces did, thus naturalistic evolutionism is true. The implications of this worldview are clear. In an essay based on the Phi Beta Kappa Oration given at Harvard University on June 3, 2008, Nobel Laureate Professor Steven Weinberg wrote that the

worldview of science is rather chilling. Not only do we not find any point to life laid out for us in nature, no objective basis for our moral principles, no correspondence between what we think is the moral law and the laws of nature. . . . the emotions that we most treasure, our love for our wives and husbands and children, are made possible by chemical processes in our brains that are what they are as a result of natural selection acting on chance mutations over millions of years. And yet we must not sink into nihilism or stifle our emotions. At our best we live on a knife-edge, between wishful thinking on one hand and, on the other, despair. Living without God isn't easy. But its very difficulty offers one other consolation — that there is a certain honor, or perhaps just a grim satisfaction, in facing up to our condition without despair and without wishful thinking — with good humor, but without God.[26]

This View in Science Is Widespread

Surveys of eminent evolutionists find that most agree with those scientists quoted above. For example, Greg Graffin completed a PhD in evolutionary biology at Cornell University under Professor William Provine. His thesis was on the religious beliefs of leading evolutionary biologists. The sample consisted of 271 scientists, with 56 percent completing the entire questionnaire (151 persons). Graffin found that, as a result of accepting the Darwinian world-view, due to evolution, almost 98.7 percent of his respondents rejected a traditional theistic worldview and, instead, became functional atheists. He defined theism as a belief in a personal creative God as taught by the Christian, Jewish, and Muslim religions. In answer to Cornell professor William Provine's question: "'Is there an intellectually honest Christian evolutionist position? . . . Or do we simply have to check our brains at the church house door?'" Graffin's answer is, "You indeed have to check your brains."[27]

More than 84 percent of the scientists that returned the questionnaire rejected *all* theistic religions and most concluded that evolution serves as a *replacement* for theism. Almost none of the scientists in this pool of world-famous scientists even tried to marry Darwinism and theism, the two popular worldviews that Judge Jones ruled "in no way conflict." Graffin found that a rare few scientists attempted to harmonize Darwinism with theism, and an even rarer few tried to claim, as did one Ivy League paleontologist, that evolution is the fruit of "God's love."[28] Almost every scientist in his study recognized the unbridgeable gap between Darwinism and theism.

Both Graffin's Cornell PhD dissertation and his book on the same topic document in detail why orthodox Neo-Darwinism (a central tenet of which is naturalism) and theism are at opposite ends of the spectrum. This is true not only for theism, but also of all major worldview questions, such as if an ultimate purpose exists in life and if we will be held accountable for our behavior in an afterlife or even if an afterlife exists. In Graffin's words, "In most evolutionary biologists' view, there is no conflict between evolution and religion on one important condition: that religion is essentially atheistic."[29] Graffin concluded his study has documented "naturalism is a young, new religion" that is now the dominant religion among almost all leading Darwinists.[30]

Most atheists and secular humanists recognize the fact that evolution commonly leads to atheism and for this reason, they are at the forefront of defending evolution.[31] In a British article subtitled "Grayling Dissects a New Defense of Intelligent Design," Grayling writes that science has proven man-to-molecules evolution is fact and, as a result, "the more science, the less religion. And this is a universal phenomenon (see the Pew polls on the decline of religion, even in the USA)."[32] This is the reason evolutionists fight so tenaciously to insure that dogmatic Darwinism is forced into the schools and that criticism of this view is, by law, censored.[33]

Evolution is Anti-Science

The chasm between evolution and theism is not the only concern of theists. Some theists object to what has now become dogmatic evolutionism for other reasons. Nobel Laureate Robert Laughlin concluded that evolution is actually anti-science. He wrote his concern is that much "present-day biological knowledge is ideological," which, he notes, involves explanations that have no implications and cannot be tested. I call such logical dead ends antitheories because they have exactly the opposite effect of real theories: they stop thinking rather than stimulate it. Evolution by natural selection, for instance, which Charles Darwin originally conceived as a great theory, has lately come to function more as an antitheory, called upon to cover up embarrassing experimental shortcomings and legitimize findings that are at best questionable and at worst not even wrong. Your protein defies the laws of mass action? Evolution did it! Your complicated mess of chemical reactions turns into a chicken? Evolution! The human brain works on logical principles no computer can emulate? Evolution is the cause! . . . Biology has plenty of theories [to explain origins]. They are just not discussed — or scrutinized — in public.[34]

In other words, Laughlin claims that evolutionism has become an explanation for events for which in fact no explanation as of yet exists. The fact that he implies an explanation does exist impedes scientific investigation to find the actual explanation.

Given the validity of the conclusions in this chapter, Judge Jones's ruling means that only one worldview, Darwinism, can be taught in public schools. Information that supports a theistic worldview would thus be illegal in state schools. Professor Todd noted, "It should be made clear in the classroom that science, including evolution, has not disproved God's existence because *it cannot be allowed to consider it.*"[35] Dr. Todd concluded that even if "all the data point to an intelligent designer, such a hypothesis is excluded from science because it is not naturalistic."[36] Professors Cobb and Coyne wrote that "science is about finding material explanations of the world," and conversely, religion is

about humans thinking that awe, wonder, and reverence are the clue to understanding a God-built Universe. . . . *There is a fundamental conflict here, one that can never be reconciled until all religions cease making claims about the nature of reality.* The scientific study of religion is indeed full of big questions that need to be addressed, such as why belief in religion is negatively correlated with an acceptance of evolution.[37]

They concluded that efforts to bring religion and science into harmony will not bring science and religion (or "spirituality") closer to one another nor bring about "advances in theological thinking" because the "only contribution that science can make to the ideas of religion is atheism."[38] In 1929, Professor Watson wrote that evolution "is accepted by zoologists, not because it has been observed to occur or . . . is supported by logically coherent evidence to be true, but because the only alternative, special creation, is clearly incredible."[39] The same is still believed to be true today by Darwinists.

For example, Oxford professor Richard Dawkins wrote that instead of "examining the evidence for and against rival theories [of the origins of life], I shall adapt a more armchair approach. My argument will be that Darwinism is the only known theory that is in principle *capable* of explaining [the origins of life] . . . even if there were no actual evidence in favor of the Darwinian theory . . . we should still be justified in preferring it over all rival theories."[40]

Dawkins believes that there is evidence for Darwinism, but nonetheless admits his bias as did Watson. This is why Professor Laughlin has concluded that Darwinism is anti-science dogma. Professor Daniel Dennett concluded that Darwinism spelled the end of theism because Darwin's idea of natural selection

> is the best idea anybody ever had, ahead of Newton, ahead of Einstein. What it does is it promises to unite the two most disparate features of all of reality. On the one side, purposeless matter and motion, jostling particles; on the other side, meaning, purpose, design. Before Darwin these were completely separate realms.[41]

Darwinism united the "most disparate features of all reality," meaning now that the main evidence for God, purpose, and design, can be explained by natural selection, the need to consider God is negated.

This View Existed from the Beginning of Darwinism

Nagel wrote that from the commencement of the Darwinian revolution

> it has been commonplace to present the theory of evolution by random mutation and natural selection as an alternative to intentional design as an explanation of the functional organization of living organisms. . . . Its defining element is the claim that all this happened as the result of the appearance of random and purposeless mutations in the genetic material followed by natural selection due to the resulting heritable variations in reproductive fitness. It displaces design by proposing an alternative.[42]

As noted in chapter 1, Darwin himself made it very clear that his theory displaced God but he felt that an indirect approach was a more effective route to atheism. Darwin had murdered God, at least in the minds of many scientists. Cornell University biology professor William B. Provine made this very clear:

> When Darwin deduced the theory of natural selection to explain the adaptations in which he had previously seen the handiwork of God, he knew that he was committing cultural murder. He understood immediately that if natural selection explained adaptations, and evolution by descent were true, then the argument from design was dead and all that went with it, namely the existence of a personal god, free will, life after death, immutable moral laws, and ultimate meaning in life. The immediate reactions to Darwin's *On the Origin of Species* exhibit, in addition to favorable and admiring responses from a relatively few scientists, [was] an understandable fear and disgust that has never disappeared from Western culture.[43]

So confident are Darwinists that evolution has destroyed theism that some scientists predict theistic religion will eventually die out as knowledge of evolution spreads. University of Pennsylvania professor Anthony Wallace wrote in 1966 that religion, due to the assault of science, by which he means evolution, has been increasingly restricted in its influence, and he predicts that the

evolutionary future of religion is extinction. Belief in supernatural beings and in supernatural forces that affect nature without obeying nature's laws will erode and become only an interesting historical memory. To be sure, this event is not likely to occur in the next generation; the process will likely take several hundred years . . . but as a cultural trait, belief in supernatural powers is doomed to die out all over the world, as a result of the increasing adequacy and diffusion of scientific knowledge . . . the process is inevitable.[44]

Why do many "scientists publicly deny the implications of modern science, and promulgate the compatibility of religion and science"? Provine answered the reason is due to

wishful thinking, religious training, and intellectual dishonesty are all important factors. Perhaps the most important motivation in the United States, however, is fear about federal funding for science. Almost all members of Congress profess to being very religious. Will Congress continue to fund science that is inconsistent with religion? Scientists are trading intellectual honesty for political considerations.[45]

Conclusions

It is well established that the most eminent life scientists of our age agree, and have expressed themselves in the strongest terms on the matter, that a clear unbridgeable contradiction exists between Darwinism and theism. As Nick Lane of University College, London, wrote:

Evolution has no foresight, and does not plan for the future. There is no inventor, no intelligent design. . . . Design is all around us, the product of blind but ingenious processes. Evolutionists often talk informally of inventions, and there is no better word to convey the astonishing creativity of nature.[46]

Claims such as Judge Jones's that no contradiction exists between theism and Darwinism are not only naïve but, as documented above, are grossly uninformed and contradict the testimony of many of the world's most eminent scientists who document that a chasm exists between modern neo-Darwinism and Orthodox Biblical Christianity.

Endnotes

1. *Kitzmiller et al. v. Dover Area School District et, al.*, case No. 04cv2688, December 20, 2005, U.S. District Court for the Middle District of Pennsylvania, p. 135.

2. Jerry A. Coyne, "Creationism for Liberals," *The New Republic* (August 12, 2009): 34.

3. Jerry A. Coyne, "Seeing and Believing," *The New Republic* (February 4, 2009): 34.

4. Stephen Gould, *Bully for Brontosaurus* (New York: W.W. Norton, 1991), p. 15.

5. Ibid., p. 18.

6. Carl Zimmer, *Evolution: The Triumph of an Idea,* Introduction by Stephen Gould (New York: Harper Collins, 2001), p. 11.

7. Gould, *Bully for Brontosaurus,* p. 13.

8. Zimmer, *Evolution: The Triumph of an Idea,* p. xiii.

9. Scott C. Todd, "A View from Kansas on that Evolution Debate," *Nature* 401 (September 30, 1999): 423.

10. Steve Stewart-Williams, "Can An Evolutionist Believe in God?" *Philosophy Now* (August/September 2004): 19.

11. Nigel Williams, "Darwin Celebrations Begin," *Current Biology* 18(14) (2008): R579.

12. Francisco J. Ayala, "Darwin's Greatest Discovery: Design Without Designer," *Proceedings of the National Academy of Sciences* 104 (May 15, 2007): 8567.

13. I. Bernard Cohen, *Revolution in Science* (Cambridge, MA: Harvard University Press, 1985), p. 285, 299.

14. Charles Darwin, edited by F. Burkhardt, *The Correspondence of Charles Darwin,* Volume 7, "Letter to Charles Darwin, November 21, 1859," by Hewett C. Watson (New York: Cambridge University Press, 1991), p. 385.

15. Ernst Mayr, *Evolution and the Diversity of Life* (Cambridge, MA: Harvard University Press, 1976), p. 291.

16. Ayala, "Darwin's Greatest Discovery: Design Without Designer," p. 8567.

17. Ibid., p. 8568.

18. Stewart-Williams, "Can An Evolutionist Believe in God?" p. 19.

19. Hiram Caton, *The Darwin Legend* (Queensland: Institute of Medical Research, 2008), p. 3.

20. Edward B. Aveling, *The Religious Views of Charles Darwin* (London: Freethought Publishing Company, 1883), p. 4–5.

21. Ibid., p. 5.

22. Bryan Appleyard, "The Delusion Is All Yours," *New Scientist* (March 3, 2007): 47.

23. Coyne, "Creationism for Liberals," p. 33.

24. William Provine, "Scientists, Face it! Science and Religion Are Incompatible," *The Scientist* 2(16):10 (September 5, 1988): 10.

25. Jesse Preston and Nicholas Epley, "Science and God: An Automatic Opposition Between Ultimate Explanations," *Journal of Experimental Social Psychology* 45 (2009): 238

26. Steven Weinberg, "Without God," *The New York Review of Books* 55(14):1 (September 25, 2008): 1.

27. Provine, "Scientists, Face it! Science and Religion Are Incompatible," p. 10.

28. Gregory W. Graffin, *Evolution, Monism, Atheism, and the Naturalist World-View* (Ithaca, NY: Polypterus Press, 2004), p. 78.

29. Ibid., p. 21–22.

30. Ibid., p. 38.

31. Doug Sharp and Jerry Bergman, editors, *Persuaded by the Evidence* (Green Forest, AR: Master Books, 2008).

32. A.C. Grayling, "Origin of the Specious; A.C. Grayling Dissects a New Defense of Intelligent Design," *New Humanists* 123(5) (September/October 2008): 27–29.

33. Phillip Johnson and John Mark Reynolds, *Against All Gods* (Downers Grove, IL: InterVarsity Press, 2010).

34. Robert B. Laughlin, *A Different Universe* (New York: Basic Books, 2005), p. 168–169.

35. Todd, "A View from Kansas on that Evolution Debate," p. 423, emphasis added.

36. Ibid., p. 423.

37. Mathew Cobb and Jerry Coyne, "Atheism Could Be Science's Contribution to Religion," *Nature* 454 (2008): 1049, emphasis added.

38. Ibid.

39. D.M.S. Watson, "Adaptation," *Nature* 124 (1929): 231–233.

40. Richard Dawkins, *The Blind Watchmaker* (New York: Norton, 1986), p. 287.

41. Anatoly Ruvinsky, *Genetics and Randomness* (Boca Raton, FL: CRC Press, 2009), p. 146.

42. Thomas Nagel, "Public Education and Intelligent Design," *Philosophy & Public Affairs* 36(2) (2008): 188.

43. John Marks Templeton, editor, *Evidence of Purpose: Scientists Discover Creativity,* "Dare a Scientist Believe in Design," by William B. Provine (New York: Continuum, 1994), p. 30.

44. Anthony Wallace, *Religion: An Anthropological View* (New York: Random House, 1966), p. 264–265.

45. Provine, "Scientists, Face it! Science and Religion Are Incompatible," p. 10.

46. Nick Lane, *Life Ascending* (New York, NY: Norton, 2009), p. 5.

CHAPTER 3

Darwin's Religious Views

Chapter Synopsis

The history of Darwin's religious development was reviewed, concluding that for most of his life Darwin was likely an agnostic, one who doubts that God exists but does not know for sure. His scientific work and life experiences, particularly the loss of his daughter Anna, were all important factors in causing him to develop an agnostic worldview. Other important factors that influenced Darwin's worldview include the contradiction he perceived between the evil in the world and his conception of a living, caring, loving Creator God, which he felt could not be answered satisfactorily by the clergy of his day. Darwin's father, Robert, his brother Erasmus, and his grandfather Erasmus, all well-known students of science in their own right, were also likely agnostics. Consequently, in the area of religion, Darwin was following his family tradition more than rebelling against his social background.

Introduction

The man who in the popular mind is credited with discovering the theory of evolution by natural selection, Charles Darwin, is consistently rated by modern scientists as one of the greatest scientists who ever lived. Darwin is invariably included in the top 10 scientists, or at least in the top 20. Simmons ranks Darwin fourth out of his selection of the top 100 scientists that ever lived.[1] Darwin's work had a major influence in the area of science and religion because Darwin's theory opened a whole "new relationship between man and nature," which, as a result, took history on a "dramatic and secular turn."[2]

Furthermore, Darwin's "theories of evolution and natural selection have had an exceptionally direct influence in western culture," radically changing the world forever. Some have even suggested that we rank our age the "post-Darwin era." Not only did Darwin radically change his generation, but his work permanently changed our worldview in ways that are still being resisted by many persons and organizations today. This conflict was illustrated by the hundreds of articles that were generated worldwide after the decision by the Kansas State Board of Education to no longer use questions on macroevolution for their state-wide testing.[3]

Darwin's Religious Development

Although as a young man Darwin's "religious views remained decidedly lukewarm and passively conventional, simply because he had never given the matter any extensive thought," evidence indicates that he did not firmly hold to the typical view of his time, that of God as a loving Father and Creator responsible for the existence of the world around us.[4] Indeed, "Darwin himself was inconsistent on the whole question of his conversion, with the result that authors with differing viewpoints have been able to see somewhat in his writings a conformation of their own particular views."[5] Nonetheless, a careful examination of Darwin's extant writings can give us a fairly accurate picture of his religious views.

One of several critical incidents that influenced the development of Darwin's antagonism to a theological worldview besides the death of his daughter, Anna, [6] involved his reading of books by both skeptics and the so-called "higher criticism" advocate. Darwin attended the University of Edinburgh and no doubt was influenced by the higher criticism taught there that caused David Hume to "become a thorough going skeptic" a century earlier.[7] Darwin's doubts about the reliability of the Scriptures, especially the miracles and what he saw as contradictions, were both important in his progress to agnosticism.[8]

Even as a young man, Darwin's "religious views must have been very much in flux . . . carrying him rapidly toward agnosticism."[9] In the end, his theism did die "along with any semblance of orthodox Christianity," no doubt influenced by his reading of so-called skeptics such as David Hume and militant anti-Christians, such as the founder of the field of sociology, Auguste Comte, who wrote, "All real science stands in radical and necessary opposition to all theology."[10]

Darwin's ideas on religion were also partly a reflection of his upper-class British social milieu. His views for the most part were not all that radical or highly original in his social circle; his achievement was primarily to elaborate and publicize them through his best-selling books. Darwin's family and social network included many liberal Unitarians, freethinkers, agnostics, and atheists.

Although the major focus of Darwin's *Beagle* trip was biology, of the 2,530 pages of notes Darwin took during his 57-month voyage, his geological notes totaled 1,383 pages compared to only 368 pages of zoological notes. The educated public likewise also had much interest in geology, partly because the major occupation of the time was farming, which involved tilling the land. Herbert claims that between 1820 and 1840 more books on geology were sold than novels.[11]

Geology was once firmly based on a biblical framework, but after the Bible's hold on the educated scientific population was lost, people began to look at the field of geology for support of their new non-biblical worldviews. A major research motivation of many of the leading geologists, biologists, and other scientists was to refute the basis for the supernatural interventionist worldview. The views of the leading agnostic scientists soon became the general views of secular educated society.

As documented in chapter 8, the theory of evolution was not original with Charles Darwin but was gleaned from his social milieu.

Darwin's grandfather Erasmus (1731–1802), concluded in one of his books titled *Zoonomia*:

> All warm-blooded animals have arisen from one living filament [a simple cell], which THE GREAT FIRST CAUSE endued with animality, with the power of acquiring new parts, attended new propensities . . . and thus possessing the faculty of continuing to improve by its own inherent activity, and of delivering down those improvements by generation to its posterity, world without end.[12]

Darwin was no-doubt highly influenced by his grandfather's book "which he thoroughly enjoyed." *Zoonomia* enjoyed wide circulation and support, but was not without opposition: Samuel Coleridge referred to it as the orangutan "theology of the human race substituted for the first chapters of the Book of Genesis."[13] Herbert noted that Darwin "spoke with a great deal of pride that *Zoonomia* had been placed on the *Index Librorum Prohibitorum*" in 1817.[14] Bynum argued that Erasmus Darwin's conclusions about evolution "were based on an appreciation of the fossil record, the reality of biological extinction and the immense age of the earth."[15]

Darwin was also heavily influenced by the intellectual climate of his time that included putative intellectual giants such as the French thinker Voltaire who argued for a form of agnosticism. He also had a close association with Dr. Robert Grant, an "outspoken evolutionist" who openly argued against the veracity of the biblical record and the supernatural worldview. Dr. Grant "made a lasting impression" on young Darwin.[16] A naturalist of Grant's stature and knowledge no doubt influenced young Darwin to move away from the theistic perspective of origins.[17]

Another person who had an enormous influence on Darwin was Robert Chambers (1802–1871), who wrote *Vestiges of Natural History of Creation*,[18] the first full-length presentation of an evolutionary theory of the species in English. Darwin was especially impressed by the work of lawyer Charles Lyell, an ardent deist who wrote a bestseller arguing for uniformitarianism, an idea that was critical in the eventual widespread acceptance of macro-evolution. Uniformitarianism concluded that the present is the key to the past and that all history could be explained by the operation of natural law.

Evidently, the last time Darwin expressed confidence in historical Christianity in writing was in a letter dated April 23, 1829. Darwin once claimed that he had accepted most orthodox religious beliefs until the early 1840s.[19] Even while on his *Beagle* trip, Darwin still accepted the Bible as an "authority" on points of morality. In Darwin's own words, his loss of the religious faith of his youth was gradual and related to unanswered questions about nature. He wrote while on

> board the *Beagle* I was quite orthodox, and I remember being heartily laughed at by several of the officers (though themselves orthodox) for quoting the Bible as an unanswerable authority on some point of morality. I supposed it was the novelty of the argument that amused them. But I had gradually come by this time, *i.e.*, 1836 to 1839, to see that the Old Testament was no more to be trusted than the sacred books of the Hindoos (sic). The question then continually rose before my mind and would not be banished, is it credible that if God were now to make a revelation to the Hindoos (sic), he would permit it to be connected with the belief in Vishnu, Siva, &c., as Christianity is connected with the Old Testament? This appeared to me utterly incredible.[20]

Darwin's wife, Emma Wedgewood, was a devout Unitarian. After she married Darwin, she moved to a home called Down House south of Downe, a village southeast of London. There she and the children, but not her husband, attended the local Anglican Church until she died. Unitarians of the middle 1800s were very similar to many conservative Protestant denominations today. It is of interest that in the

Emma Darwin
From Henrietta Litchfield, editor, *Emma Darwin, a Century of Family Letters, 1792–1896* (London: John Murray, 1915).

19th century they stressed "restoring authentic Christianity by discovering God's design in nature."[21]

Emma's personal letters show that she held the Bible in reverence, frequently read it, and expressed "anxiety over her husband's renunciation of the Bible." Furthermore, her concerns over Charles' disbelief persisted after their marriage, and were expressed in several letters written during their marriage. Emma consistently expressed "loving concern" to all of her loved ones, a sentiment that deeply touched Charles.

It is often assumed that his discovery of evolution was a major factor in producing his agnosticism, his conclusion that the Bible was wrong, and therefore was not inspired, but probably was more important in his rebellion against Christianity and, eventually, God.[22] Another important factor was the tragic loss of his favorite child, Anne, at the tender age of ten, evidently from tuberculosis, and his coincidental reading of certain works by Cardinal John Henry Newman at about this time.

Most of Darwin's colleagues, even Rev. Adam Sedgwick, president of the Geological Society and professor of geology at Cambridge, accepted many of the uniformitarianist naturalistic beliefs that were then in vogue in British academic society.[23] This is true in spite of the fact that Professor Sedgwick disagreed with Darwin's totally naturalistic worldview, describing Darwin's theory as "a dish of rank materialism cleverly cooked and served up . . . to make us independent of a Creator."[24]

Conversely, several individuals who were prominent in Darwin's life were "deeply religious," such as his good friend Rev. John Henslow, who was a professor of botany at Cambridge. In college, although Darwin detested lectures, he did attend many of Henslow's botany classes and found them to be intellectually stimulating.[25] Others include his cousin Rev. Fox and Rev. Bodie Innes, a devout Christian and the vicar of the parish adjoining Down. Darwin corresponded with Rev. Innes for almost 40 years, and although he was a dedicated naturalist as was Darwin, he was unable to convince Innes of evolution.[26] As noted, Darwin's wife, Emma, was also a creationist and deeply religious.

Darwin's agnostic and atheistic friends and colleagues, his devoutly religious wife, and some of his important professors, especially Professor Henslow, produced in him an ambivalence that has given scholars much latitude in trying to determine his personal religious persuasion. Darwin wrote about Professor Henslow that he showed such deep concerns about others that Darwin concluded, "I fully believe a better man never walked this earth."[27]

The conclusions about Darwin's religious faith "span from his being a theist [more correctly a deist] to atheist or even agnostic."[28] The agnostic label is probably the most accurate, although some argue that his writings that touch on religion indicate he never fully abandoned the view that a Creator who governed by natural law was the uncaused *First Cause*.

Examples of what may appear to be Darwin's ambivalence are many. His famous words in *The Origin*, namely the statement that "there is grandeur in this view of life, with its several powers, having been originally breathed by the Creator into a few forms or into one ... from so simple a beginning endless forms most beautiful and most wonderful have been, and are being evolved" may have been a concession to theists.[29] He later removed them from *Origin* and stated he regretted including them in previous editions.

In a letter to Hooker dated March 1863, Darwin discussed this incident, noting that, "It will be sometime before we see slime, snot, or protoplasm generating a new animal. But I have long regretted that I truckled to public opinion & used the Pentateuchal term of creation, by which I really meant 'appeared' by some wholly unknown process."[30]

Yet in his autobiography Darwin categorically stated that he believed in God — and he often used the term *First Cause* — consequently some people have concluded that he should be at least called a deist.[31] He even once stated, "I cannot think that the world, as we see it, is the result of chance."[32] Although he was not consistent in expressing his own personal beliefs, it is clear that Darwin lived his life as if God did not exist.

Darwin also claimed that he had not "thought deeply enough to justify" publication of his thoughts on religion, and in response to a request that he write an article on religion and science, he stated that he had "never systematically thought much on religion in relation to science, or on morals in relation to society; and without steadily keeping my mind on such subjects for a long period, I am really incapable of writing anything worth sending to the *Index*."[33] When he grew older, Darwin said that in his

> most extreme fluctuations I have never been an Atheist in the sense of denying the existence of a God. I think that generally (and more and more as I grow older), but not always, that an Agnostic would be the more correct description of my state of mind.[34]

A concern is that his denial of atheism could well be an effort to please his wife and the many Christians he counted as his friends. As to Darwin's alleged deathbed religious conversion told to Lady Hope, several careful studies by both evolutionists and creationists indicate that this story is unsupported and very likely apocryphal.[35]

His Doubts about God's Existence

To the end, Darwin expressed uncertainty about God, even once admitting as to God's existence, "I just don't know," and as to religion, "My judgment often fluctuates."[36] He often alluded to the "design problem" argument against creationism, such as, if we were created, why would males have "rudimentary mammae," whose purpose should have been very obvious to him as a male.[37] He admitted, however, that he could not "keep out of the question" theology and origins.[38] Herbert concludes that Darwin's vacillation provides scholars with evidence for the diversity of opinion held today regarding Darwin's religious views.[39]

It also illustrates the sociological conclusion that even alleged revolution makers such as Darwin were profoundly influenced by their social environment and circumstances. Had Darwin lived today, no doubt he would be an atheist. In 1900, only an estimated 0.2 percent of the world's population were atheists, and the number is now estimated at 21.3 percent.[40] Furthermore, as documented in chapter 2, a recent survey reveals that almost 99 percent of the National Science Academy members were atheists, and surely Darwin would fit in this category of esteemed scientists.

He becomes More Negative Toward Christianity

Although Darwin ended up an agnostic, the record is clear that he gradually became more negative toward Christianity, and according to his autobiography, he later eventually concluded that the Christian faith is "manifestly false," the Bible "false" (even stating that the Christian God was a "revengeful tyrant"), and that the Christian Scriptures were "no more to be trusted than . . . the beliefs of any barbarian."[41] He even claimed the gospels differed in so many important details that they were worse than the inaccuracies that would be expected from actual eyewitnesses.[42]

In the area of support for the charitable works of churches, his behavior was contradictory. For example, in spite of Darwin's skeptical, even antagonistic, religious views, he openly supported Christian moral and social work — at the age of 58 he was still mailing money in support of Christian missionary work.[43] Yet he pressed on with his crusade against Christianity in spite of his support for the considerable charitable work of the various Christian organizations of his day.

Both naturalism and Christianity are concerned with where we came from, why we are here, and where we are going. As a belief system, naturalism required evolution, just as Christianity required some form of creationism. Darwin often argued in favor of naturalism and against supernaturalism in a strongly polemical manner. He accepted his main contribution to evolution, natural selection, as valid not because he could prove it, but because it explained much data from a naturalistic framework.[44]

Darwin also was confident that his work would disprove the Bible and he realized that the process of overthrowing the theistic worldview was slow and he had to be discreet. In a letter to Lyell he debated the best approach to get his book accepted:

> Would you advise me to tell Murray that my book is not more *un*-orthodox than the subject makes inevitable. That I do not discuss the origin of man. That I do not bring in any discussion about Genesis, &c., &c., and only give facts, and such conclusions from them as seem to me fair. Or had I better say *nothing* to Murray, and assume that he cannot object to his much unorthodoxy, which in fact is not more than any Geological Treatise which runs slap counter to Genesis.[45]

Actually, Darwin was very active in propagating his ideas about creation.[46] In a letter dated August 11, 1858, to Asa Gray, Darwin noted that a person he had been working on converting had finally accepted his ideas. As a result "Darwin could hardly contain himself, and his glee even now seems to jump right off the page when he declared our best British botanist . . . is a full convert and is now going immediately to publish his confession of faith; and I expect daily to see proof sheets."[47] The extent of his efforts at converting others is best shown by the fact that in a half century he exchanged over 14,000 letters with some 1,800 correspondents, and "just managing his voluminous mail was truly an astounding feat."[48]

In spite of some of Darwin's contradictory statements about God, Wiker argued that, in the end

> Darwin's triumph has been to set ideological atheism as the default position of science; as the prism through which scientists are supposed to see the world and conduct their work. It is just as distorting to science as ideological Marxism is to the study of economics. It offers an answer for everything; it is an answer to which facts are twisted to conform.[49]

Wiker concluded that scientists have cast "Darwin as the apostle of light" leading us away from the superstition of theism. The result of this

> has had the unfortunate effect of ruling out of order, as sheer reactionary ignorance, any questioning of whether Darwin might be leading us down another, opposite path of superstition. What is certain is that Charles Darwin, despite his fine personal qualities, was dishonest in this regard.[50]

Conclusions

In the end, most Darwin scholars have concluded that while Darwin personally was an agnostic, he insisted his theory of "evolution *must* be godless to be scientific" which Wiker called "the Darwin Myth," that is

> so profoundly misleading that it must be called a great lie, one that is unfortunately at the heart of his life and legacy. I cannot ultimately explain why Darwin himself so strongly, so implacably insisted on evolution being entirely incompatible with belief in God.[51]

One answer to Wiker's question is found in the conclusion that at his core Darwin was in fact an atheist even though he denied this, no doubt in deference to his devout wife and his scientific friends who were believers. In contrast to the common belief, Darwin's theory was not so much a result of the evidence but was accepted *in spite* of the evidence. Sulloway noted the conclusion that "Darwin was somehow *un*prejudiced toward the evidence [for evolution] is both unsatisfactory and misleading" and it was Darwin "and not the evidence per se, that ultimately" caused him to accept the "unorthodox interpretations that led him to embrace the theory of evolution."[52] The following chapters will document this observation in more detail.

Endnotes

1. John Simmons, *The Giant Book of Scientists: the Hundred Greatest Minds of all Time* (London: Magpie Books, 1997).

2. Ibid., p. 21.

3. Rex Dalton, "Kansas Kicks Evolution Out of the Classroom," *Nature* 400 (August 1999): 701.

4. Stephen J. Gould, *Rocks of Ages; Science and Religion in the Fullness of Life* (New York: Ballantine, 1999), p. 30.

5. Frank J. Sulloway, "Darwin's Conversion: The Beagle Voyage and Its Aftermath," *Journal of the History of Biology* 15 (1982): 326.

6. Randal Keynes, *Darwin, His Daughter and Human Evolution* (New York: Riverhead Books, 2002).

7. William Phipps, *Darwin's Religious Odyssey* (Harrisburg, PA: Trinity Press International, 2002), p. 3.

8. Maurice Mandelbaum, "Darwin's Religious Views," *Journal of the History of Ideas* 19(3) (1958):363–378.

9. Frank Birch Brown, *The Evolution of Darwin's Religious Views* (Macon, GA: Mercer University Press, 1986), p. 12.

10. Ibid., p. 12, 15.

11. David Herbert, *Charles Darwin's Religious Views: From Creationist to Evolutionist*, revised and expanded edition (Guelph, Ontario, Canada: Joshua Press, 2009), p. 35.

12. Erasmus Darwin, *Zoonomia, or the Laws of Organic Life* (New York: Ams Press, 1794), p. 505, emphasis in original, spelling modernized.

13. David Herbert, *Charles Darwin's Religious Views: From Creationist to Evolutionist* (London, Ontario: Hersil Publishing, 1990), p. 5.

14. Ibid.

15. W.F. Bynum, "Heritable Traits of a Grandfather," *Nature* 401(6753) (1999): 528.

16. Herbert, *Charles Darwin's Religious Views*, p. 16.

17. Ibid.

18. Robert Chambers, *Vestiges of Natural History of Creation* (New York: Humanities Press, 1969), first published in 1844.

19. Brown, *The Evolution of Darwin's Religious Views*.

20. Charles Darwin, edited by Francis Darwin, *Charles Darwin, His life Told in an Autobiographical Chapter and in a Selected Series of His Published Letters* (New York: D. Appleton and Company, 1892), p. 62.

21. Phipps, *Darwin's Religious Odyssey*, p. 1.

22. Benjamin Warfield, "Charles Darwin's Religious Life: A Sketch in Spiritual Biography," *The Presbyterian Review* 9 (1888): 569–601.

23. Herbert, *Charles Darwin's Religious Views*, p. 22.

24. John Willis Clark, *The Life and Letters of the Rev. Adam Sedgwick*, Vol. 2 (Cambridge, MA: Cambridge University Press, 1890), p. 360.

25. Herbert, *Charles Darwin's Religious Views*, p. 20.

26. Robert M. Stecher, "The Darwin-Innes Letters: The Correspondence of an Evolutionist with His Vicar, 1848–1884," *Annals of Science* 17 (1961): 201–258.

27. Phipps, *Darwin's Religious Odyssey*, p. 10

28. Herbert, *Charles Darwin's Religious Views*, p. 49.

29. Charles Darwin, *The Origin of Species* (London: John Murray, 1859), p. 374; Herbert, *Charles Darwin's Religious Views*, p. 69.

30. Charles Darwin, edited by F. Burkhardt, *The Correspondence of Charles Darwin 1863*, Volume 11 (New York: Cambridge University Press, 2000), p. 278.

31. Herbert, *Charles Darwin's Religious Views*, p. 77.

32. Darwin, *Charles Darwin, His life Told in an Autobiographical Chapter and in a Selected Series of His Published Letters*, p. 61.

33. Ibid., p. 59.

34. Ibid.

35. James R. Moore, *The Darwin Legend* (Grand Rapids, MI: Baker, 1994); Wilbert H. Rusch and John W. Koltz, *Did Charles Darwin Become a Christian?* (Kansas City, MO: Creation Research Society Books, 1988).

36. Darwin, *Charles Darwin, His life Told in an Autobiographical Chapter and in a Selected Series of His Published Letters*, p. 59.

37. Jerry Bergman, "Is the Human Male Nipple Vestigial," *TJ Technical Journal* 15(2) (2001): 38–41.

38. Charles Darwin, edited by Francis Darwin, *The Life and Letters of Charles Darwin*, Volume 2 (New York: D. Appleton and Company, 1896), p. 174–175.

39. Herbert, *Charles Darwin's Religious Views*, p. 79.

40. David Barrett, *World Christian Encyclopedia* (New York: Oxford, 1982).

41. Charles Darwin, edited by Nora Barlow, *The Autobiography of Charles Darwin 1809–1882* (New York: Norton, 1958), p. 85.

42. Phipps, *Darwin's Religious Odyssey*, p. 34.

43. Herbert, *Charles Darwin's Religious Views*, p. 33.

44. Ibid., p. 61.

45. Charles Darwin, edited by F. Burkhardt, *The Correspondence of Charles Darwin*, Volume 7 (New York: Cambridge University Press, 1992), p. 270.

46. James R. Moore, "Charles Darwin and the Doctrine of Man," *Evangelical Quarterly* 44(4) (1972): 196–217.

47. Herbert, *Charles Darwin's Religious Views*, p. 60

48. Ibid., p. 59.

49. Benjamin Wiker, *The Darwin Myth: The Life and Lies of Charles Darwin* (Washington, DC: Regnery Publishing, Inc., 2009), p. xi.

50. Ibid.

51. Ibid.

52. Sulloway, "Darwin's Conversion: The Beagle Voyage and Its Aftermath," p. 389.

CHAPTER 4

Darwin's Religion of Purposelessness

Chapter Synopsis

The conclusion that no ultimate purpose exists in the universe is a logical result of Darwinism held by many, if not most, orthodox evolutionists today. This lack of ultimate purpose also applies to all life, including human life. Evolution stresses only proximate purpose exists, primarily to do what is needed to survive and pass on life to the next generation. In the end the earth and all life will perish forever. This chapter elaborates on this worldview and documents how pervasive it is in our public education system.

Introduction

Darwin's theory of evolution is "deceptively simple yet utterly profound in its implications."[1] Its first profound implication is that living creatures "differ from one another, and those variations arise at random, *without a plan or purpose.*"[2] Evolution must be without plan or purpose because, at its core, is selection of the more fit that were produced by random copying errors called mutations. Darwin "was keenly aware that *admitting any purposefulness* whatsoever to the question of the origin of species would put his theory of natural selection on a very slippery slope."[3] This fact of evolution is obvious, but few outsiders

> could see it, so trapped were they by the human . . . *desire to find design and purpose in the world.* . . . Darwin's brilliance

was in seeing beyond the appearance of design, and understanding the *purposeless, merciless process of natural selection*, of life and death in the wild, and how it culled all but the most successful organisms from the tree of life, thereby creating the illusion that a master intellect had designed the world. But close inspection of the watch-like 'perfection' of honeybees' combs or ant trails . . . reveals that they are a product of random, repetitive, unconscious behaviors, not conscious design.[4]

The fact that evolution teaches life is purposeless except to aid survival is not lost on teachers. One teacher testified that when she taught evolution it significantly impacted her students' consciences because it moved them away from the "idea that they were born for a purpose . . . something completely counter to their mind-set and beliefs."[5]

Yale psychologists Bloom and Weisberg concluded in a study on why children resist accepting evolution, that the evolutionary view of the world, which the authors call "promiscuous teleology," makes it difficult for children to accept evolution. Children "naturally see the world in terms of design and purpose" and they have to be indoctrinated to see the world in another way.[6] The ultimate purposelessness of evolution, and thus its products including life, was eloquently expressed by Professor Lawrence Krauss as follows: "We're just a bit of pollution. . . . If you got rid of us . . . the universe would be largely the same. We're completely irrelevant."[7] As Oxford Professor Richard Dawkins concluded, although "humans have always wondered about the meaning of life" the fact is "life has no higher purpose [other] than to perpetuate the survival of DNA."[8]

The Textbooks

To determine what schools are teaching about religious questions, such as the purpose of life, a set of leading current science textbooks were surveyed. The clear trend found is they teach the view that evolution is both nihilistic and atheistic. One of today's most widely used textbooks stated that "evolution works without either plan or purpose. . . . **Evolution is random and undirected.**"[9] Another text by the same authors added that Darwin knew his theory

> required believing in *philosophical materialism*, the conviction that matter is the stuff of all existence and that all mental and spiritual phenomena are its by-products. Darwinian evolution was not only purposeless but also heartless — a process in which . . . nature ruthlessly eliminates the unfit. Suddenly, humanity was reduced to just one more species in a world that cared nothing for us. The great human mind was no more than a mass of evolving neurons. Worst of all, there was no divine plan to guide us.[10]

One text taught that humans are just "a tiny, largely fortuitous, and late-arising twig on the enormously arborescent bush of life" and the belief that a "progressive, guiding force, consistently pushing evolution to move in a single direction" is now known to be "misguided."[11] Many texts teach that evolution is purposeless and goal-less except to achieve brute survival: the "idea that evolution is not directed towards a final goal or state has been more difficult for many people to accept than the process of evolution itself."[12] One major textbook openly teaches that humans were created by a blind, deaf, and dumb watchmaker, namely natural selection, a process which is

> totally blind to the future. . . . Humans . . . came from the same evolutionary source as every other species. It is natural selection of selfish genes that has given us our bodies and our brains. . . . Natural selection . . . explains . . . the whole of life, the diversity of life, the complexity of life, [and] the apparent design in life (from an interview with Richard Dawkins).[13]

The same claim of purposelessness that results from evolution is related in the mass media as well. For example, *Newsweek* relates that Darwin knew full well the

> consequences of his theory. Mankind was no longer the culmination of life but merely part of it; creation was mechanistic and purposeless. In a letter to a fellow scientist, Darwin wrote that confiding his theory was "like confessing a murder."[14]

The Implications of Darwin

Many school textbooks are very open about the implications of Darwinism for theism. One teaches that Darwin's "immeasurably important" contribution to science was to show that, despite life's apparent evidence of design and purpose, purely mechanistic causes explain all biological phenomena. The text adds that by coupling "undirected, purposeless variation to the blind, uncaring process of natural selection, Darwin made theological or spiritual explanations of the life processes superfluous."[15] Futuyma concluded by adding that "it was Darwin's theory of evolution that provided a crucial plank to the platform of mechanisms and materialism . . . that has been the stage of most western thought."[16]

Another text even stated that humans were created by a random process, not a loving, purposeful God, and the "real difficulty in accepting Darwin's theory has always been that it" diminishes our significance because evolution requires "us to accept the proposition that, like all other organisms, we too are the products of a random process that, as far as science can show, we are not created for any special purpose or as part of any universal design."[17]

These texts all clearly teach worldviews, not science. An excellent example is a textbook that openly ruled out not only theistic evolution but *any role* for God in nature, noting that Darwinism threatened theism by showing that humans and all life "could be explained by natural selection without the intervention of a god":

Evolutionary randomness and uncertainty had replaced a deity having conscious, purposeful, human characteristics. The Darwinian view that . . . present-type organisms were not created spontaneously but formed in a succession of selective events that occurred in the past, contradicted the common religious view that there could be no design, biological or otherwise, without an intelligent designer. . . . In this scheme a god of design and purpose is not necessary. . . . Religion has been bolstered by . . . the comforting idea that humanity was created in the image of a god to rule over the world and its creatures. Religion provided emotional solace, a set of ethical and moral values.vNevertheless, faith in religious dogma has been eroded by natural explanations of its mysteries. . . . The positions of the creationists and the scientific world appear irreconcilable.[18]

These texts are only following Darwin, who also taught a totally atheistic, naturalistic view of origins. He once proclaimed, "I would give nothing for the theory of natural selection if it requires miraculous additions at any one stage of descent."[19] And his disciples have faithfully followed him. Alcock concluded that, as an evolutionary biologist, he believes that "we exist solely to propagate the genes within us."[20]

Leading Darwin scholar Janet Browne makes it very clear that Darwin's goal was the "arduous task of reorienting the way Victorians looked at nature." To do this, Darwin had to convince the world that "ideas about a benevolent, nearly perfect natural world" and

beauty was given to things for a purpose, were wrong — that the idea of a loving God who created all living things and brought men and women into existence was . . . a fable. The world . . . steeped in moral meaning which helped mankind seek out higher goals in life, was not Darwin's. Darwin's view of nature was dark — black. . . . Where most men and women generally believed in some kind of design in nature

— some kind of plan and order — and felt a deep-seated, mostly inexpressible belief that their existence had meaning, Darwin wanted them to see all life as empty of any divine purpose.[21]

Darwin knew how difficult it was to abandon such a view because, for evolution to work, nature must ultimately be

governed entirely by chance. The pleasant outward face of nature was precisely that — only an outward face. Underneath was perpetual struggle, species against species, individual against individual. Life was ruled by death . . . destruction was the key to reproductive success. All the theological meaning was thus stripped out by Darwin and replaced by the concept of competition. All the *telos*, the purpose, on which natural theologians based their ideas of perfect adaptation was redirected into Malthusian — Darwinian — struggle. What most people saw as God-given design he saw as mere adaptations to circumstance, adaptations that were meaningless except for the way in which they helped an animal or plant to survive.[22]

Dawkins made it crystal clear that the implications of a purposeless universe means

some people are going to get hurt, other people are going to get lucky, and you won't find any rhyme or reason in it, nor any justice. The universe we observe has precisely the properties we should expect if there is, at bottom, no design, no purpose, no evil and no good, nothing but blind, pitiless indifference.[23]

How widely is this view held by scientists? One study of 149 leading biologists found that 89.9 percent believed that evolution has no ultimate purpose or goal except survival, and that humans are a cosmic accident existing at the whim of time and chance. Only a mere 6 percent believed that evolution has a purpose beyond survival.[24] Most all of those who believed evolution had no purpose were hard core atheists. Brown University professor Kenneth Miller noted:

> If life itself was given to us by evolutionary random chance, then we shouldn't bother searching for meaning in our own existence because we're not going to find any. We are just the products of random molecules and physical forces. We have no reason to regard our existence as anything but a pointless byproduct of nature.[25]

He adds that some of his scientific colleagues have even

> argued that the question of life's purpose is not even worth asking ... the question of meaning is itself without meaning ... and that we humans ask such questions only because our evolutionary heritage programs us to look for a hidden significance to events, perhaps as a survival trait.[26]

This is only one example of what Sommers and Rosenberg call the "destructive power of Darwinian theory."[27] Many people have concluded that there is nothing worth living for or no cause worth dying for. This reflects itself in the fact that, especially among the young, a major cause of death is suicide. Miller adds that he, personally, has concluded the purpose of life is only to live and enjoy life as much as possible, and this gives life enough purpose. This echoes Paul's lament, "If there is no resurrection, 'Let's feast and drink, for tomorrow we die'" (1 Corinthians 15:32, NLT).

Purpose and Christianity

Christianity teaches that God made the universe to serve as a home for humans, but if the universe evolved purely by time, chance, and the outworking of natural law means, it just exists and no reason beyond this exists for its existence. Any "purpose" for its existence can only be that which *humans* decide to attribute to the universe. This negates the fact that the similarity of human-constructed machines and the universe is the *basis* of the design argument. Just as a machine requires a designer and a builder, so too a universe requires a designer and builder. If the universe was not designed for a purpose, then the major reason most people believe in God is negated as well as the reason to accept the conclusion that the universe was made for a purpose, as were humans.

Determining the purpose of something depends on the observer's worldview. To a non-theist the question "What is the *purpose* of a living organism's structure?" means only "How does it aid survival?" Orthodox neo-Darwinism views everything as either an unfortunate or a fortuitous event as judged by survival goals due to the outworking of natural law and mutations selected by natural selection. In this view, eyes and legs have nothing to do with purpose or the enjoyment of life; rather, they are merely an unintended byproduct of evolution because they aid survival. Biologists consistently explain everything from coloration to sexual habits solely on the basis of how it contributes to the survival of the fittest.

Conversely, creationists interpret all reality according to beliefs about God's purpose for creating humans and everything else. Evolutionists can usually explain even contradictory behavior by the survival of the fittest idea, but creationists look beyond this and try to determine what role it plays in God's plan. Susskind wrote that the origins conflict is primarily between those

> who are convinced that the world must have been created or designed by an intelligent agent with a benevolent purpose [and] . . . the hard-nosed, scientific types who feel certain that the universe is the product of impersonal, disinterested laws of physics, mathematics, and probability — a world without a purpose, so to speak. By the first group, I . . . am talking about thoughtful, intelligent people who look around at the world and have a hard time believing that it was just dumb luck that made the world so accommodating

to human beings. I don't think these people are being stupid; they have a real point.[28]

He concludes:

The argument is not between science and religion but between two warring factions of science — those who believe, on one hand, that the laws of nature are determined by mathematical relations, which by mere chance happen to allow life, and those who believe that the Laws of Physics have, in some way, been determined by the requirement that intelligent life be possible.[29]

Conclusions

Orthodox evolution teaches that the living world has no plan or purpose except survival, and is random, undirected, and heartless. Humans live in a world that cares nothing for us, our mind is simply a mass of meat, and no divine plan exists to guide us or anything else. These teachings are hardly neutral, but openly teach a religion, the religion of atheism and ultimate nihilism. The courts have consistently approved teaching this anti-Christian religion in public schools and have blocked all attempts to neutralize these clearly religious ideas as the constitution requires. Judge Jones' decision (recapped in chapter 2) is only the latest example.

Endnotes

1. Edward Humes, *Monkey Girl: Evolution, Education, Religion, and the Battle for America's Soul* (New York: Ecco, 2007), p. 119.

2. Ibid., p. 119, emphasis added.

3. J. Scott Turner, *The Tinker's Accomplice: How Design Emerges from Life Itself* (Cambridge, MA: Harvard University Press, 2007), p. 206, emphasis added.

4. Humes, *Monkey Girl: Evolution, Education, Religion, and the Battle for America's Soul*, p. 119, emphasis added.

5. Ibid., p. 172.

6. Paul Bloom and Deena Skolnick Weisberg, "Childhood Origins to Adult Resistance to Science," *Science* 316 (2007): 996.

7. Richard Panek, "Out There," *New York Times Magazine* (March 11, 2007): 56.

8. Liam Scheff, "The Dawkins Delusion," *Salvo* 2 (2007): 94.

9. Kenneth R. Miller and Joseph S. Levine, *Biology*, fourth edition (Englewood Cliffs, NJ: Prentice Hall, 1998), p. 658, emphasis in original.

10. Joseph S. Levine and Kenneth R. Miller, *Biology: Discovering Life*, second edition (Lexington, MA: D.C. Heath, 1994), p. 161, emphasis in original.

11. Peter H. Raven and George B Johnson, *Biology*, sixth edition (Boston, MA: McGraw Hill, 2002), p. 16, 443.

12. William K. Purves, David Sadava, Gordon H. Orians, and H. Craig Keller, *Life: The Science of Biology*, sixth edition (Sunderland, MA: Sinauer Associates, 2001), p. 3.

13. Neil A. Campbell, Jane B. Reece, and Lawrence G. Mitchell, *Biology*, fifth edition (Menlo Park, CA: Addison Wesley Longman, 1999), p. 412–413.

14. Malcolm Jones, "Who Was More Important: Lincoln or Darwin?" *Newsweek* (July 7–July 14, 2008): 32.

15. Douglas J. Futuyma, *Evolutionary Biology*, third edition (Sunderland, MA: Sinauer Associates, 1998), p. 5.

16. Ibid., p. 5.

17. Helena Curtis and N. Sue Barnes, *Invitation to Biology*, third edition (New York, NY: Worth, 1981), p. 475.

18. Monroe W. Strickberger, *Evolution*, third edition (Sudbury, MA: Jones & Bartlett, 2000), p. 70–71.

19. Charles Darwin, edited by Francis Darwin, *The Life and Letters of Charles Darwin* (London: John Murray, 1888), p. 210.

20. John Alcock, *Animal Behavior: An Evolutionary Approach* (Sunderland, MA: Sinauer Associates, 1998), p. 16, 609.

21. Janet Browne, *Charles Darwin: A Biography, Volume 1, Voyaging* (Princeton, NJ: Princeton University Press, 1995), p. 542.

22. Ibid., p. 542.

23. Richard Dawkins, *River Out of Eden* (New York: Basic Books, 1995), p. 133.

24. Gregory W. Graffin, *Evolution, Monism, Atheism, and the Naturalist World-View* (Ithaca, NY: Polypterus Press, 2004), p. 42.

25. Kenneth R. Miller, *Only a Theory: Evolution and the Battle for America's Soul* (New York: Viking, 2008), p. 134.

26. Ibid., p. 157.

27. Tamler Sommers and Alex Rosenberg, "Darwin's Nihilistic Idea: Evolution and the Meaningless of Life," *Biology and Philosophy* 18 (2003): 653.

28. Leonard Susskind, *The Cosmic Landscape: String Theory and the Illusion of Intelligent Design* (New York: Back Bay Books, 2007), p. 6.

29. Ibid., p. 6–7.

PART TWO

Darwin and Mental Health

CHAPTER 5

Was Darwin Psychotic?
A Study of His Mental Health

Chapter Synopsis

Darwin's mental health was reviewed, concluding that he suffered from several mental health problems, including agoraphobia, the fear of crowds, and was possibly psychotic. His mental problems were described in some detail, focusing on his symptoms and efforts to deal with them. Last, it was stressed that understanding Darwin's theory requires understanding his motivations and person.

Introduction

For most of his adult life Darwin suffered from various combinations of psychological, or psychologically influenced, physical health symptoms. These included severe depression; insomnia; incapacitating anxiety; fits of hysterical crying; depersonalization; vision alterations (such as seeing spots and other visual hallucinations); malaise; vertigo; shaking; tachycardia; fainting spells; shortness of breath; trembling; nausea; vomiting; dizziness; muscle twitches, spasms, and tremors; cramps and colics; bloating and nocturnal flatulence; headaches; nervous exhaustion; dyspnea; skin problems (including scalp blisters and eczema); tinnitus; and sensations of loss of consciousness and impending death.[1]

Colp concluded that "much of Darwin's daily life was lived" in pain that was sometimes "distressingly" severe.[2] Darwin's mental problems were considered so severe that UCLA School of Medicine Professor Robert Picover included Darwin in his collection of persons he labeled "strange brains ... eccentric scientists, and madmen."[3] That Darwin suffered from several severely disabling maladies is not debated, the only debate is the cause.[4] Although Darwin consulted more than 20 doctors, the medical knowledge of his time prevented a definitive diagnosis. Furthermore, the treatments available then were, at best, only temporarily successful.

Fortunately, Darwin described in great length (and in extreme clinical detail) his suffering in his diaries, but it is difficult to determine how accurate his subjective observations were. He even recorded the daily volume and quality of his tinnitus! Darwin stated that his health problems began as early as 1825 when he was only 16 years old, and he became incapacitated around age 28.[5] Horan concluded that Darwin was "ill and reclusively confined to his home in Kent for forty years."[6] George Pickering, in an extensive study of Darwin's illness, concluded that, after around age 30, Darwin became an "invalid recluse,"[7] and Darwin scholar Michael Ruse also concluded that Darwin "was an invalid from the age of 30" until he died.[8]

Darwin's lifelong serious medical complaints have been the subject of much research and speculation for more than a century. Dozens of scholarly articles and at least three books have been penned on Darwin's incapacitating health problems. Unfortunately, most Darwin biographers have shied away from this topic, partly because Darwin is now openly idolized by many scientists and secularists. His supporters are no doubt concerned that his health problems could diminish his iconic status in science and among the public. Often listed as one of the greatest scientists of the 19th century, if not the greatest scientist that ever lived, Darwin is one of the few scientists known to most Americans. To understand Darwin's work and his motivations, though, his mental condition must be evaluated to help determine if and how it affected his conclusions about God, worldviews, and life's origin.

Agoraphobia

The most widely accepted conclusion is that Darwin suffered from several seriously incapacitating psychiatric disorders including agoraphobia. *Agoraphobia* is characterized by fear of panic attacks, or actual panic attacks, when not in a psychologically safe environment.[9] The current *American Psychiatric Association Diagnostic Manual* (DSM) defines agoraphobia as

> anxiety about being in places or situations from which escape might be difficult (or embarrassing) or in which help may not be available in the event of having an unexpected or situationally predisposed Panic Attack or panic-like symptoms. Agoraphobic fears typically involve characteristic clusters of situations that include being outside the home alone; being in a crowd. . . . The situations are avoided (e.g., travel is restricted) or else are endured with marked distress or with anxiety about having a Panic Attack or panic-like symptoms, or require the presence of a companion.[10]

Barloon and Noyes concluded that Darwin's symptoms fit the DSM clinical picture.[11] Darwin also suffered from all of the common agoraphobia phobias — including being in crowds, being alone, or leaving home unless accompanied by his wife.[12] He refused to sleep anywhere but a "safe house," such as a close relative's home.[13]

Darwin's condition is today considered symptomatic of both social phobias (fear of social gatherings or visitors outside a defined space that the phobic feels in control of) and a panic disorder. Darwin's premorbid vulnerability was attributed to his sensitivity to stress that results from guilt and criticism. The variable intensity of his symptoms, and the prolonged chronic course of his illness without physical deterioration, indicate that his problem was psychiatric.[14]

Panic disorder usually first appears in the teens or early adulthood, and is often associated with stressful life transitions.

Panic disorder patient histories often include separation from a person who is emotionally important, which may be significant, because Darwin's mother died when he was only eight. Although Darwin apparently had an overall happy childhood, and was emotionally supported by his siblings, separation anxiety may have contributed to his panic disorder as an adult.[15] Darwin's illness often followed situations such as the "excitement" of attending meetings.

Darwin's anxiety disorders were so severe that they limited his ability to leave his home, even just to meet with colleagues or friends. When Darwin left his home, it was mostly to visit friends or relatives, although he did endeavor to fulfill his scientific meeting obligations. The agoraphobic diagnosis explains Darwin's very secluded, hermit-like adult lifestyle.[16] It also helps to explain the title of Desmond and Moore's 1991 biography of Darwin: *Darwin: The Life of a Tormented Evolutionist*. Agoraphobia does not totally explain Darwin's condition, because he experienced abnormal fears even in the safety of his own home. For example, Darwin seldom lingered at the dinner table after dinner because

> too active a conversation would often provoke a nervous attack that would spoil the next day's work altogether. He played two games of backgammon with Emma, read scientific books for a while and then listened to Emma playing the piano. He then retired but seldom slept well.[17]

That Darwin "seldom slept well" is a fact that indicates much about Darwin. Darwin also suffered depersonalization — a feeling of being detached from, and outside of, one's body.[18] He also had sudden and discrete attacks involving heart "palpitations, shortness of breathe (air fatigues), light headedness (head swimming), trembling, crying, dying sensations, abdominal distress, and depersonalization (treading on air and vision)."[19]

These attacks were so common that Darwin wrote in a letter dated March 2, 1878, to Hooker that he had "constant attacks of swimming of the head which makes life an intolerable bother & stops all work."[20] In 1849 he wrote, "All this winter I have been bad enough, with dreadful vomiting every week, and my nervous system began to be affected, so that my hands trembled and head was often swimming."[21]

Having moved from smoky, dirty London to a country home, a former parsonage at Downe, Kent, Darwin became so reclusive that he actually installed a mirror outside his house so that he could withdraw to his bedroom when he saw visitors coming around the corner.[22] Whenever Darwin expected a weekend guest, he often invited another guest to keep the first one company because he knew that, "after talking for a few minutes, he would become too ill" to visit much longer.[23] Darwin wrote to Wallace on August 19, 1868, requesting him to invite several persons when he came to visit Darwin because Darwin "found it impossible to talk with any human being for more than half an hour, except on extraordinarily good days."[24] Darwin's son Francis wrote that about half an hour of conversation could cause his father a sleepless night, and the loss of half of the next day's work.[25]

The Panic Disorder Diagnosis

Persons afflicted with panic disorder are likely to use avoidance (social withdrawal) as a coping mechanism.[26] Darwin was neither socially aggressive nor even assertive — Huxley served as "Darwin's bulldog." Although Darwin had great confidence in himself, he became nervous when his routine was altered, such as by holiday changes, trips, or unexpected visitors.[27] By 1839 he was "living a life of extreme quietness" and had "given up all parties" even dinner parties.[28]

Evidence against the agoraphobia diagnosis include when Darwin was a member of the Royal Society Council from 1855 to 1856, he attended meetings on 16 occasions, and he was away from home about 2,000 days between 1842 and his death in 1882.[29] Colp's conclusion that this behavior indicates Darwin was merely balancing work and leisure and does not fit the agoraphobia diagnosis: 2,000 days in 40 years is around only three days a month, a minuscule amount for an active, internationally famous scientist. The fact is, Darwin left home very infrequently, and, when he did, he was usually accompanied by his wife.[30] In Darwin's words, in a letter to Rev. Fox dated October 29, 1872, he complained, "I have long found it impossible to visit anywhere; the novelty and excitement would annihilate me."[31]

From his study of Darwin's illness, Sorsby concluded that Darwin suffered from "an anxiety state with obsessive features and psychosomatic manifestations" and that anxiety "clearly precipitated much of his physical trouble." He provided the following evidence for this diagnosis:

> Darwin exhibited the obsessional's trait of having everything "just so"; he kept meticulous records of his health and symptoms like many obsessional hypochondriacs. Everything had to be in its place; he even had a special drawer for the sponge which he used in bathing. . . . The obsessive nature of his make-up comes out more clearly in his son's reminiscences. . . . Surely the obsessive, compulsive driving force which made him do this must have been one of very considerable intensity. Then there is the health diary he kept. Days and nights were given a score according to how good they were; the score was added up at the end of each week, and there is evidence of frequent changing of mind in deciding whether a night was very good or just good.[32]

Darwin's Youth

Darwin's mental health problems date back to his early youth when he displayed "strange, locked-away somnambulistic" mental behaviors and a mind that others could not access. As a very young boy, Darwin had "a strong taste for long solitary walks; but what I thought about I know not." Once he became so absorbed that he fell seven or eight feet to the ground, off the truncated walls. . . . The lonely intensity of his childhood fantasizing was to be matched twenty-five years later by the lonely intensity of his scientific speculations.[33]

As a young man, Darwin had "episodes of abdominal distress, especially in stressful situations."[34] Like many panic disorder patients, as a youth Darwin had a "premorbid vulnerability" and an abnormal sensitivity to criticism. Panic disorder usually appears in the teens or early adulthood, and is associated with stressful life transitions, often some type of separation from an emotionally important person.

Darwin, who was eight when his mother died in July of 1817, said that he could not "remember hardly anything about her except her death-bed, her black velvet gown, and her curiously constructed work-table."[35] Some speculate that this experience may have had adverse psychological effects on Darwin. Although young, he was old enough to have had many memories of his mother, yet this part of his life was evidently totally repressed. After Darwin's mother died, he was boarded at Shrewsbury Grammar School.

Relationship with His Father

Agoraphobic patients frequently describe their parents as dominant, controlling, critical, frightening, rejecting, or overprotective, which matches the claims that Darwin's father (the physician Robert Darwin) was tyrannical. Psychoanalyst Edward J. Rempf believed that Charles Darwin's "complete submission" to a tyrannical father prevented Charles from expressing anger toward his father and then, subsequently, toward others. Huxley and Kettlewell wrote the "predisposing cause of any psychoneurosis which Charles Darwin displayed seems to have been the conflict and emotional tension springing from his ambivalent relations with his father, Robert, whom he both revered and subconsciously resented."[36]

John Chancellor concluded Darwin's "obsessive desire to work and achieve something was prompted by hatred and resentment of his father, who called him an idler and good-for-nothing during his youth." An example of one of Darwin's father's more strident comments to Darwin was: "You care for nothing but shooting, dogs, and rat catching, and you will be a disgrace to yourself and all your family!"[37]

English psychiatrist Dr. Rankine Good claimed that, "If Darwin did not slay his father in the flesh, then he certainly slew the Heavenly Father in the realm of natural history," suffering for his "unconscious patricide" which accounted for "almost forty years of severe and crippling neurotic suffering."[38] The conclusions remain controversial because they are based primarily on Darwin's writings, not on clinical evaluations.

Darwin's relationship to his father wasn't as horrendous as the above claim indicates. In his autobiography, Darwin contradicted the tyrannical father hypothesis, noting his father "was a little unjust to me when I was young, but afterwards I . . . became a prime favourite with him." Darwin's father may have had some harsh things to say about his son — but authoritarianism was fairly common for Victorian fathers. Also, his harshness was more than balanced by the constructive things that Darwin's father did for him, which helps to explain why Darwin is said to revere his father who Darwin once said was the "kindest man I ever knew, and whose memory I love with all my heart."[39] Darwin also reportedly had a very happy childhood. Furthermore, the tendency in psychology to blame adult unhappiness on fathers or mothers is controversial.

Development of His Symptoms

As a medical student at Edinburgh University, Darwin dealt poorly with the sight of blood and the brutality of surgery. He then turned to natural history, an interest that he developed when studying to qualify as a clergyman at Cambridge. In his unpaid job on the *Beagle* survey expedition, he suffered greatly from seasickness during the 18 months he was at sea. He was able to spend almost three years on land in strenuous exploration, but in October of 1833 he collapsed in Argentina. After spending two days in bed with a fever he took a boat to Buenos Aires, staying in his cabin until his fever passed. On September 20, 1834, while returning from a horseback expedition in the Andes Mountains, Darwin fell ill and spent a whole month in bed in Valparaiso.

His *Beagle* voyage ended on October 2, 1836. On September 20, 1837, he suffered uncomfortable heart palpitations and was "strongly" advised by his doctors to spend a month in the countryside recuperating. By the spring of 1838 he suffered from stomach upsets, worry, and headaches that laid him up for days. As his symptoms intensified, his heart troubles returned. In June, he felt fully recuperated and went "geologising" in Scotland, but later that year bouts of illness returned, a pattern that would continue until he died. He married his cousin Emma Wedgwood on January 29, 1839 and, in December of that year, as Emma's first pregnancy progressed, he fell ill and accomplished little during the following year.

Relationship with Wife, Nervousness about Being Left Alone

As analysis of Darwin's letters reveal that Darwin's wife, Emma, was "always the mother, never the child, Darwin always the child, never the father." Darwin gave his wife the nickname "mammy," writing, "My dearest old Mammy . . . Without you, when sick I feel most desolate. . . . Oh Mammy, I do long to be with you and under your protection for then I feel safe."[40] This response is more typical of a young child writing to his mother than a 39-year-old man writing to his wife.[41] Darwin's admission of "nervousness when Emma leaves me" is evidence of a fear of being alone associated with panic disorder.[42]

His personality aberrations were so severe that Ledgin concluded Darwin also suffered from a form of autism called Asperger's Disease.[43] Asperger's (after Viennese pediatrician Hans Asperger) patients often have severe difficulties in developing normal social relationships, experience trouble communicating, and have obsessive behavior.

Darwin's Other Psychiatric and Medical Problems

Most of Darwin's physical symptoms — including headaches, cardiac palpitations, "ringing in ears" (tinnitus), painful flatulence, and gastric upsets — all commonly have a psychological origin.[44] Rarely did a day go by when Darwin did not have in "varying degrees of severity and in many combinations" medical symptoms including nausea, severe vomiting, flatulence, alimentary canal pain, skin eruptions, and nervous exhaustion.[45]

Darwin also wrote that his "nervous system began to be so affected that my hands trembled and my head was often swimming . . . involuntary twitching of the muscle . . . fainting seeing black spots before the eyes."[46] Colp noted that behind these symptoms was a core of anxiety and depression.[47]

In a letter to Joseph Hooker dated April 23, 1861, Darwin complained that speaking for only "a few minutes" to the Linnean Society "brought on 24 hours of vomiting."[48] At another time, Darwin had a "house full of guests," and then visited his parish church for a christening. As a result of the stress he was "back to square one" — his good health "had vanished 'like a flash of lightning' " and his sickness (including the vomiting) returned.[49] He vomited so often that he actually had a porcelain vomitatorium installed in his study behind a curtain![50]

Heredity Factors

Several of Darwin's children suffered from similarly vague illnesses for much of their early lives,[51] but this may have been partly because Darwin lived in a household where sickness engendered much sympathetic attention. Charles' illness supplied a means to get his father's attention, support, and sympathy.[52] Darwin worried that he had passed his condition to his children, and was especially concerned about his marriage to his first cousin, Emma Wedgwood. Some speculate that his interest in the effects of inbreeding may also have been motivated by his marriage to his first cousin.

Alvarez wrote that much insanity and depression existed in the Darwin family, and the "extreme degrees of asthenia such as Darwin suffered from are commonly equivalents of melancholia."[53] Much of the "nervous defect probably came through Charles' paternal grandfather, the famous Dr. Erasmus Darwin, who stammered badly and in other ways was odd."[54] The first wife of Darwin's grandfather, Erasmus,

> was always sickly, and died at the age of 30. Their first son, Charles, stammered. The second, Erasmus, was a listless, hypersensitive, and melancholy dreamer who finally committed suicide. His father is reported to have called him "that poor insane coward." The third son, Robert, the father of the great Charles Darwin, was able but "sensitive to an abnormal degree."[55]

Alvarez adds:

> Charles Darwin inherited a tendency to melancholia also from his mother's stock. According to Pearson [1914], her father had at least one short nervous breakdown. One of her brothers, Tom Wedgwood, suffered terribly from fits of depression with great abdominal distress. According to Litchfield, his biographer, toward the close of his short life "his condition [was] hardly distinguishable from insanity."[56]

Arguments for Psychic Diagnosis

Some authorities concluded that Darwin's mental disturbance bordered on a full-blown psychosis, a severe incapacitating mental disorder often requiring hospitalization. Evidence for this diagnosis include entries in his diaries describing fits of depersonalization, hallucinations, suicide thoughts, obsessive-compulsiveness, bizarre behavior, sadism (such as his inordinate love of killing animals), and evidence that he suffered from an anti-social personality disorder and an immature relationship with his children.[57] Some of Darwin's statements to others also cast doubt on his mental stability. In February 1875, he wrote the following words to fellow scientist Robert Hooker: "You ask about my book, & all that I can say is that I am ready to commit suicide: I thought it was decently written, but find so much wants rewriting. . . . I begin to think that every one who publishes a book is a fool."[58]

Regardless of the diagnosis, Darwin's condition was clearly incapacitating, staying in bed much of the day, often for months at a time, rendering him an invalid for much of his life, especially during the prime of his life. Toward the end of his life he became so out of touch with reality that he worried he "might lose his mind."[59]

Barloon and Noyes conclude that Darwin was "preoccupied with his illness and excessively worried about its manifestations and consequences."[60] As evidence of this, they point to the fact that Darwin kept a detailed diary on his health problems and many complaints.[61] He also frequently discussed his health problems both in his letters and in his autobiography. Darwin's own description of his condition included the following: "I am forced to live . . . very quietly and am able to see scarcely anybody and cannot even talk long with my nearest relations."[62] When Darwin was 56 years old he wrote a note on May 20, 1865, to one of his many medical advisors summarizing the health problems that he had experienced for 25 years, including the following:

> Extreme spasmodic daily & nightly flatulence: occasional vomiting, on two occasions prolonged during months. . . . Vomiting preceded by shivering, hysterical crying, dying sensations or half-faint & copious and very pallid urine. Now vomiting & every passage paroxys[m] of flatulence preceded by ringing of ears, treading on air & vision. Focus & black dots, air fatigues, specially reading, brings on the Head symptoms.[63]

He added that the "nervousness" he experienced when his wife Emma left him for too long caused his "intensely acid, slimy (sometimes bitter)" vomit to corrode his teeth.[64] In 1837, he wrote "of late, anything which flurries me completely knocks me up afterwards and brings on a bad palpitation of the heart."[65] In 1849, he wrote he was

> so unwell that I was unable to travel, which added to my misery. Indeed all this winter I have been bad enough, with dreadful vomiting every week, and my nervous system began to be affected, so that my hands trembled and head was often swimming.[66]

Darwin's Treatment of Others

Darwin's behavior also indicates that he suffered from a serious mental disorder. Although devoted to his wife and daughters, he treated them like children, even after his daughters became adults.[67] Darwin's son, Leonard, claimed that his father's psychological illness interfered with his feelings for his children. For example, Leonard noted that as a young man he once tried to talk to his father who "turned away as if quite incapable of carrying on any conversation. Then there suddenly shot through my mind the conviction that he wished he was no longer alive."[68]

Combined Causes

Darwin may have suffered from more than one mental and/or physical disease, such as multiple allergies, or his psychosomatic complications and phobias may have resulted from this condition.[69] Severe panic disorders are usually accompanied by hypochondria. The psychological aspects of Darwin's illness might have been both a cause and an effect of his illness. Physical causes of Darwin's mental and physical disorders, including Chaga's disease, a parasitic infection spread by a South American insect, arsenic poisoning, epilepsy, multiple allergy, Lupus Erythematosus, and possibly even an inner ear disorder have all been refuted.[70] The psychogenic view of Darwin's sickness is now the most widely accepted cause.[71]

As in all forensic diagnosis, there is no way of empirically testing these theories because Charles Darwin is no longer available for personal analysis.

Darwin's Attempt to Treat His Illness

Darwin tried many of the therapies available in the limited medical science armamentarium of the time. The numerous medicines that he tried included bismuth compounds and laudanum. He even attempted quack therapies, such as electrical stimulation of the abdomen with a shocking belt.

The only procedure that had any beneficial effect, and to which he once adhered to enthusiastically, was Dr. James Gully's Water Cure. The treatment consisted of cold showers, vigorous rubbing and body strapping with wet towels, and drinking lots of water. He began treatment in March of 1848, and, despite his early suspicions, the cure worked for a while. After 16 weeks at the spa, he continued the treatment at home, but the excitement of a British Science Association meeting brought back the sickness and he returned for further treatment, a cycle that was repeated several times.

In June of 1850, his fears that his illness might be hereditary were reawakened when his nine-year-old daughter, Anne, suffered a long illness. She was also treated at the spa, but died on April 23, 1851. Darwin kept records of the effects of his water treatment until he finally ended it in 1852. Although it helped him relax, the treatment had no significant long-term effects, indicating that it served only to decrease his psychosomatic symptomatology.

Illness Contributes to Darwin's Work

Darwin's maladies may have contributed to what many believe was a long and fruitful creative life in science.[72] Pickering wrote that, isolated from the social life and many obligations of a "normal" scientist, such as administrative and teaching requirements, Darwin had ample time and the material comforts for researching, thinking, and writing.[73]

Darwin often complained that his malady robbed him of half a lifetime, but he was still able to conduct much research and completed a prodigious amount of writing. Darwin wrote in 1876 that he has enjoyed "ample leisure from not having to earn my own bread. Even ill-health, though it has annihilated several years of my life, has saved me from the distractions of society and amusement."[74]

In spite of Darwin's psychological problems, he was responsible for his staff of maids, cooks, gardeners, and his other employees.[75] Darwin also successfully managed his finances and the estate left by his father and also participated in the local church council. He wrote tens of thousands of pages, both scientific and personal, and over 14,000 letters to friends, relatives, colleagues, and even scientific rivals and opponents. Darwin was also described as cautious, responsible, thoughtful, work-oriented, curiosity-driven, and studious.[76]

Conclusions

Darwin was clearly a very troubled man, and suffered from severe emotional problems for most of his adult life, especially from about age 28 until his middle fifties. The causes of his many mental and physical problems have been much debated and may never be known with absolute certainty.[77] Historical investigations increasingly support the diagnosis that the main cause of his illness was psychological. Since Darwin wrote extensively about his mental and physical problems, we have much material on which to base reasonable conclusions about this area of his life. The diagnosis of his mental and physical problems included a variety of debilitating conditions, but agoraphobia complicated by psychoneurosis was most probably correct.

Endnotes

1. Clifford A. Picover, *Strange Brains and Genius: The Secret Lives of Eccentric Scientists and Madmen* (New York: Quill William Morrow, 1998), p. 290;

Thomas Barloon and Russel Noyes Jr., "Charles Darwin and Panic Disorder," *JAMA*, 277 (2) (1997): 138–141; William B. Bean, "The Illness of Charles Darwin," *The American Journal of Medicine* 65(4) (October 1978): 572–574; Ralph Colp Jr., *To Be an Invalid: The Illness of Charles Darwin* (Chicago, IL: The University of Chicago Press, 1977), p. 97; Ralph Colp Jr., *Darwin's Illness* (Gainesville, FL: The University Press of Florida, 2008); Gordon C. Sauer, "Charles Darwin Consults a Dermatologist," *International Journal of Dermatology*, 39(6) (2000): 474–478; Peter B. Medawar, "Darwin's Illness," in *The Art of the Soluble: Creativity and Originality in Science* (Harmondsworth, Middlesex, England: Penguin Books, 1969), p. 71–78.

2. Colp Jr., *To Be an Invalid: The Illness of Charles Darwin*, p. 97.

3. Picover, *Strange Brains and Genius: The Secret Lives of Eccentric Scientists and Madmen.*

4. Rachel J. Katz-Sidlow, "In the Darwin Family Tradition: Another Look at Charles Darwin's Ill Health," *Journal of the Royal Society of Medicine* 91(9) (September 1998): 484–488.

5. Barloon and Noyes Jr., "Charles Darwin and Panic Disorder," p. 138.

6. Charles Darwin, *The Origin of Species* (New York: Gramercy Books, 1979), foreword, p. ix.

7. George Pickering, *Creative Malady* (New York: Oxford University Press, 1974), p. 34.

8. Michael Ruse, "Is Evolution a Secular Religion?" *Science* 299 (2003): 1523.

9. D.L. Chambless and J. Mason, "Sex, Sex-Role Stereotyping and Agoraphobia," *Behaviour Research and Therapy* 24(2) (1986): 231–235.

10. American Psychiatric Association, *Diagnostic and Statistical Manual of Mental Disorders* (Washington, DC: American Psychiatric Association, 2000), p. 433.

11. Barloon and Noyes Jr., "Charles Darwin and Panic Disorder," p. 139.

12. Harold I. Kaplan and Benjamin J. Sadock, editors, *Comprehensive Textbook of Psychiatry*, fifth edition (New York: Williams and Wilkins, 1990), p. 958–959.

13. Adrian Desmond and James Moore, *Darwin: The Life of a Tormented Evolutionist* (New York: Warner Books, 1991).

14. Barloon and Noyes Jr., "Charles Darwin and Panic Disorder," p. 139.

15. John Bowlby, *Charles Darwin: A New Life* (New York: Norton, 1990).

16. Barloon and Noyes Jr., "Charles Darwin and Panic Disorder," p. 139.

17. Peter J. Bowler, *Charles Darwin: The Man and His Influence* (Cambridge, MA: Basil Blackwell, 1990), p. 93.

18. Kaplan and Sadock, *Comprehensive Textbook of Psychiatry*.

19. Barloon and Noyes Jr., "Charles Darwin and Panic Disorder," p. 138.

20. Colp Jr., *Darwin's Illness*, p. 109.

21. Charles Darwin, edited by F. Burkhardt, D. Porter, J. Harvey, and M. Richmond, *The Correspondence of Charles Darwin*, Volume 8 (Cambridge, England: Cambridge University Press, 1988), p. 277.

22. Desmond and Moore, *Darwin: The Life of a Tormented Evolutionist*, p. xix.

23. Walter C. Alvarez, *Nervousness Indigestion and Pain* (New York: Harper and Brothers, 1943), p. 240.

24. Charles Darwin, *More Letters of Charles Darwin*, Volume 2 (New York: D. Appleton and Co., 1903), p. 84.

25. Charles Darwin, *The Life and Letters of Charles Darwin*, Volume 1 (New York: D. Appleton, 1896), p. 110.

26. Chambless and Mason, "Sex, Sex-Role Stereotyping and Agoraphobia."

27. Darwin, *The Life and Letters of Charles Darwin*, Volume 1, p. 105–108.

28. Ibid., Volume 1, p. 65, 269.

29. Ralph Colp Jr., "The Dueling Diagnosis of Darwin," *JAMA* 8;277(2) (Jan. 1997):138–41.

30. Barloon and Noyes Jr., "Charles Darwin and Panic Disorder."

31. Anthony Larkum, *A Natural Calling: Life and Diaries of Charles Darwin and William Darwin Fox* (New York: Springer, 2009), p. 388.

32. Arnold Sorsby, editor, *Tenements of Clay* (New York: Charles Scribner's Sons, 1974), p. 228.

33. Peter Brent, *Charles Darwin: A Man of Enlarged Curiosity* (New York, NY: Harper and Row, 1981), p. 30–31.

34. Barloon and Noyes Jr., "Charles Darwin and Panic Disorder," p. 138.

35. Charles Darwin, edited by Nora Barlow, *The Autobiography of Charles Darwin 1809–1882* (New York: Norton, 1958), p. 22.

36. Julian Huxley and H. B. D. Kettlewell, Charles Darwin and His World (New York: The Viking Press, 1965), p. 66.

37. Darwin, *The Autobiography of Charles Darwin 1809–1882*, p. 28.

38. Colp Jr., *To Be an Invalid: The Illness of Charles Darwin*, p. 32.

39. Darwin, *The Autobiography of Charles Darwin 1809–1882*, p. 28.

40. Darwin, *The Correspondence of Charles Darwin*, Volume 8, p. 147.

41. Brent, *Charles Darwin: A Man of Enlarged Curiosity*, p. 316.

42. Barloon and Noyes Jr., "Charles Darwin and Panic Disorder," p. 139.

43. Norm Ledgin, *Asperger's and Self-Esteem: Insight and Hope through Famous Role Models* (Arlington, TX: Future Horizons, 2002), p. 57–63.

44. Robert O. Pasnau, "Darwin's Illness: A Biopsychosocial Perspective," *Psychosomatics* 31(2) (1990): 121–128.

45. Bean, "The Illness of Charles Darwin," p. 573.

46. Ibid., p. 573.

47. Colp Jr., *To Be an Invalid: The Illness of Charles Darwin*, p. 97.

48. Charles Darwin, edited by F. Burkhardt, D. Porter, J. Harvey, and M. Richmond, *The Correspondence of Charles Darwin*, Volume 9 (Cambridge, England: Cambridge University Press, 1994), p. 98–99.

49. Desmond and Moore, *Darwin: The Life of a Tormented Evolutionist*, p. 456.

50. John Darnton, "Darwin Suffered Spiritual Crisis," *The Journal Gazette* (September 25, 2005): p. 17A.

51. Katz-Sidlow, "In the Darwin Family Tradition: Another Look at Charles Darwin's Ill Health."

52. Ibid.

53. Alvarez, *Nervousness Indigestion and Pain*, p. 241.

54. Ibid., p. 241.

55. Ibid., p. 242.

56. Ibid., p. 242.

57. David Adler, "Darwin's Illness," *Israel Journal of Medical Sciences* 25(4) (April 1989): 218–221.

58. Colp Jr., *To Be an Invalid: The Illness of Charles Darwin*, p. 228.

59. Keith Stewart Thomson, "Laying Bare Darwin's Secrets," *American Scientist* 91(1) (2003): 75.

60. Barloon and Noyes Jr., "Charles Darwin and Panic Disorder," p. 140.

61. Colp Jr., *To Be an Invalid: The Illness of Charles Darwin*, p. 136.

62. Bowlby, *Charles Darwin: A New Life*, p. 240.

63. Charles Darwin, edited by Frederick Burkhardt et al., *The Correspondence of Charles Darwin, 1865, Supplement to the Correspondence 1822–1864*, Volume 13 (New York: Cambridge University Press, 2002), p. 482.

64. Ibid., p. 482.

65. Charles Darwin, edited by F. Burkhardt, *The Correspondence of Charles Darwin*, Volume 2 (Cambridge, England: Cambridge University Press, 1986), p. 51–52.

66. Darwin, *The Correspondence of Charles Darwin*, Volume 8, p. 227.

67. Picover, *Strange Brains and Genius: The Secret Lives of Eccentric Scientists and Madmen*, p. 289.

68. Colp Jr., *To Be an Invalid: The Illness of Charles Darwin*, p. 100.

69. Fabienne Smith, "Charles Darwin's Ill Health," *Journal of the History of Biology* 23(3) (1990): 443–459.

70. Saul Adler, "Darwin's Illness," *Nature* 184 (1959): 1102–1103; Picover, *Strange Brains and Genius: The Secret Lives of Eccentric Scientists and Madmen*, p. 290; Smith, "Charles Darwin's Ill Health"; D.A. Young, "Darwin's Illness and Systemic Lupus Erythematosus," *Notes Rec Royal Society of London* 51(1)

(January 1997): 77–86; Pasnau, "Darwin's Illness: A Biopsychosocial Perspective"; Jared Haft Goldstein, "Darwin, Chagas', Mind, and Body," *Perspectives in Biological Medicine* 32(4) (1989): 586–601.

71. Young, "Darwin's Illness and Systemic Lupus Erythematosus"; Jerry Bergman, "Was Charles Darwin Psychotic? A Study of His Mental Health," *Impact* #367 (2004).

72. Edward J. Rempf, "Charles Darwin: The Affective Sources of His Inspiration and Anxiety-Neurosis," *Psychoanalytic Review* 5 (1918): 151–192.

73. Pickering, *Creative Malady.*

74. Charles Darwin, edited by Nora Barlow, *The Autobiography of Charles Darwin 1809–1882* (New York: Norton, 1958), p. 144.

75. Richard Milner, "Putting Darwin in His Place," *Scientific American* 287(4) (October 2002): 103–104.

76. Medawar, "Darwin's Illness."

77. Colp Jr., *Darwin's Illness*; A.K. Campbell and S.B. Matthews, "Darwin's Illness Revealed," *Postgraduate Medicine Journal* 81(954) (April 2005): 248–251.

CHAPTER 6

Were Darwin's Mental Health Problems Due to His Conflicts with Theism?

Chapter Synopsis

The severe and varied mental health problems that Charles Darwin experienced as an adult were briefly reviewed. It was concluded that his religious conflicts, especially over the doctrine of evolution that he spent much of his life developing, likely played an integral role in his serious health and life difficulties. He likely had much guilt over his theory developed to, in his words, "murder God" by destroying the major reason for belief in God.

Introduction

As documented in chapter 5, for much of his adult life Charles Darwin suffered from various combinations of severe psychological (or psychologically influenced) health problems, including severe depression, fits of hysterical crying, shaking, severe anxiety, insomnia, fainting spells, muscle twitches, trembling, nausea, vomiting, depersonalization, visual hallucinations, malaise, vertigo, cramps, bloating and nocturnal flatulence, headaches, nervous exhaustion, dyspnea, tachycardia, tinnitus, and sensations of loss of consciousness and impending death.[1]

In an extensive study of Darwin's illness, George Pickering concluded that Darwin's mental problems became so severe as an adult that he became an "invalid recluse" after around age 30 and was largely confined to his home for almost a half century.[2] Of note is that Darwin's major symptoms began when he started to work on his evolution theory.[3]

That Darwin suffered from several severely disabling health problems is not debated; the only debate is over their exact cause.[4] Although Darwin consulted with over 20 doctors, the level of medical knowledge of his day prevented a definitive diagnosis. Furthermore, the treatments available then had only limited or temporary success.[5]

Unfortunately, most Darwin biographers have shied away from this topic, partly because Darwin is now idolized by most scientists and historians. Often listed as one of the greatest scientists of the 19th century, or even the greatest scientist that ever lived, Darwin is one of the few scientists known to most Americans. Nonetheless, Darwin's lifelong serious medical complaints have been the subject of much research and speculation for over a century. Dozens of scholarly articles and at least four books have detailed Darwin's many incapacitating health problems. The factor explored in this chapter is the influence of his loss of religious faith and acceptance of a materialistic, atheistic evolution theory on his mental and physical health.

The first clear evidence of his loss of belief in God was in his famous "notebooks" about biological transmutation, written from 1837 to 1840, which he filled with his thoughts about biological origins. In notebook "C" Darwin wrote that after he considered all of the evidence he had gathered up to that time, he "argued excitedly" that "the fabric falls." The "fabric was natural theology," the main evidence for God, today called the "cosmological argument" or "creationism."[6] Quammen asked, "Did it [his conclusion about natural theology and God] make him physically sick?" Evidence for this conclusion included the fact that "Darwin's work on the transmutation notebooks coincided with his early complaints about what became chronic bad health."[7]

Early Religious Tension

Charles Darwin's religious background was complex. Although the Darwin–Wedgwood family members were all reared as nominal Unitarians, Darwin's grandfather, Erasmus Darwin, and his father, Robert, both left the faith and became agnostic free-thinkers. Although Darwin's father complied with all of the Anglican (Church of England) requirements, and even reared his children in the faith, he did so only to conform to the early 19th century social climate.

As a youth, Darwin was a nominal orthodox Christian. Darwin also evidently accepted much of Paley's *Natural Theology* that argued for the existence of God from design. In a letter to John Lubbock dated November 22, 1859, Darwin wrote, "I do not think I hardly ever admired a book more than Paley's *Natural Theology*. I could almost formerly have said it by heart."[8]

As a young man, Darwin had considered becoming a country clergyman, and before studying at the University of Cambridge he claims that he "did not then in the least doubt the strict and literal truth of every word in the Bible," and even persuaded himself that the Church's creed must be fully accepted.[9]

However, Darwin was not a very diligent student at Cambridge, partly because he spent a great deal of his time shooting, collecting beetles, reading fiction, and partying with friends. Conversely, most of the clergyman biology professors at Cambridge who became Darwin's lifelong friends accepted an ancient earth but opposed evolutionism for reasons that included the fact that they felt the theory would undermine the stability of the social order. Although Darwin also had an Anglican education at Edinburgh University, he joined a student society where his tutors espoused Lamarckian biology and materialism.

Even on his five-year *HMS Beagle* voyage, Darwin at times still appealed to biblical authority to support Christian morality. While on the *Beagle*, Darwin also studied Lyell's book on geology, which advocated long-age, uniformitarian geology and this book likely began to change his thinking on theology. Nonetheless, he struggled religiously to the degree that Milner wrote Darwin "dreamt of being beheaded or hanged" due to his theory, and once even stated that evolution was a "belief that went so contrary to biblical authority [that it] was 'like confessing a murder,'" the murder of God.[10]

He read a great deal on religion and did much thinking on the topic when dealing with his religious crisis.[11] He struggled for decades over the conflicts in his mind over replacing faith in the Creator with faith in naturalism in order to explain all that exists. He wrote that this struggle was "a painful experience" that left him in a constant state of "bewilderment."[12] As late as January 11, 1844, Darwin still had doubts about his evolution theory when he wrote to his friend Joseph Hooker, stating that he was "almost convinced . . . that species are not . . . immutable."[13]

Darwin's belief in Christianity was also very shallow and slowly drifted away during this time, eventually dying completely. In his autobiography, Darwin wrote about his struggle to retain his religious beliefs, claiming that he was once very unwilling to give up these beliefs:

> I can well remember . . . inventing day-dreams of old letters between distinguished Romans and manuscripts being discovered at Pompeii or elsewhere which confirmed in the most striking manner all that was written in the Gospels. But I found it more and more difficult, with free scope given to my imagination, to invent evidence which would suffice to convince me. Thus disbelief crept over me at a very slow rate, but was at last complete. The rate was so slow that I felt no distress, and have never since doubted even for a single second that my conclusion was correct.[14]

One wonders how accurate his claim was about not feeling distress over his loss of faith.

Darwin's Loses the Comfort of God

Although he claimed that his loss of Christianity was so slow that it caused no distress, Brentnall and Grigg concluded that one "immediate effect of Darwin's rejection of the Bible was his loss of all comfort from it. The hopeless grief of his later letters to the bereaved contrasts sharply with the earlier letter of condolence."[15] On April 23, 1829, Darwin wrote the following touching words to his cousin to console him over the loss of his recently deceased sister: "I am assured [that you] well know where to look for ... support ... [namely in] the pure & holy a comfort as the Bible."[16]

When his favorite daughter Anne died in 1851, 22 years later, though, Darwin did not refer to the comfort found in the Bible, but rather of despair — there "was no life beyond the grave; Anne was gone forever."[17]

There was at this time for Darwin "no straw to clutch, no promised resurrection. Christian faith was futile."[18] For example, Darwin wrote on April 29, 1851, about his daughter Anne that "Thank God she suffered hardly at all. . . . Our only consolation is, that she passed a short, though joyous life."[19] He added, "We have lost the joy of the household, and the solace of our old age."[20]

Two years after Anne died, Darwin stoically wrote on August 10, 1853, to a close friend — his second cousin Rev. Fox, who had also lost a child — that "time softens and deadens . . . one's feelings and regrets."[21] No words of condolence or encouragement, only a mundane "you will get over it" response. Barbour noted that Darwin approached his life in his autobiography "as if examining a scientific specimen that demonstrates universal laws."[22] When Hooker's wife died unexpectedly, all Darwin could do was to encourage him to try to cover his harrowing thoughts by hard work.[23] This advice was not very helpful: Hooker had six children, three were then still very young.

Fanny had held the household together, helped him write and proof-read, and escorted dignitaries around Kew, being a botanical Henslow herself. She had been the perfect partner for twenty-three years. . . . Now he felt as though he were wandering again in the Himalayas, cut off, desperately alone. He entered "a sort of trance," scarcely able to fathom the calamity. The prospect of returning home after the funeral stunned him, and he begged refuge at Downe. The house . . . turned into a hospice, with Hooker staying for a few days and leaving the children to Emma's care. Returning home he was unable to function. "Utter desolation" overcame him as he stepped into his house at Kew, and his first impulse was to return to the Darwins.[24]

Darwin's loss of religion's comfort was also illustrated by the situation of his close friend Charles Lyell. Close to blind and in very poor health when his wife died, Darwin could "offer little comfort" to his close lifelong friend.[25] Darwin "knew that if he were blind and without Emma 'facing the end, the problem of the hereafter would recur in the dead of the night with painful force.' "[26]

Darwin's Marriage to a Devout Christian

Both Darwin's mother and his wife, Emma, were devout Unitarians. Darwin's father, speaking from experience, warned Charles before he proposed to Emma that "some women suffered miserably by doubting about the salvation of their husbands, thus making them likewise to suffer."[27] When Darwin informed Emma about his religious doubts, she became deeply concerned about the dangers of his agnosticism to his afterlife as expressed in the Gospel: "If a man abide not in me . . . they are burned" (John 15:6; KJV). Darwin wrote that even as a young adult he was a skeptic, and that before he was engaged to Emma, his father advised him to carefully conceal his religious doubts because he had known the "extreme misery" that this had caused married couples:

My father added that he had known during his whole life only three women who were skeptics; and it should be remembered that he knew well a multitude of persons. . . . When I asked him who the three women were, he had to own with respect to one of them, his sister-in-law Kitty Wedgwood, that he had no good evidence, only the vaguest hints, aided by the conviction that so clear-sighted a woman could not be a believer. At the present time, with my small acquaintance, I know (or have known) several married ladies, who believe very little more than their husbands.[28]

Nonetheless, Emma married him even though Darwin felt he as a man was physically "repellently plain." Emma, a spinster a few months older than Darwin, was at that time very eager to get married.[29] Darwin's anxiety was also "related to the fact that his wife, Emma, strongly disapproved of the religious consequences of his theory" of evolution.[30] Her disapproval of his evolutionist ideas was an indication of what the public reaction would be to his books, a fact that must have increased Darwin's "anxiety and torment" over his theory.[31]

Nonetheless, Emma remained fully supportive of her husband's research throughout their marriage. She even read to him and helped him in his work by reviewing his writings, making notes in the margins to point out unclear passages, and noting where she disagreed. As Charles' illness progressed, she nursed him, ensured that he did not overwork, made him take holiday breaks, and always helped him to continue with his lifelong work of proving evolution. However, Emma suffered due to Darwin's loss of faith. Browne writes that Emma received

> consolation in Christian assurances about immortality. Her church's doctrines assured her that she would meet her children and other loved ones in heaven. Darwin confronted mortality in solitude and isolation. Old or young, death came knocking. In retrospect, it seems possible that Emma may have suffered twice over from not being able to share religious consolation with her doubting husband.[32]

In view of Darwin's blatant materialism, how can we explain Darwin's accommodations to theism in his public writings? West notes, "Some of his comments were undoubtedly designed to disarm popular prejudices."[33] An example is Darwin's concluding sentence in *The Origin of Species*, where he wrote "life . . . having been originally breathed by the Creator into a few forms or into one"[34] was written to make his work more palatable to the general public.

We know this because after a hostile reviewer attempted to use this passage from Darwin's book to defend his belief in a Creator, Darwin wrote to a friend, "I have long regretted that I truckled to public opinion, and used the Pentateuchal term of creation, by which I really meant 'appeared' by some wholly unknown process."[35]

Darwin's observation in *The Descent of Man* that the existence of "a Creator and Ruler of the universe" had been affirmed "by the highest intellects that have ever lived," was undercut by Darwin's rejection of the divine origin of religion. Rather, he believed that religion had evolved.[36] The statement may also reflect the judicious editing of Darwin's daughter Henrietta, who was charged by her father with toning down *The Descent of Man* manuscript.[37] In fact, Darwin replaced sectarian religion with secular religion, a change that revolutionized society in ways that neither Darwin nor his early disciples could imagine.

Guilt Over His Writings

Darwin's great-great-grandson, Randal Keynes, concluded from unpublished family documents that, underlying Darwin's health concerns "were his anxieties about the theory of evolution, the strain of living with the secret, and his anticipation of the attacks when he announced it and people saw the implications. When he completed the text of *The Origin of Species*, he wrote in a letter to Rev. Fox dated February 12, 1859 that this book was the cause of 'the main part of the ills which my flesh is heir to.' "[38] Bowler added that during the period when Darwin's illness flared up he could do no work and was completely dependent on Emma to nurse him. He had genuine fears that he would not live to complete his work and, as we shall see, took steps to ensure that Emma would arrange for publication of the theory [of evolution] in the event of his death.[39]

The rapid onset of his sickness is strong evidence that his incapacitating illness was psychological in origin. His health problems "invariably flared up in times of stress" and, significantly, his writing on evolution especially "produced illness and collapse."[40] This fact indicates Darwin may have had internal conflicts over his materialistic theory of origins and/or his loss of belief in God. Criticism of his work by scientists caused mental and physical problems, such as faintness and severe anxiety that interfered with his work and sleep.[41]

For a combination of reasons, including guilt over his work and opposition he expected he would face from scientists and others, Darwin was also in acute emotional turmoil around the time he published his *Origin of Species* in 1859. Darwin's anxiety was so great that he corrected the proofs of this book

> amid fits of vomiting. During that whole time he had rarely been able to write free of stomach pains for more than twenty minutes at a stretch. The next day . . . Darwin felt a cold shudder surge through him once more. The howling wind was as nothing to the storm of self-doubt, his nagging, gnawing fear that "I have devoted my life to a fantasy and a dangerous one. . . ." God knows what the public will think.[42]

As Bean concluded, Darwin's psychoneurosis was "provoked and exaggerated by his evolutionary ideas."[43] Darwin was clearly worried by the implications of his ideas and wanted to avoid distressing not only his wife, but also his friends. At both universities Darwin attended, he saw how evolution was associated with radicals seeking to overthrow society and how publicly supporting such ideas could lead to problems in society.

As expected, Darwin's evolutionary theory set off a firestorm of controversy that Darwin followed closely while allowing his disciples, including Thomas Huxley and Joseph Hooker, to defend his ideas for him. Darwin's concern was indicated by the fact that "he clipped, cataloged and indexed hundreds of offprints, about 350 reviews and 1,600 articles," plus satires, parodies, and caricatures with which he filled several large scrapbooks.[44]

That criticism of his work greatly troubled Darwin is illustrated by the fact that, after Charles Lyell published a very weak endorsement of his *Antiquity of Man,* "Darwin's disappointment brought on 10 days of vomiting, faintness and stomach distress." When anatomist St. George Mivart attacked *The Descent of Man,* it "triggered two months of 'giddiness' and inability to work."[45] Darwin's writings at the time of the publication of his theory suggest he was experiencing much emotional turmoil. What is not clear is if his anxiety was due largely to concerns that his theory would disgrace him and his friends, or if it was more a result of his loss of faith in theism and Christianity.

The fact that his friends supported him, as did many scientists and even clergy, supports the view that his own personal conflicts were more important. In fact, his book was favorably reviewed in many journals and newspapers and sold out to book dealers on the first day it was released. Even after his theory was widely accepted, Darwin still suffered from major health problems due to his own doubts. Even Darwin's facial eczema was attributed to the controversies over his evolutionist ideas.[46]

When Hooker, "who is our best British biologist and perhaps the best in the world," finally accepted evolution as a result of Darwin's working on him, Darwin wrote that he was "a full convert, and is now going immediately to publish his confession of faith."[47] Although Darwin seemed happy at this turn of events, as an avid proselytizer of his theory, he may also have felt guilt over his goal to convert the world to his pessimistic view.

Guilt Over His Life Work

Other observers, including Darwin's own wife, also concluded that his mental problem stemmed in part from guilt over his life's goal to refute the argument for God from design.[48] Darwin realized his writing argued that the "natural world has no moral validity or purpose.... Animals and plants are not the product of special design or special creation," and, as a result of this teaching, could destroy "all hope of heavenly reunion with loved ones" for countless men and women and the "consolation in the idea of an afterlife."[49] He wrote in his autobiography that "all the planets will in time grow too cold for life ... it is an intolerable thought that [humans] ... and all other sentient beings are doomed to complete annihilation," adding that, to those who believe in the "immorality of the human soul, the destruction of our world will not appear so dreadful."[50]

However, he was not fully convinced of his own theory as revealed by a letter he wrote on November 26, 1860 to Asa Gray about the problem of design, noting that he was "in an utterly hopeless muddle. I cannot think that the world, as we see it, is the result of chance; & yet I cannot look at each separate thing as a result of Design."[51]

His nagging, gnawing fear about murdering God caused a "cold shudder to run through" him because of his fear that he had devoted his "life to a fantasy ... an illusion," and a "dangerous one" at that.[52] He feared that if his theory was false and there, in fact, was a divine Creator, he not only wasted his life, but may have forfeited his afterlife as his wife had feared. The psychoanalytic studies on Darwin have often argued that his problems were a result of his "slaying of his heavenly father" by his theory.[53]

Darwin even wrote that his theory was "a mere rag of an hypothesis with as many flaws & holes as sound parts."[54] In a December 24, 1859, letter to Asa Gray, Darwin wrote, "I am *sure* to be in error in many parts; but my general view, I conclude, must have some truth in it — There are however many *bitter* opponents."[55]

Darwin wrote that, although he was a "strong" believer in the "general truth" of his evolutionary ideas, he still had doubts as late as 1860. In February of 1860, he wrote to Asa Gray, "About the weak points I agree. The eye to this day gives me a cold shudder, but when I think of the fine known gradations, my reason tells me I ought to conquer the cold shudder."[56]

In April of 1860, Darwin again wrote to Asa Gray about his doubts: "I remember well the time when the thought of the eye made me cold all over, but I have got over this stage of the complaint, & now small trifling particulars of structure often make me feel uncomfortable. The sight of a feather in a peacock's tail, whenever I gaze at it, makes me sick!"[57] Also in April of 1860, Darwin wrote to Charles Lyell, "For the life of me I cannot see any difficulty in Natural selection producing the most exquisite structure, *if such structure can be arrived at by gradation*; & I know from experience how hard it is to name any structure towards which at least some gradations are not known."[58] The eye still creates trouble for those who hold to the evolutionist position of origins:

> It's one of the oldest riddles in evolutionary biology: How does natural selection gradually create an eye, or any complex organ for that matter? The puzzle troubled Charles Darwin, who nevertheless gamely nailed together a just-so story of how it might have happened — from photoreceptor cells to highly refined orbits — by drawing examples from living organisms such as mollusks and arthropods. But holes in this progression have persistently bothered evolutionary biologists and left openings that creationists have been only too happy to exploit.[59]

Lastly, in his biography Darwin wrote the following about his publicly stated position on agnosticism:

> Formerly I was led . . . to the firm conviction of the existence of God, and of the immortality of the soul. In my Journal I

wrote that whilst standing in the midst of the grandeur of a Brazilian forest, "it is not possible to give an adequate idea of the higher feelings of wonder, admiration, and devotion, which fill and elevate the mind." I well remember my conviction that there is more in man than the mere breath of his body. But now the grandest scenes would not cause any such convictions and feelings to rise in my mind.[60]

As late as February 28, 1882, only six weeks before he died, Darwin wrote to geologist Daniel Mackintosh that proof of God from the design argument that he had fought for most of his life to destroy "was a perplexing subject, on which I often thought, but could not see my way clearly."[61]

Conclusions

Darwin was clearly a very troubled man and suffered from severe emotional problems for most of his adult life, especially when he was actively developing his evolution theory. The exact cause of his many mental and physical problems has been much debated and may never be known for certain.[62] One factor that clearly adversely influenced his mental and physical problems was the conflict in his mind about both the truth and the implications of his evolution theory for theism. Since Darwin wrote extensively about his mental and physical problems, we have much material on which to base a reasonable conclusion about this area of his life.

Darwin clearly was a complex, but very troubled man. Recent historical investigations increasingly support the conclusion that psychological factors related to his doubts were likely a major cause of his illness. Herbert wrote that Darwin's evolutionary worldview was responsible for his pessimistic outlook on life, specifically because Darwin "had come to believe that the universe, and even himself, would be annihilated — everything would cease to exist!"[63]

Some argue that Darwin's admirers were slow to recognize the seriousness of his psychological problems because of the social stigma of psychologically related illnesses. Darwin's fame is such that Michael White opined that, for biologists today, "Darwin is second only to God, and for many he might rank still higher."[64] Steven Jay Gould wrote that all early theories of origins cited God for their support, and "Darwin comes close to this status [a god] among evolutionary biologists."[65] Admitting Darwin's own doubts and misgivings about his theory and life no doubt would detract considerably from Darwin's godlike image. Yet he founded a religion, the secular religion of evolution that, for many, replaced the theistic religions.[66] McKie summarized Darwin's legacy, writing:

> Darwin's eyes had been opened to the unforgiving processes that drive evolution . . . as he wrote elsewhere: "All Nature is war." This pitiless vision — which stressed blind chance as the main determiner in the struggle for survival and the course of evolution — was upsetting for Victorians. . . . Nevertheless, this is the version of natural selection which has since been supported by a century and a half of observation and which is now accepted by virtually every scientist on earth. It has not been a happy process, of course. Even today, natural selection holds a special status among scientific theories as being the one that it is still routinely rejected and attacked . . . [and] adamantly reject the idea that humanity . . . descended from ape-like ancestors.[67]

Such is the sad legacy of Charles Robert Darwin. We have learned much about Darwin in the last decade, thanks to a number of intrepid researchers who have doggedly researched Darwin's voluminous correspondence, and the picture emerging has increasingly supported the view documented here.[68]

Endnotes

1. Clifford A. Picover, *Strange Brains and Genius: The Secret Lives of Eccentric Scientists and Madmen* (New York: Quill William Morrow, 1998), p. 290; Thomas Barloon and Russel Noyes Jr., "Charles Darwin and Panic Disorder," *JAMA*, 277(2) (1997):138–141; William B. Bean, "The Illness of Charles

Darwin," *The American Journal of Medicine*, 65(4) (October 1978):572–574; Ralph Colp Jr., *To Be an Invalid: The Illness of Charles Darwin* (Chicago, IL: University of Chicago Press, 1977), p. 97; Peter Brent, *Charles Darwin: A Man of Enlarged Curiosity* (New York, NY: Harper and Row, 1981).

2. George Pickering, *Creative Malady* (New York: Oxford University Press, 1974), p. 34.

3. David Herbert, *Charles Darwin's Religious Views: From Creationist to Evolutionist*, revised and expanded edition (Guelph, Ontario, Canada: Joshua Press, 2009), p. 99.

4. R.O. Pasnau, "Darwin's Illness: A Biopsychosocial Perspective," *Psychosomatics* 31(2) (1990):121–128; Norm Ledgin, *Asperger's and Self-Esteem: Insight and Hope through Famous Role Models* (Arlington, TX: Future Horizons, 2002).

5. A.W. Woodruff, "Darwin's Illness," *Israel Journal of Medical Sciences* 26(3) (March 1990):163–164.

6. David Quammen, *The Kiwi's Egg, Charles Darwin & Natural Selection* (London: Weidenfeld & Nicolson, 2007), p. 37.

7. Ibid., p. 37.

8. Charles Darwin, edited by F. Burkhardt, *The Correspondence of Charles Darwin*, Volume 7 (New York: Cambridge University Press, 1991), p. 388.

9. Charles Darwin, Nora Barlow, *The Autobiography of Charles Darwin 1809–1882* (New York: Norton, 1958), p. 57.

10. Richard Milner, *Encyclopedia of Evolution* (New York: Facts on File, 1990), p. 113.

11. John Bowlby, *Charles Darwin; A New Life* (New York: Norton, 1990), p. 226.

12. Charles Darwin, *The Life and Letters of Charles Darwin* (New York, NY: Appleton, 1896), 1:274.

13. Charles Darwin, edited by F. Burkhardt, *The Correspondence of Charles Darwin*, Volume 3 (New York: Cambridge University Press, 1987), p. 2.

14. Charles Darwin, edited by Nora Barlow, *The Autobiography of Charles Darwin 1809–1882* (New York: Norton, 1958), p. 86–87.

15. John M. Brentnall and Russell M. Grigg, "Darwin's Slippery Slide into Unbelief," *Creation* 18(1) (December 1995): p. 35.

16. Charles Darwin, edited by F. Burkhardt, *The Correspondence of Charles Darwin*, Volume 5 (New York: Cambridge University Press, 1989), Vol. 1, p. 84.

17. Herbert, *Charles Darwin's Religious Views: From Creationist to Evolutionist*, p. 97.

18. Adrian Desmond and James Moore, *Darwin: The life of a Tormented Evolutionist* (New York: Warner Books, 1991), p. 384.

19. Darwin, *The Correspondence of Charles Darwin*, p. 32.

20. Ibid., p. 542.

21. Ibid., p. 151.

22. John D. Barbour, *Versions of Deconversion: Autobiography and the Loss of Faith* (Charlottesville, VA: University Press of Virginia, 1994), p. 59.

23. Desmond and Moore, *Darwin: The life of a Tormented Evolutionist*, p. 612.

24. Ibid., p. 612.

25. Ibid., p. 612.

26. Ibid., p. 612.

27. Darwin, *The Autobiography of Charles Darwin 1809–1882*, p. 95.

28. Ibid., p. 95–96.

29. Bowlby, *Charles Darwin; A New Life*, p. 226.

30. Bean, "The Illness of Charles Darwin," p. 574.

31. Ibid., p. 574.

32. Janet Browne, *The Power of Place: Charles Darwin* (New York: Knopf, 2002), p. 45.

33. John West, *Darwin Day in America: How our Politics and Culture Have Been Dehumanized in the Name of Science* (Wilmington, DE: Intercollegiate Studies Institute, 2007), p. 37.

34. Charles Darwin, *The Origin of Species* (London: John Murray, 1859), p. 490.

35. Charles Darwin, *More Letters of Charles Darwin* (New York, NY: Appleton, 1903), p. 272.

36. Charles Darwin, *The Descent of Man, and Selection in Relation to Sex*, Volume 1 (London: John Murray, 1871), p. 65.

37. Desmond and Moore, Darwin: The life of a Tormented Evolutionist, p. 573.

38. Darwin, *The Correspondence of Charles Darwin*, Volume 7, p. 247.

39. Peter J. Bowler, *Charles Darwin: The Man and His Influence* (Cambridge, MA: Basil Blackwell, 1990), p. 93.

40. Keith Stewart Thomson, "Laying Bare Darwin's Secrets," *American Scientist* 91(1) (2003): 72–73.

41. Ralph Colp Jr., *Darwin's Illness* (Gainesville, FL: University Press of Florida, 2008), p. 85–86.

42. Desmond and Moore, *Darwin: The life of a Tormented Evolutionist*, p. 476–477.

43. Bean, "The Illness of Charles Darwin," p. 574.

44. Richard Milner, 2002. "Putting Darwin in His Place," *Scientific American* 287(4) (October 2002): 103.

45. Ibid., p. 104.

46. Colp Jr., *To Be an Invalid: The Illness of Charles Darwin.*

47. Darwin, *More Letters of Charles Darwin*, p. 1:119.

48. Russell Grigg, "Darwin's Mystery Illness," *Creation Ex Nihilo* 17(4) (1995): 28; Pasnau, "Darwin's Illness: A Biopsychosocial Perspective," p. 126.

49. Browne, *The Power of Place: Charles Darwin*, p. 54, 67.

50. Darwin, *The Autobiography of Charles Darwin 1809–1882*, p. 92.

51. Charles Darwin, edited by F. Burkhardt, *The Correspondence of Charles Darwin*, Volume 8 (New York: Cambridge University Press, 1993), p. 496.

52. Darwin, *The Correspondence of Charles Darwin*, Volume 7, p. 392; Desmond and Moore, *Darwin: The life of a Tormented Evolutionist*, p. 477.

53. Pasnau, "Darwin's Illness: A Biopsychosocial Perspective," p. 122.

54. Darwin, *More Letters of Charles Darwin*, p. 64.

55. Darwin, *The Correspondence of Charles Darwin*, Volume 7, p. 446, emphasis in original.

56. Darwin, *The Correspondence of Charles Darwin*, Volume 8, p. 75.

57. Ibid., p. 140.

58. Ibid., p. 161, emphasis in original.

59. Virginia Morell, "Placentas May Nourish Complexity Studies," *Science* 298 (November 1, 2002):945.

60. Darwin, *The Life and Letters of Charles Darwin*, p. 281.

61. Darwin, *More Letters of Charles Darwin*, p. 2:171.

62. Ralph Colp Jr., "The Dueling Diagnosis of Darwin," *JAMA*, 8;277(2) (January 1997):138–41; Ralph Colp Jr., "More on Darwin's illness," *History of Science* 38(120 Pt 2) (June 2000):219–36; Colp Jr., *Darwin's Illness*.

63. Herbert, *Charles Darwin's Religious Views: From Creationist to Evolutionist*, p. 136.

64. Michael White, *Rivals: Conflict as the Fuel of Science* (London: Vintage, 2002), p. 131.

65. Steven Jay Gould, "Sociobiology: The Art of Storytelling," *New Scientist* 80(1129) (November 16, 1978):531.

66. Michael Ruse, "Is Evolution a Secular Religion?" *Science* 299 (2003):1523–1524.

67. Robin McKie, "How Darwin Won the Evolution Race," *The Observer*, June 22, 2008.

68. Thomson, "Laying Bare Darwin's Secrets."

CHAPTER 7

Darwin's Passion for Hunting and Killing

Chapter Synopsis

This chapter documents Darwin's sadistic side, especially his inordinate love of killing animals. Later in life he acknowledged his abnormal behavior. This sadistic drive of Darwin was then related to the development of his theory of the origins of life that involved death as the creator called natural selection. It is ironic that Darwin condemned God for the behavior that he displayed as a youth and young man.

Introduction

One side of Charles Darwin rarely discussed in either the popular or the scientific literature was his powerful sadistic bent. One of his passions reflecting this was his love for killing animals, hunting, and guns. Shooting and hunting were not unusual activities in 19th-century England, but Darwin carried it far beyond that of most of his contemporaries. Many people hunt for food and/or for sport, then as well as now, but rarely engage in wanton killing purely for the pleasure of killing as Darwin did. With Darwin it was an obsession that involved behavior which, at the least, bordered on sadism.

Early hints of this dark side included Darwin's propensity to lie and steal in order to create excitement and get attention. In his own words, "As a little boy I was much given to inventing deliberate falsehoods, and this was always done for the sake of causing excitement."[1] Darwin also admitted to stealing solely for fun.[2] A clearer example of his sadistic impulse was when, as a young boy, Darwin "beat a puppy . . . simply from enjoying the sense of power." He even admitted that he later felt much guilt over his behavior, indicating that he knew his actions were wrong.[3] At this time, he still had a strong faith in God, and this fact may partly explain his guilt.[4]

Darwin's Sadistic Impulses

Although Darwin first learned to handle a gun before he was 15 years old, it evidently did not become a passion for him until he killed his first animal. He was then hooked. His "passion for shooting . . . would stay with him through all the years of his formal schooling and some years beyond."[5] Darwin loved killing so much that when he killed his first bird, he literally trembled with excitement. His own words, recorded in his biography, provide a vivid illustration of just how important killing animals was to him:

> In the latter part of my school life I became passionately fond of shooting, and *I do not believe that anyone could have shown more zeal for the most holy cause than I did for shooting birds.* How well I remember killing my first snipe, and my excitement was so great that I had much difficulty in reloading my gun from the trembling of my hands. This taste long continued and I became a very good shot.[6]

He also wrote in his autobiography, "How I did enjoy shooting,"[7] and "If there is bliss on earth, that is it."[8] He even declared: "My zeal was so great that I used to place my shooting boots open by my bed-side when I went to bed, so as not to lose half-a-minute in putting them on in the morning" to enable him to rush outside to kill something with minimal delay.[9] Darwin's cousin, Bessy Galton, discussed the beginning of Charles' love of guns and shooting:

> When about 15, he was staying with us and went out with my Father to practice shooting. On his return we asked if he

had been successful. "Oh," said my Father, "the birds sat upon the tree and laughed at him." Some time after my Father and Brothers went to Shrewsbury. My Father had hardly sat down, when Charles begged him to come out on the lawn, where he threw up a glove and hit it shooting, without missing, two or three times.[10]

Croft wrote that on the one hand, Darwin

presented himself as a humane naturalist, yet at the same time, he could still enjoy a passion for killing game with the shot-gun. He also enjoyed exhibiting his skill at being able to kill birds and rabbits by hurling stones.[11]

Evidently, William Owen taught him to shoot.[12] By 1828, his ambitions for killing animals had outgrown his equipment. He wanted a more powerful double-barreled gun, and so petitioned his family for the funds to purchase a new one. He threatened them with dire consequences if he was forced to continue using his old gun, which he claimed could, at any moment, "destroy the aforesaid Charles Darwin's legs, arms, body & brains."[13] Not long thereafter he was given a new gun. His gun became his best friend, which he took with him as a student at Cambridge University to practice. When he was not able to go outside, he practiced shooting in his room! While at Cambridge, he joined the "sporting set" and "did a good deal of drinking, hunting, and riding."[14]

Harvard Professor Browne claimed that after about 1826, every summer and autumn of Darwin's youth was dedicated to killing animals. Non-shooting months were passed by "studying handbooks about guns and in writing down useful information about the diameter of shot" needed to kill different animals.[15] Darwin gleaned numerous books, such as *Instructions for Young Sportsmen by an Old Sportsman*, for their advice to help him improve his already considerable skills in killing animals. His "beloved shooting" clearly came first in his life.[16]

His passion for hunting was so great that Darwin had much difficulty waiting until hunting season to stalk his prey. To solve this problem he weighed "the financial penalties for killing game out of season" and, after considering the fact that "no common person or gamekeeper can demand your certificate without producing his own," he thought about ignoring the law and hunting out of season.[17] He was also very aware of his obsession with shooting and killing animals because, as he once said, "I must have been half-consciously ashamed of my zeal, for I tried to persuade myself that shooting was almost an intellectual employment."[18]

His passion for shooting was well-known and, as a young man, was greater than for any other activity, although later in life his love for science became more important. Browne noted:

> The only object that could possibly have matched a microscope in Darwin's affections at that time was a gun; and a gun he already had. Shooting completely dominated those thoughts not given over to beetles.[19]

Darwin admitted that shooting animals was for a long time even more important than science:

> I visited Barmouth to see some Cambridge friends who were reading there, and thence returned to Shrewsbury and to Maer for shooting; for at that time I should have thought myself mad to give up the first days of partridge-shooting for geology or any other science.[20]

Darwin even compiled an elaborate system to accurately record his numerous killings. His list was subdivided into groups such as partridges, hares, and pheasants in order to keep a running total of everything he killed each season.[21] The importance of killing animals was also indicated by Darwin's following experience:

> I kept an exact record of every bird which I shot throughout the whole season. One day when shooting at Woodhouse with Captain Owen, the eldest son and Major Hill, his

cousin . . . I thought myself shamefully used, for every time after I had fired and thought that I had killed a bird, one of the two acted as if loading his gun and cried out, "You must not count that bird, for I fired at the same time," and the gamekeeper perceiving the joke, backed them up. After some hours they told me the joke, but it was no joke to me for I had shot a large number of birds, but did not know how many, and could not add them to my list. . . . This my wicked friends had perceived.[22]

Browne concluded that his sporting ledger was as important to him emotionally as was shooting itself, indicating an obsession similar to a murderer who notches his gun after each killing. Even Darwin's own father saw his obsession as a problem. He once said that Charles cared "for nothing but shooting, dogs, and rat-catching," and, as a result, was a "disgrace" to himself and his entire family.[23]

He not only gave shooting his wholehearted attention," but as a young man all kinds of "undiluted enjoyment was uppermost in his mind" such as drinking and partying.[24] Later in life Darwin had some regrets about spending so much time shooting as a youth, but he never expressed any regrets for his sadistic behavior, only his obsession with it. According to Bowler, Darwin's passion for shooting survived into his "university days, to be repudiated eventually as useless slaughter."[25] Croft claimed his shooting was not just useless slaughter, but much worse. In his home in the city of Down, England, Darwin

performed extensive experimentation on rabbits, so much so, that in one of his letters he referred to his laboratory as his "chamber of horrors" going on to describe how he

murdered an angelic little fantail and a pouter at ten days old. I tried to chloroform and ether for the first and though evidently a perfectly easy death it was prolonged; for the second I tried putting lumps of cyanide of potassium in a large damp bottle, half an hour before putting in the pigeon.

He apparently had no qualms regarding this sort of cruelty because he believed that the progress of scientific investigation justified it. In a letter to professor Holmgren of Uppsala, he explained his philosophy:

> Physiology cannot possibly progress except by means of experiments on living animals, and I feel he who retards the progress of physiology commits a crime against mankind.[26]

When Darwin was on his five-year-long *H.M.S. Beagle* voyage he continued to actively shoot animals whenever the opportunity arose. For example, when the ship landed on the Brazilian coast, Darwin had a "marvelous morning . . . whooping and killing birds with abandon."[27] He thought gannet and tern were so stupid that he said, "I could have killed any number of them with my geological hammer," behavior that reminds one of the behavior that lead to the extinction of one of the most common birds in America, the American passenger pigeon.[28]

How many birds Darwin killed with his hammer he did not say but, regardless of the number, this is a brutal way to kill any animal. FitzRoy wrote that Darwin "picked up his hammer and began killing the peaceful birds and away went the hammer, with all the force of his own right arm."[29] On this trip Darwin

> displayed particular delight in harassing the sea and land iguanas. Both types struck him as "stupid." . . . He pulled a land iguana by the tail simply to see its shocked reaction. "I opened the stomach of several," Darwin wrote of both types, "and found them full of vegetable fibers."[30]

Darwin also would kill small mammals, such as rabbits, by throwing rocks at them, and his son Francis noted that he was "good at killing animals in this way."[31]

Darwin's love of killing even extended to humans, at least those persons that he regarded as primitive humans or what he called "cannibals." When Darwin learned he was able to go on the exploration trip on the *Beagle* he excitedly told a school friend, "It is such capital fun ordering things, today I ordered a Rifle & 2 pair of pistols; for we shall have plenty of fighting with those d--- Cannibals: It would be something to shoot the king of the Cannibals Islands."[32]

On his *H.M.S. Beagle* trip a guard ship fired a blank at their ship. Unaware that it was a blank, Captain Fitzroy threatened to sink the ship. Fitzroy complained to the captain of another ship, the *H.M.S. Druid*, and promised to sail to the ship that fired at the *H.M.S. Beagle* and demand an apology. Darwin, anxious for violence, hoped that the guard ship would likewise fire at the *H.M.S. Druid*, so that the *Druid* would fire back and sink the guard ship!

A little while later the chief of police begged FitzRoy to help quell a riot by the local Negroes. FitzRoy sent 50 well-armed soldiers to make peace with them. Darwin followed and "secretly longed to swish a cutlass or put a dagger between his teeth" and join in the fighting. The Negroes, though, capitulated easily, way too easily for Darwin. Darwin was very "disappointed in not seeing any gunfire" or violence.[33]

His "sporting enthusiasms" even included one of the most violent and inhumane of all sports, fox hunting, using killer dogs.[34] One wonders if Darwin's "passion" for killing and death might have played a part in developing his ruthless "survival of the fittest" red-tooth-and-claw theory of natural selection in which death became a positive force for good:

> Darwin clearly viewed death and destruction as an engine of evolutionary progress, as we see in the penultimate sentence of *The Origin of Species*: "Thus, from the war of nature, from famine and death, the most exalted object which we are capable of conceiving, namely, the production of the higher animals, directly follows."[35]

He thus glorified death, and instead of the biblical "enemy," death became our creator, a force for evolutionary progress. Furthermore, death was also significant because Darwin taught that the elimination of the weak was required to promote the progress of every species.[36] Did Darwin think that by his actions, he was doing his part to kill off the weaker animals and further the upward progress of evolution?

His Family's Attitude Toward Killing

Charles' attitude toward killing contrasts greatly with that of several members of his family. His sister concluded it was not proper even to kill insects for collections, and that "dead ones would have to do."[37] Darwin acquiesced to her ideals, once stating that it "was not right to kill insects for the sake of making a collection."[38]

Darwin ignored this ideal and collected with abandon.[39] Darwin's attitude toward killing for collections also contrasts with that of certain renowned biologists. For example, Professor August Forel said that as a child he was allowed to collect only dead insects. Then, in 1859, he was allowed to collect living specimens after his uncle, also an entomologist, showed him how to kill the creatures painlessly.[40]

Darwin said of his father, even though a doctor, "The thought of an operation almost sickened him and he could scarcely endure to see a person bleed."[41] One wonders what to make of Darwin's claim that, while still in medical school, he sat in on two "bad operations," one on a child, but he left the class before they were completed, "this being long before the blessed days of chloroform."[42]

Darwin had no such qualms about "stuffing birds," an area in which he took lessons to develop his taxidermist skills.[43] He even "delighted in carrying out dissections . . . of living animals."[44] This was before anesthesia, when ripping out the innards of animals caused them to suffer greatly. Until about the time he married, Darwin "showed no qualms about shooting birds and animals, energetically . . . dining off turtles, alpacas, and armadillos with all the gusto of an unconcerned sailor."[45]

Darwin's behavior is especially ironic in view of his complaint that God is sadistic. In a letter to his friend Professor Hooker, dated July 13, 1856, Darwin said in reference to flower pollen "in which nature seems to us so clumsy & wasteful" that "What a book a Devil's chaplain might write on the clumsy, wasteful, blundering low & horridly cruel works of nature!"[46] In another letter Darwin sent to Professor Asa Gray, dated May 22, 1860, Darwin wrote that he could not believe in the Christian creator God because there is so much misery in the world. The example he gave was:

> I cannot persuade myself that a beneficent & omnipotent God would have designedly created the Ichneumonidae [a parasitic insect] with the express intention of their feeding within the living bodies of caterpillars or that a cat should play with mice.[47]

Some may see it as the height of irony that Darwin argued the Christian God does not exist because he thought God did the very same things that Darwin himself enjoyed doing as a youth!

Browne claims that Darwin "ultimately came to hate killing animals" yet he dissected animals until late in his life, as his many books relate in detail. Darwin claimed that he gave up shooting only when his "'primeval instincts' yielded to the acquired tastes of a civilized man."[48] In 1836, Browne wrote that by then Darwin had "virtually given up shooting, viewing his former exploits as the activities of a barbarian, or at least of an uncouth, unthinking oaf" concluding that "killing animals for pleasure [as he once did] was wrong."[49] Obviously, he recognized that his behavior was barbarian and morally wrong, if not sadistic.

Conclusions

Darwin was psychologically a very troubled man for most of his life.[50] He evidently suffered from an inordinate sadistic desire to kill animals for much of his life, especially when he was a young man in the prime of life. Unfortunately, most scholars and writers have ignored the implications of this trait of Darwin's, indicating only that he liked to hunt — hardly an accurate assessment of his behavior. Many men hunt to put food on the table, but Darwin's obsession went well beyond this. He loved to kill and, apparently, loved to see animals suffer.

One possible reason why many writers avoid this topic is because Darwin is now idolized by many scientists and others. Often listed as one of the greatest scientists of the 19th century, if not the greatest scientist that ever lived, Darwin is one of the few scientists known to most Americans.[51] To understand Darwin as a person and his motivations, though, one must evaluate his almost pathological drive to kill, and consider how it may have affected his conclusions about natural selection.

Endnotes

1. Charles Darwin, edited by Nora Barlow, *The Autobiography of Charles Darwin 1809–1882* (New York: W.W. Norton, 1958), p.23.

2. Ibid., p. 24.

3. Ibid., p. 27.

4. Ibid., p. 25.

5. Barry G. Gale, *Evolution without Evidence: Charles Darwin and the Origin of Species* (Albuquerque, NM: University of New Mexico Press, 1982), p. 9.

6. Darwin, *The Autobiography of Charles Darwin 1809–1882*, p. 44, emphasis mine.

7. Ibid., p. 55.

8. Janet Browne, *Charles Darwin: Voyaging* (Princeton, NJ: Princeton University Press, 1995), p. 109.

9. Darwin, *The Autobiography of Charles Darwin 1809–1882*, p. 54.

10. Karl Pearson, editor, *The Life, Letters, and Labours of Francis Galton*, Volume 1 (Cambridge, MA: Cambridge University Press, 1914), p. 51.

11. Laurence R. Croft, *Life and Death of Charles Darwin* (Lancashire, UK: Elmwood Books, 1989), p. 22.

12. Peter Brent, *Charles Darwin: A Man of Enlarged Curiosity* (New York, NY: Harper and Row, 1981), p. 30.

13. Browne, *Charles Darwin: Voyaging*, p. 110.

14. Gale, *Evolution without Evidence: Charles Darwin and the Origin of Species*, p. 13.

15. Browne, *Charles Darwin: Voyaging*, p. 110.

16. Gale, *Evolution without Evidence: Charles Darwin and the Origin of Species*, p. 144.

17. Browne, *Charles Darwin: Voyaging*, p. 110.

18. Darwin, *The Autobiography of Charles Darwin 1809–1882*, p. 55.

19. Browne, *Charles Darwin: Voyaging*, p. 109.

20. Darwin, *The Autobiography of Charles Darwin 1809–1882*, p. 71.

21. Browne, *Charles Darwin: Voyaging*, p. 110.

22. Darwin, *The Autobiography of Charles Darwin 1809–1882*, p. 54.

23. Ibid., p. 28.

24. Browne, *Charles Darwin: Voyaging*, p. 98.

25. Peter J. Bowler, *Charles Darwin: The Man and His Influence* (Cambridge, MA: Basil Blackwell, 1990), p. 39.

26. Croft, *Life and Death of Charles Darwin*, p. 22.

27. Browne, *Charles Darwin: Voyaging*, p. 204.

28. Charles Darwin, *Journal of Researches into the Geology and Natural History of Various Countries* (London: Henry Colburn, 1839), p. 9.

29. Robert FitzRoy, *Narrative of the surveying voyages of His Majesty's ships Adventure and Beagle, between the years 1826 and 1836, describing their examination of the southern shores of South America, and the Beagle's circumnavigation of the globe* (London: Henry Colburn, 1839), p. 26.

30. Edward J. Larson, *Evolution's Workshop: God and Science on the Galapagos Islands* (New York: Basic Books, 2001), p. 71.

31. Charles Darwin, edited by Francis Darwin, *The Life and Letters of Charles Darwin*, Volume 1 (New York: D. Appleton, 1896), p. 89.

32. Charles Darwin, edited by Frederick Burkhardt and Sydney Smith, *The Correspondence of Charles Darwin*, Volume 1, 1821–1836 (New York: Cambridge University Press, 1985), p. 150.

33. Browne, *Charles Darwin: Voyaging*, p. 217–218.

34. Ibid., p. 98.

35. Richard Weikart, *From Darwin to Hitler: Evolutionary Ethics, Eugenics, and Racism in Germany* (New York: Palgrave Macmillan, 2004), p. 73.

36. Ibid., p. 81.

37. Adrian Desmond and James Moore, *Darwin: The Life of a Tormented Evolutionist* (New York: Warner Books, 1991), p. 16.

38. Darwin, *The Autobiography of Charles Darwin 1809–1882*, p. 45.

39. Ibid., p. 62.

40. August Forel, *Out of My Life and Work* (New York: W.W. Norton, 1937), p. 33.

41. Darwin, *The Autobiography of Charles Darwin 1809–1882*, p. 30.

42. Ibid., p. 48.

43. Ibid., p. 51.

44. Browne, *Charles Darwin: Voyaging*, p. 214.

45. Ibid., p. 231.

46. Charles Darwin, edited by Frederick Burkhardt and Sydney Smith, *The Correspondence of Charles Darwin*, Volume 6, 1856–1857 (New York: Cambridge University Press, 1990), p. 178.

47. Charles Darwin, edited by Frederick Burkhardt, *The Correspondence of Charles Darwin*, Volume 8 (New York: Cambridge University Press, 1993), p. 224.

48. Browne, *Charles Darwin: Voyaging*, p. 231.

49. Ibid., p. 327.

50. Clifford A. Picover, *Strange Brains and Genius: The Secret Lives of Eccentric Scientists and Madmen* (New York: Quill William Morrow, 1998); Thomas Barloon and Russel Noyes Jr., "Charles Darwin and Panic Disorder," *JAMA* 277(2) (1997):138–141; R.O. Pasnau, "Darwin's Illness: A Biopsychosocial Perspective," *Psychosomatics* 31(2) (1990):121–128; W.B. Bean, "The Illness of Charles Darwin," *The American Journal of Medicine* 65(4) (1978):572–574; Ralph Colp Jr., *To Be an Invalid: The Illness of Charles Darwin* (Chicago, IL: The University of Chicago, 1977).

51. Michael Ruse, "Is Evolution a Secular Religion?" *Science* 299 (2003):1523–1524.

PART THREE

Darwin and His Theory

CHAPTER 8

Did Darwin Plagiarize His Evolution Theory?

Chapter Synopsis

All of the major contributions to evolution theory credited to Darwin, including natural selection, were borrowed, and some conclude plagiarized, from others. Many, if not most, of his major ideas are found in earlier writings, including those by his grandfather, Erasmus Darwin. Charles Darwin rarely gave proper credit to the many persons from whom he liberally borrowed. This review looks at the evidence for this claim, concluding that much evidence exists to support this view.

Introduction

A common (but erroneous) conclusion is that Charles Darwin alone conceived the modern theory of biological evolution, including natural selection.[1] An example of statements commonly found in the scientific literature indicating this conclusion is the claim by Michael Fitch that not "until Darwin, did anyone draw the same conclusion . . . except Alfred R. Wallace. . . . But Darwin undoubtedly preceded him in the conception of the theory" of evolution by natural selection.[2] A study of the works of pre-Darwin naturalists shows that, in contrast to this common assumption, Darwin was *not* the first modern person to develop the idea of organic evolution by natural selection.[3]

Furthermore, most (if not all) of the major ideas credited to Darwin were actually discussed in print by others before him. De Vries noted that some critics have even concluded that Darwin did not make *any* major new contributions to the theory of evolution by natural selection.[4] Even the common belief that Darwin began to actively develop his theory when on the Galapagos Islands turns out to be false — not only is there no evidence of this claim, but there is "almost no hint of evolutionary thought in the scientific notes or letters Darwin had written while on the Beagle."[5] No evidence exists that Darwin expressed much interest in evolution at this time, rather his major interest was in geology. A study by Professor Howard Gruber found by comparing the 1839 and 1845 accounts of his *Beagle* trip that Darwin altered the former account to imply that Darwin the creationist became Darwin the evolutionist, or at least was well on his way to becoming an evolutionist, as early as 1839.[6] Darwin altered his 1839 account by inserting new paragraphs and sections dealing with evolutionary ideas to give the impression that he originated the theory of evolution by natural selection while on his *Beagle* trip.[7] Waller concluded that historical research has proven beyond doubt that the belief

that humans represent the latest stage in the "transmutation" of unicellular organisms had been put forward by dozens of naturalists between 1800 and 1859. More specifically, the longstanding idea that Darwin invented the idea of evolution itself is . . . entirely fictitious.[8]

A study of the history of evolution shows that, in fact, Darwin "borrowed" all of his major ideas — some conclude plagiarized is a more accurate word — without giving proper credit to these people until he was forced by complaints from his fellow scientists to do so. A few examples are discussed below.

The Pre-Darwin Modern Theories of Biological Evolution

The modern theory of biological evolution was probably first put in print by Charles De Secondat Montesquieu (1689–1755), who concluded that "in the beginning there were very few" kinds of species, and by natural means of gradual evolution the number has "multiplied since."[9] Another important early evolutionist was Benoit de Maillet (1656–1738), whose book on evolution was published posthumously in 1748. In this book, de Maillet suggests that fish were the precursors of birds, mammals, and men.[10] Yet another pre-Darwin scientist, Pierre-Louis Maupertuis (1698–1759), concluded in his 1751 book that new species result from the fortuitous recombining of different parts of living animals.

At about this same time, the French encyclopedist Denis Diderot (1713–1784) taught that all animals evolved from one primeval organism and that this prototype organism was fashioned into all of the animal kinds alive today via natural selection. George Louis Buffon (1707–1788) expounded this idea at length, stating that not only did apes and humans have a common ancestry, but that all animals also had a common ancestor.[11] Macrone concluded that, although Darwin put evolution on a firmer scientific basis,

> he was hardly the first to propose it. A century before Darwin the French naturalist Georges Buffon wrote extensively on the resemblance among various species of birds and quadrupeds. Noting such similarities and also the prevalence in nature of seemingly useless anatomical features (such as toes on a pig), Buffon voiced doubts that every single species had been uniquely formed by God on the fifth and sixth days of creation. Buffon suggested in guarded language that at least a limited sort of evolution would account for variances among similar species and for natural anomalies.[12]

De Vries noted that evolution, which he defined as the "origin of new species by variation from ancestor species," as an explanation for the variety of life in

> the living world, had been proclaimed before Darwin by several biologist thinkers, including the poet Johann

Wolfgang Goethe, in 1795. Jean-Baptiste de Lamarck in 1809, Darwin's grandfather, the ebullient physician-naturalist-poet-philosopher Erasmus Darwin, and in Darwin's time anonymously by Robert Chambers in 1844.[13]

Even Darwin's commonly alleged major contribution to evolution, natural selection, had been developed, or at least discussed, by others before Darwin published, including William Charles Wells in 1813, Edward Blyth in 1835, 1836, and 1837, and, later, Alfred Russel Wallace (1823–1913).

Erasmus Darwin

One of the most important pre-Darwinists was Charles Darwin's own grandfather, Erasmus Darwin (1731–1802). He discussed his ideas at length in a two-volume work titled *Zoonomia*, published in 1794. This work was no obscure volume, but sold well and was even translated into German, French, and Italian. Darlington argued that Erasmus Darwin "originated almost every important idea that has since appeared in evolutionary theory," including natural selection.[14] While still a young man, Charles Darwin traveled to Edinburgh, where his grandfather had many admirers.[15] While there, Robert Grant explained Erasmus' ideas on "transmutation" (as evolution was called then) to Charles Darwin at length. However, no evidence exists that Darwin openly admitted that his grandfather had a major influence on his central idea.

Some scholars even assert that Erasmus Darwin's view was in some ways *more* developed than Charles Darwin's. Desmond King-Hele made an excellent case for the view that Charles Darwin's theory, even "in its mature form in the later editions of the *Origin of Species*, is, in some important respects, less correct than that of Erasmus."[16] Both writers stressed that evolution occurred by the accumulation of small, fortuitous changes that were selected by natural selection. Erasmus wrote the following about when the earth came into existence:

Perhaps millions of ages before the beginning of the history
of mankind . . . all warm-blooded animals have arisen from
one living filament, which THE GREAT FIRST CAUSE
endued with animality, with the power of acquiring new
parts, attended with new propensities, directed by irrita-
tions, sensations, volitions, and associations; and thus
possessing the faculty of continuing to improve by its own
inherent activity, and of delivering down those improvements by generation to its posterity.[17]

Large sections in many of Charles Darwin's books closely parallel
Erasmus' writings.[18] King-Hele even claimed that the similarity
between their two works was so close that Darwin's grandfather had
evolution "all charted in advance" for Darwin. Yet "Charles persistently
fails to note the similarity . . . an omission which sometimes leaves him
open to criticism" of plagiarizing. [19] It is not difficult to conclude that
Darwin's borrowing was on a large scale because even his terminology
and wording was similar to his grandfather's writing.[20]

An example where the conclusions of Erasmus Darwin were in
some ways more advanced than Charles Darwin's is Charles accepted
Lamarckianism to a greater extent than Erasmus, a major blunder
on Charles's part.[21] In explaining the evolution of the giraffe's long
neck, Darwin "accepted the validity of evolution by use and disuse,"
theory, even though he had relied on natural selection as the major
explanation for giraffe neck evolution.[22]

And last, for both Erasmus and Charles Darwin, "The theory of
Evolution was no mere scientific hypothesis but the very basis of
life."[23] The closest that Darwin came to admitting the enormous
influences of his grandfather was in his autobiography where he
admitted that he had read the *Zoönomia* in which views similar to
his were espoused, but he claimed that his grandfather's advice produced no

effect on me. Nevertheless it is probable that the hearing
rather early in life such views maintained and praised may

have favored my upholding them under a different form in my *Origin of Species*. At this time I admired greatly the *Zoönomia*; but on reading it a second time after an interval of ten or fifteen years, I was much disappointed, the proportion of speculation being so large to the facts given.[24]

Our review supports the following conclusion by Margulis and Sagan:

Darwin would have us believe that the entire concept of evolution originated with him. He consistently failed to credit his energetic paternal grandfather, Erasmus Darwin. The contribution of Erasmus . . . who wrote (in *Zoonomia*, 1794–1796) about evolution by natural selection, was taken as less than serious by his grandson.[25]

Jean Baptiste Lamarck

Jean Baptiste Lamarck (1744–1929) is regarded as the "first modern naturalist to publish a great body of literature that argued for the evolution of all modern life from ancestral predecessors."[26] Darwin's idea that pangenesis (see chapter 10) was the major source of biological variation was purely Lamarckian.[27] Darwin borrowed so heavily from Lamarck that he could accurately be said to be a Neo-Lamarckian, yet today Darwin is lionized and Lamarck vilified. Margulis and Sagan note that Lamarck was actually commonly assumed to have

made a negative contribution to science with his erroneous claim that characteristics acquired by an animal or plant may be inherited in the descendants of the acquirer. "Inheritance of the acquired characteristics," the phrase inseparable from the name of Lamarck, is taught as equivalent to "Lamarckianism" — and "wrong."[28]

They concluded that, like Lamarck, Darwin

struggled with the problem of the ultimate source of heritable variation — and came up with wrong answers. That

Darwin invented, in the end, a Lamarckian explanation — his "pangenesis" hypothesis to explain how heritable variations arise — tends to be forgotten. . . . By his reckoning, "gemmules," theoretical particles borne by all living beings and subject to experience during the lifetime of their bearers, send representatives into the offspring of the next generation. Darwin's view, scarcely distinguishable from Lamarck's was absolutely a statement for "the inheritance of acquired characteristics." Ultimately, however, Darwin equivocated on where these "sports," "mutants," or "heritable variants" came from. He simply did not know.[29]

Darwin never acknowledged his enormous debt to Lamarck, nor do most historians today. He even claimed that he did not obtain a single "fact or idea from" Lamarck's work![30]

Robert Chambers

Another important pre-Darwinian forerunner was Robert Chambers (1802–1871). His book *Vestiges of the Natural History of Creation* was first published in 1844.[31] Crookshank concluded in a summary of this work that Chambers believed the extant varieties of humans were a product of evolutionary advances and regressions. *Vestiges* not only advanced an evolutionary hypothesis, but also argued that the natural world "could best be understood by appeal to natural law rather than by flight to an intervening deity."[32]

Without Chambers' book, Darwin admitted that he might never have written *The Origin of Species*.[33] Millhauser claimed that Chambers' work was critically important in the Darwinian revolution for other reasons, including the fact that Chambers' popularizing his evolution theory in *Vestiges* helped prepare the way for Darwin. Middle-class consumers "took up the book with the same enthusiasm they felt for the latest novels."[34] *Vestiges* went through four editions in only six months, ten editions a decade later, and is still in print today.[35]

Many radical reformers were especially enthusiastic about the book but, ironically, scientists "quite generally dismissed its shoddy zoology and botany."[36] Nonetheless, *Vestiges* and Chamber's other works on the same subject were read or discussed by most all segments of British society.[37] Equally important was the fact that Robert Chambers' works were a major stimulus for Thomas Henry Huxley, who became "Darwin's Bulldog" and one of the most active and important of all of Darwin's disciples.[38]

Patrick Matthew

Yet another naturalist who discussed major aspects of evolution, specifically natural selection, long before Darwin was Patrick Matthew, whose priority was later acknowledged both by Charles Darwin and Edward Blyth.[39] Matthew actually

> anticipated Darwin's main conclusions by twenty-eight years, yet he thought them so little important that he published them as an appendix to his book . . . and did not feel the need to give substance to them by continuous work. Darwin's incessant application, on the other hand, makes one think that he had found in evolution and its related concepts, not merely a scientific theory about the world, but a vocation.[40]

Matthew even wrote to Darwin to "express his frustration at Darwin's non-citation" of his work.[41] In response to Matthew's evidently valid concern, Darwin merely "offered some diplomatic palliation in the historical introduction added to later editions of the *Origin*." Darwin was forced to respond to Matthew's ire in the *Gardener's Chronicle* for April 21, 1860 as follows: "I freely acknowledge that Mr. Matthew has anticipated by many years the explanation which I have offered of *the origin of species*, under the name of natural selection."[42]

This statement indicates Darwin's guilt, yet Gould tries to justify Darwin with the excuse that Darwin was not aware of Matthew's views on natural selection because they only appeared in the appendix of Matthew's book on timber and arboriculture. This could well be, but it does not justify the slight Matthew was given ever since.

His priority is rarely acknowledged even today, but instead he is largely ignored.

Did Darwin Get His Main Idea from Creationist Edward Blyth?

Loren Eiseley invested decades tracing the origins of the ideas commonly credited to Darwin. He summarized his research in his 1979 book titled, *Darwin and the Mysterious Mr. X.* Eiseley reached the conclusion that Darwin "borrowed" heavily from the works of others, and never publicly acknowledged most of these persons. According to Eiseley, one of these persons, English naturalist Edward Blyth (1810–1873), originated many of the ideas for which Darwin was given credit. Less-charitable evaluators may be inclined to label Darwin's many unacknowledged borrowing infractions as plagiarism:

> No less a scientific giant than Charles Darwin has been accused of failing to acknowledge his intellectual debts to researchers who preceded him. Loren Eiseley . . . argues that Blyth wrote on natural selection and species evolution in two separate papers published in 1835 and 1837, years before Darwin's *Origin of Species* was published in 1859. Eiseley details similarities in phrasing, the use of rare words, and the choice of examples between Blyth's and Darwin's work. While Darwin quotes Blyth on a number of points, he doesn't reference Blyth's papers that directly discussed natural selection.[43]

Eiseley concluded that Blyth's and Darwin's evolution ideas were so similar that "the main difference between Blyth and Darwin lies in the fact that one was a special creationist and the other was an evolutionist."[44] Specifically, Eiseley claimed that Blyth discussed in detail all Darwin's major ideas before Darwin, including natural and sexual selection, the importance of variation in selection, and the struggle for existence. Blyth interpreted these concepts as part of the in-built design of the Creator, concluding they supported divine creationism.

Even Darwin's magnum opus *The Descent of Man* (1871), Eiseley argues, was largely a repeat of the ideas of others, such as Carl Vogt's 1864 book *Lectures on Man*. Eiseley states that Darwin's ideas on human evolution in this book were "scarcely new. . . . Nevertheless, the world wanted to hear what the author of the *Origin* had to say on the evolution of man."[45] Although the fact that many naturalists preceded Darwin is now widely recognized, some die-hard defenders of Darwin — such as the late Stephen J. Gould — have tried, unsuccessfully in this reviewer's opinion, to justify (or even deny) Darwin's lack of candor in acknowledging the origin of his evolutionary theory.

Gould claims that Darwin was influenced by many people and could have developed his ideas tangentially (as evidently occurred with Wallace). Although Gould claims that "all good biologists" discussed natural selection "in the generations before Darwin," he argues that the plagiarism charges are not all valid because certain aspects of Darwin's theory were unique to him.[46] This may well be, but a cloud of suspicion still hangs over Darwin.

The close similarity of Darwin's ideas to many of his forerunners — even the wording Darwin used — argues that "suspicion" is a charitable interpretation of the situation. It is true, as Gould notes that Darwin's and Blyth's ideas did differ in certain minor details. Specifically, Gould claims that Darwin saw natural selection as a creative force and an agent of change, but Blyth saw it primarily as a force that removed the less fit to reduce devolution. Blyth's theory of natural selection has turned out to be much closer to the findings of empirical research, both in the 1800s and today, than was Darwin's.

Darwin's argument that natural selection did not just eliminate traits, but was "*the creative* force for evolutionary *change*"[47] has been carefully refuted by others and will not be reviewed here (see chapter 14). Suffice it to say that natural selection cannot create new traits but only eliminate traits by eliminating those organisms with them and opening up new ecological niches. This fact was recognized even in Darwin's day. For example, Richard Owen wrote much about this concern. In one letter Owen used an analogy to restate the

> basic objections he had expressed when Darwin's *Origin of Species* was first published in 1859: that although natural selection is a valid mechanism to explain species diversification through time, *it did not answer the more basic question of the origin of the inheritable individual differences* subsequently "naturally selected" for survival in a surrounding and changing environment. Without an answer to the problem of inherited variations, Owen believed that the origins of species were not fully understood. Darwin himself confessed: "Our ignorance of the laws of variation is profound."[48]

Darwin read at least one paper by Blyth, the one published in 1837, because Darwin's personal copy contained annotations in Darwin's handwriting.[49] Schwartz noted that the 1937 paper asked, might "a large proportion of what are considered species have descended from a common parentage?"

Others Also Charged Darwin with Plagiarism

Although some feel that it is inappropriate to judge Darwin by today's plagiarism standards, accusations of plagiarism were first made by Darwin's peers only a few years after Darwin published his classic work *Origin of Species*. Broad and Wade note:

> Eiseley is not the only critic of Darwin's acknowledgement practices. He was accused by a contemporary, the acerbic man of letters Samuel Butler, of passing over in silence those who had developed similar ideas. Indeed, when Darwin's *On the Origin of Species* first appeared in 1859, he made little mention of predecessors.[50]

When essayist and novelist Samuel Butler (1835–1902) "accused Darwin of slighting the evolutionary speculations of Buffon, Lamarck, and his own grandfather, Erasmus," Gould reported that

Darwin reacted to these accusations with "silence."[51] Evidently aware that these charges may have some merit, Darwin provided a few more details about his sources in later editions of his *Origin* book. Nonetheless, "under continued attack, he added [acknowledgments of his predecessors] to the historical sketch in three subsequent editions" of the *Origin*.[52] This concession, though, was

> still not enough to satisfy all his critics. In 1879, Butler published a book entitled *Evolution Old and New* in which he accused Darwin of slighting the evolutionary speculations of Buffon, Lamarck, and Darwin's own grandfather Erasmus. Remarked Darwin's son Francis: "The affair gave my father much pain."[53]

In 1858, Wallace sent Darwin a copy of his paper describing his independently developed theory of evolution by natural selection. Although Leslie noted some scholars have concluded that "Darwin conspired to rob Wallace of credit for natural selection,"[54] others argue Darwin was backed into a corner and was left with no choice but to co-author his first paper on natural selection with Wallace. Gunther Stent concluded that it was not Darwin's sense of fair play that required the simultaneous publication with Wallace, but rather Darwin's fear of getting scooped.[55]

Brackman claims that Darwin's putative plagiarizing from Wallace was "one of the greatest wrongs in the history of science." He adds that "Darwin and two eminent scientific friends conspired to secure priority and credit" of evolution theory for Charles Darwin, specifically the mechanism of evolution, natural selection (from the introduction on the book jacket).[56] Zoologist Williams uses even stronger words, arguing that Brackman demonstrated that "Darwin stole (not too harsh a word) the theory from Wallace" (parenthetical comments his). Williams concludes:

> Broad and Wade include an excellent discussion of Darwin's appropriation of the work of Blyth and others. Evidence for

this is similarities in phrasing, the choice of specific examples to support the theory and the use of certain uncommonly used words. Broad and Wade bring out that even contemporaries of Darwin such as Samuel Butler criticized Darwin "passing over in silence those who had developed similar ideas [before he did]."[57]

The famous so-called joint paper by Darwin and Wallace was in fact presented without Wallace's prior knowledge![58] Regardless of whether Darwin appropriated some of Wallace's ideas, Darwin still managed to receive most of the credit for the theory. Wallace is largely unknown today except among a small group of Darwinian scholars. Brooks relates that his interest in Wallace was aroused only when he was preparing to teach a course on evolution organized around a study of the original scientific contributions to the theory. Each year the course began with a

> reading of Wallace's 1855 "law" paper, the joint Darwin-Wallace papers, and Darwin's *On the Origin of Species*. Over several annual cycles the similarities between the concepts, *even the wording*, in Wallace's papers and several chapters, but especially chapter IV, in Darwin's 1859 book had become *increasingly apparent and disturbing*. Were these really coincidences of two totally independent conceptions? Or did Darwin somehow profit from Wallace's papers and manuscript? — a possibility to which Darwin gave no recognition, not even a hint. A nagging doubt remained; there were too many similarities . . . but, as noted in the preceding chapter, there is no mention of Wallace's work anywhere in chapter IV.[59]

After his extensive study of Wallace and Darwin, Brooks concluded that "Wallace's ideas emerged, without any attribution, as the core of chapter IV of the *Origin of Species*, a chapter which Darwin himself cited as central to his work."[60] Rhawn is even more direct about Darwin's alleged plagiarism:

Although glossed over by Darwin and his acolytes, Darwin had in fact abandoned the field of "evolution" early in his career. In fact, prior to receiving Wallace's landmark paper, Darwin had spent 15 years studying and writing about barnacles, not evolution. However, upon reading Wallace's brilliant paper, Darwin proclaimed that he had been studying evolution all along, and had been writing an identical paper, and then spent the next 8 months rewriting, and in some places, repeating the works of others without citation, including the brilliant and revolutionary work of Wallace.[61]

One can certainly understand why the affair gave Darwin "much pain." Others have concluded that Darwin's plagiarism went well beyond copying sentences or borrowing ideas without giving credit. Rhawn concluded the following about Darwin when the fame that he desired repeatedly eluded him he

> became increasingly withdrawn and depressed. He dabbled in this area and that, and then spent 15 years devoted to the study of barnacles, about which he wrote four short papers. And then, on June 8, 1858, Darwin received a letter from Alfred Russel Wallace, accompanied by a 12 page summary of Wallace's ideas on evolution; i.e., natural selection. Wallace was a renowned naturalist and has published a number of papers on evolution, which Darwin had read and expressed interest in. From an island near Borneo, Wallace had forwarded his monograph to Darwin. The paper was utterly brilliant! Darwin then claimed to have recently arrived at identical conclusions, and thus claimed Wallace's theory as his own.[62]

Rhawn concludes that, as a result of this paper, Darwin abandoned his study of

> barnacles and began feverishly working on a book, a synthesis of the words of Blyth, Wells, Pritchard, Lawrence, Naudin,

and Buffon: *On the Origin of Species by Means of Natural Selection* which he published in November of 1859, almost 18 months after receiving the paper by Wallace.[63]

Although Darwin had written as early as 1838 that "favorable variations would tend to be preserved and unfavorable ones . . . destroyed" and by this means a "new species" could evolve,[64] Rhawn concluded that Darwin relied heavily on Wallace's paper in producing his famous 1859 work.

McKinney, when doing a PhD thesis on Wallace at Yale, discovered that Wallace was not only on the path to the modern evolution theory much earlier than Darwin but, contrary to popular assumption, most of the time Wallace's ideas were ahead of Darwin's by as much as five years.[65] When Darwin read Wallace's 1856 papers, he admitted that he feared his ideas were "threadbare, implausible or out of date."[66]

Copying ideas and giving credit is common and appropriate, but there is no "indication that Darwin admitted to any of his friends that he paid any attention whatsoever to Wallace."[67] The fact is, once Wallace's 1855 paper was published, Darwin's thoughts about the origin of "species question, as recorded in his notebooks, began to move in an entirely different direction."[68] Rhawn speculated that Darwin's motivation to plagiarize was the same as that by scientists today:

> As Darwin well knew, this "synthesis" and the theory of "natural selection" would garner him world fame. Darwin, his well connected friends in the scientific community, and his acolytes have gone to extraordinary lengths to rewrite history and to spin myths regarding Darwin's utterly insignificant observations when as a youth he sailed on the *Beagle* — observations which were little different from numerous naturalists writing and publishing at the time.[69]

A key element in Rhawn's argument is his conclusion that, until receiving Wallace's paper, Darwin had published "absolutely nothing of significance on evolution, and had spent the previous 15 years studying and writing about 'barnacles.' Not evolution. Barnacles!"[70] Rhawn concluded:

> It could also be argued that Darwin's claim to fame, and the crux of his thesis, the theory of "natural section," was devised, originated and first penned and distributed by Wallace and Wallace alone, which is why knowledgeable sources grudgingly credit Wallace as the "co-founder" of the theory of evolution.[71]

Why Wallace received only second billing and why so many 19th century scientists "find it acceptable to attribute the work of Wallace to Darwin" could be because, as Darwin claimed,

> he had been writing an identical paper on "natural selection" where he made the same exact arguments and came to the same exact conclusions as Wallace, and was thus shocked and dismayed to discover that Wallace had came to the same conclusions. An amazing coincidence! Thus Darwin rightly deserves credit as being the co-discoverer. However, if that does not seem plausible, the reader might consider the following: Darwin, the former secretary of the Geological Society, was the son of a rich and well known man and part of a circle of exceedingly influential scientists. Wallace was an outsider.[72]

There remain many issues surrounding Darwin's most famous work that need to be resolved. How commonly evolution was believed is indicated by Waller, who wrote that an

> eighteenth-century Scot, Lord Monboddo, argued that the orangutan represents an earlier stage in human evolution. During the 1820s and 1830s, the newly founded University College London became notorious as a den for radical believers in human evolution. In France, such ideas were even more energetically and systematically pursued.[73]

One of the most detailed studies of Darwin's "crime" was by Roy Davies, the producer of the BBC history series "Timewatch." Davies, who produced a segment on Charles Darwin titled *The Devils Chaplain,* wrote, "If I had known then what I know now, the Devils Chaplain would never have been made."[74] He concluded the common story that Wallace sent Darwin a letter that inspired Darwin to publish his original conclusions is misleading.

Davies tries to answer the question "how did Darwin manufacture so much fame for himself and how has Wallace been denied his place in the pantheon of great British scientists so completely, despite the fact that both men were credited at the same time and on the same day with having discovered" what Davies calls "one of the most important truths about the natural world?"[75] Davies concluded the communication system among scholars was critical in allowing Darwin to prevail in what he called "Darwin's rivalry, ambition and subsequent plagiarism."[76]

Deceit

Numerous researchers have concluded that Darwin was guilty of blatant deceit. Zoologist Beddall determined that the critical correspondence between Wallace and Darwin was intentionally destroyed to "deliberately obscure the story of how Darwin arrived at his theory."[77] Darlington concluded that Darwin simply edited together other people's ideas, not only Wallace's, but also Lyell's and Hooker's.[78] Ospovat concluded that "Darwin's conception of Natural Selection" in his 1844 essay "was entirely different from that outlined in *On the Origin of Species*" published 15 years later.[79]

One example is that Darwin received a letter from Wallace that contained the critical parts of what Darwin claimed was the theory that he had originated. Even the terminology Darwin used was copied from Wallace. Darwin, though, claimed the critical letter arrived three months later than it actually did, thus allowing Darwin to claim priority.[80] The excellent records kept by the Post Office Museum in

London proved Darwin's claim that the letter at issue arrived late in April 1857 to be false. It was delivered on January 12, 1857.[81]

Another letter from Wallace that Darwin claimed arrived on June 18 in fact arrived on June 3, 1858.[82] The time difference evidently allowed Darwin to get away with plagiarizing from Wallace until several intrepid researchers uncovered his deception. Although some feel that plagiarism is too strong of a word in this case, and the plagiarism case against Darwin is inconclusive, at the least, Darwin did not properly acknowledge those many persons from whom he borrowed his ideas.[83]

Darwin did fill five notebooks, especially the last two, written from 1837 to 1840, with notes that provide some evidence of his ideas about what he called transmutation, even before he married Emma. It is not clear what ideas in these notebooks were his and what ideas he gleaned from others and never gave credit or even appropriate acknowledgment.

Darwin did acknowledge in a letter to Baden Powell dated January 18, 1860, that he did not originate the "doctrine" of evolution and the "only novelty in my work is the attempt to explain *how* species became modified" — an attempt that largely failed. Even here, evidence exists that Darwin relied on others, as documented above, even though he claimed that he "received no assistance from my predecessors."[84]

Conclusions

Although Charles Darwin was highly successful in popularizing the theory of organic evolution by natural selection, especially among the scientific community, evidence exists that he was not the originator of the major parts of the theory as is commonly supposed. Nor was Darwin the originator of even those aspects of evolution for which he most often is given credit today, including natural and sexual selection. Yet he implied that these and other ideas were his own creation. In a study of Darwin, Gould concluded:

Darwin clearly loved his distinctive theory of natural selection — the powerful idea that he often identified in letters as his dear "child." But, like any good parent, he understood limits and imposed discipline. He knew that the complex and comprehensive phenomena of evolution could not be fully rendered by any single cause, even one so ubiquitous and powerful as his own brainchild.[85]

Good evidence now exists to support the conclusion that Darwin "borrowed" — and some claim in a few cases plagiarized — all or most of his "dear child" from other researchers, especially his own grandfather. They were not "his own brainchild," nor his child, as he claimed, but that of others which he appropriated, often without giving them proper credit, especially Wallace, specifically his March 1858 4,000-word manuscript.[86]

The fact is, Darwin "had a long career of taking credit" for the work of others and "making dishonest claims" about his theory.[87] Some even argue that his major exposition of evolution, *The Origin of Species*, was "laced with hesitancies, contradictions, and possible prevarication."[88] As Davies concludes, "Charles Darwin was a very secretive man with a driving ambition . . . Charles Darwin — British national hero, hailed as the greatest naturalist the world has ever known, the originator of one of the greatest ideas of the nineteenth century — lied, cheated and plagiarized in order to be recognized as the man who discovered the theory of evolution."[89]

The account documented in this chapter is "light-years away from the established orthodoxy, which states that a letter from Wallace caused Darwin to rush to establish his claim to be the first to outline the theory of evolution." In fact, it is now well documented that the

evidence contradicts the received view of Charles Darwin as a benevolent man who, alone, unaided and without precursors, was inspired to write *On the Origin of Species*. At the heart of that famous historical event lies a deliberate and iniquitous case of intellectual theft, deceit and lies perpetrated by Charles Darwin. This book will also argue that two of the greatest Victorian scientists were willing accomplices.[90]

Davies concluded in his carefully documented work that the facts document that "there is little doubt that a compelling case can be made against Darwin that would allow any person to conclude [that] it is likely he committed one of the greatest thefts of intellectual property in the history of science."[91] If a compelling case exists, I will let the reader decide. Darwin himself must have felt that he did not give proper credit to his intellectual predecessors because "in response to accusations that he was taking credit for ideas that others had published before him" he added a section in the third edition of the *Origin* acknowledging those he borrowed from, and in the fourth edition he added another two pages of further credits.[92]

Summary

It is widely recognized that all of the major ideas on biological evolution Darwin discussed predated his published writings. As Kitcher noted, "Creationists propounded a 'creation model' of the origins of life on earth. . . . The trouble with this proposal is that it was abandoned, for excellent reasons . . . *decades* before Charles Darwin wrote *The Origin of Species*."[93] One Oxford-trained historian of science went further and concluded that, in contrast to the common

> view, none of the concepts from which Darwin pieced together his theory of evolution by natural selection was at all novel. Historians now recognize that the core principles of evolution — struggle for survival, selection, heritability, adaptation, even the appearance of random changes to the hereditary makeup — were fairly common themes in Victorian botany and zoology.[94]

Endnotes

1. Malcolm Bowden, *The Rise of the Evolution Fraud* (Bromley, Kent, Great Britain: Sovereign Publications, 1982), p. 1.

2. Michael Fitch, *Universal Evolution* (Boston, MA: Gorham Press, 1913), p. 68.

3. Bert Thompson, *The History of Evolutionary Thought* (Fort Worth, TX: Star Bible & Tract Corp, 1981); Bentley Glass, Owsel Temkin, and William Straus, *Forerunners of Darwin: 1745–1895* (Baltimore, MD: The Johns Hopkins Press, 1959).

4. Andre De Vries, "The Enigma of Darwin," *Clio Medica* 19(1–2) (1984): p. 145.

5. Roy Davies, *The Darwin Conspiracy: Origins of a Scientific Crime* (London, England: GoldenSquare Books, 2008), p. 31.

6. Howard E. Gruber, *Darwin on Man: A Psychological Study of Scientific Creativity* (Chicago, IL: University of Chicago Press, 1974).

7. Davies, *The Darwin Conspiracy: Origins of a Scientific Crime*, p. 34.

8. John Waller, *Fabulous Science: Fact and Fiction in the History of Scientific Discovery* (New York: Oxford, 2002), p. 181.

9. Robert Chambers, *Vestiges of the Natural History of Creation* (Leicester, UK: Leicester University Press, 1969), introduction by Gavin De Beer, p. 11.

10. Ibid., p. 12.

11. Ibid., p. 14.

12. Michael Macrone, *Eureka!* (New York: Barnes & Noble, 1994), p. 150.

13. De Vries, "The Enigma of Darwin," p. 145.

14. Cyril D. Darlington, "The Origin of Darwinism," *Scientific American* 200(5) (1959): p. 62.

15. Carl Zimmer, *Evolution: The Triumph of an Idea* (New York: Harper Collins, 2001), p. 14.

16. Desmond King-Hele, *Erasmus Darwin* (New York: Charles Scribner's Sons, 1963), p. 81.

17. Erasmus Darwin, *Zoonomia: Or the Laws of Organic Life* (London: J. Johnson, 1794), p. 505, reprinted by AMS Press, New York, 1974, spelling and punctuation modernized, emphasis in original.

18. King-Hele, *Erasmus Darwin*, p. 99.

19. Ibid., p. 89.

20. Ibid., p. 87.

21. Ibid., p. 81–82.

22. Stephen Jay Gould, *Leonardo's Mountain of Clams and the Diet of Worms* (New York: Harmony Books, 1989), p. 312.

23. King-Hele, *Erasmus Darwin*, p. 90.

24. Charles Darwin, edited by Nora Barlow, *The Autobiography of Charles Darwin* (New York: Norton, 1969), p. 49.

25. Lynn Margulis and Dorion Sagan, *Acquiring Genomes: A Theory of the Origin of Species* (New York: Basic Books, 2002), p. 27.

26. Ibid., p. 27.

27. De Vries, "The Enigma of Darwin," p. 140.

28. Margulis and Sagan, *Acquiring Genomes: A Theory of the Origin of Species*, p. 27–28.

29. Ibid., p. 27–28.

30. Darwin, *The Autobiography of Charles Darwin*, p. 153.

31. Milton Millhauser, *Just Before Darwin* (Middletown, CT: Wesleyan University Press, 1959).

32. Robert J. Richards, "Commotion Over Evolution Before Darwin," *American Scientist* 89(5) (2001):454.

33. F.G. Crookshank, *The Mongol in Our Midst* (New York: E.P. Dutton & Company, 1924), p. 1.

34. Richards, "Commotion Over Evolution Before Darwin," p. 455.

35. Ibid., p. 454.

36. Ibid., p. 455.

37. Robert Chambers, *Explanations: A Sequel to "Vestiges of the Natural History of Creation&rdquo*; (Philadelphia, PA: Carey & Hart, 1845); James A. Secord, *Victorian Sensation: The Extraordinary Publication, Reception, and Secret Authorship of Vestiges of the Natural History of Creation* (Chicago, IL: University of Chicago Press, 2001).

38. Chambers, *Vestiges of the Natural History of Creation*, p. 35.

39. Cyril D. Darlington, *Darwin's Place in History* (Oxford: Blackwell, 1959), p. 53; Stephen Jay Gould, "Darwin Vindicated!" *New York Review of Books* 26(1) (July 1979): p. 38.

40. Francis Huxley, "A Reappraisal of Charles Darwin," *The American Scholar* (Autumn 1959): p. 489.

41. Stephen Jay Gould, *The Structure of Evolutionary Theory* (Cambridge, MA: Harvard University Press, 2002), p. 183.

42. Ibid., p. 138.

43. Eugene Garfield, "From Citation Amnesia to Bibliographic Plagiarism," *Current Contents* 23 (June 9, 1980): p. 504–505.

44. Loren Eiseley, *Darwin and the Mysterious Mr. X* (New York: Dutton, 1979), p. 68–69.

45. Ibid., p. 201.

46. Gould, *The Structure of Evolutionary Theory*, p. 137–138.

47. Ibid., p. 139.

48. Jacob Gruber, "Owen was Right, as Darwin's Work Continues," *Nature* 413 (2001): p. 669, emphasis added.

49. Joel Schwartz, "Charles Darwin's Debt to Malthus and Edward Blyth," *Journal of the History of Biology* 7(2) (1974): p. 316.

50. William Broad and Nicholas Wade, *Betrayers of the Truth: Fraud and Deceit in the Halls of Science* (New York: Simon and Schuster, 1982), p. 31.

51. Gould, "Darwin Vindicated!" p. 36.

52. Ibid., p. 36.

53. Broad and Wade, *Betrayers of the Truth: Fraud and Deceit in the Halls of Science*, p. 31.

54. Mitch Leslie, "Into the Limelight," *Science* 294(5549) (2001):2059.

55. Gunther Stent, *Paradox of Progress* (San Francisco, CA: W.H. Freeman, 1978), p. 84.

56. Arnold Brackman, *A Delicate Arrangement: The Strange Case of Charles Darwin and Alfred Russel Wallace* (New York: Times Books, 1980).

57. Kenneth Williams, "The Origin of Darwinism," *The New Republic* 187(17)4 (1982): p. 31.

58. Alice Kenyon, "Darwin's 'Joint Paper,'" *Cen T.J.* 14(3) (2000):72–73.

59. John Langdon Brooks, *Just Before the Origin: Alfred Russel Wallace's Theory of Evolution* (New York: Columbia University Press, 1984), p. 239, emphasis mine.

60. Ibid., quoted from book jacket.

61. Joseph Rhawn, *Astrobiology, the Origin of Life and Death of Darwinism* (San Jose, CA: University of California, 2000), p. 223.

62. Ibid., p. 223–226.

63. Ibid., p. 223–226.

64. Stephen Jay Gould, "Darwin's Delay," *Natural History* 83(10) (1974): p. 68.

65. H. Lewis McKinney, *Wallace and Natural Selection* (New Haven, CT: Yale University Press, 1972).

66. Davies, *The Darwin Conspiracy: Origins of a Scientific Crime*, p. 68.

67. Ibid., p. 69.

68. Ibid., p. 63.

69. Rhawn, *Astrobiology, the Origin of Life and Death of Darwinism*, p. 223–226.

70. Ibid., p. 223–226.

71. Ibid., p. 223–226.

72. Ibid., p. 223–226.

73. Waller, *Fabulous Science: Fact and Fiction in the History of Scientific Discovery*, p. 181.

74. Davies, *The Darwin Conspiracy: Origins of a Scientific Crime*, preface.

75. Ibid., p. xvii.

76. Ibid., p. xvii-xviii.

77. Ibid., p. 168.

78. Darlington, *Darwin's Place in History*.

79. Davies, *The Darwin Conspiracy: Origins of a Scientific Crime*, p. 169; Dov Ospovat, *The Development of Darwin's Theory: Natural History, Natural Theology, and Natural Selection 1838–1859* (New York: Cambridge University Press, 1981).

80. Ibid., p. 138.

81. Ibid., p. 140.

82. Ibid., p. 147.

83. Todd Charles Wood, "There Is No Darwin Conspiracy," *Answers Research Journal* 2(1) (2009): p. 11.

84. Charles Darwin, edited by Frederick Burkhardt, *The Correspondence of Charles Darwin*, Volume 8 (Cambridge, MA: Cambridge University Press, 1993), p. 39.

85. Stephen Jay Gould, "Darwinian Fundamentalism," *New York Review of Books* (June 12, 1997): p. 1.

86. Laurence Croft, *The Life and Death of Charles Darwin* (Lancaster, England: Elmwood, 1989).

87. Davies, *The Darwin Conspiracy: Origins of a Scientific Crime*, p. 163.

88. Margulis and Sagan, *Acquiring Genomes: A Theory of the Origin of Species*, p. 26.

89. Davies, *The Darwin Conspiracy: Origins of a Scientific Crime*, p. 160, 162.

90. Ibid., p. xix.

91. Ibid., p. xix.

92. David Quammen, *The Kiwi's Egg: Charles Darwin & Natural Selection* (London: Weidenfeld & Nicolson, 2007), p. 179.

93. Philip Kitcher, "Should Evolution be Taught in Schools?" 1999, www.slate.com/id/33241/entry/33286, p. 1, emphasis mine.

94. Waller, *Fabulous Science: Fact and Fiction in the History of Scientific Discovery*, p. 180.

CHAPTER 9

Darwin's Faulty Scholarship
— a Review

Chapter Synopsis

Charles Darwin is widely regarded as one of the greatest scientists in history. However, a review of the quality of Darwin's scholarship reveals numerous examples of fraudulent, unethical, or very sloppy work. Many more examples of Darwin's faulty research exist, but the few instances cited in this brief review indicate that the high level of trust still put in Darwin's work is misplaced.

Introduction

Few other persons in recent history have had such a profound effect on the world as Charles Darwin, the man who popularized a naturalistic theory of evolution as outlined in his *The Origin of Species*.[1] Darwin has been credited with having the "single best idea that anyone has ever had . . . ahead of Newton and Einstein and everyone else . . . my admiration for Darwin's magnificent idea is unbounded."[2] Although Darwin was a prolific writer, subsequent research has found that many of his arguments in *The Origin* were superficial or clearly wrong. As a result, he arrived at many incorrect and invalid conclusions.

Research on Darwin's Many Errors

Darwin made thousands of changes to correct errors and to improve the accuracy in his *The Origin* book alone. One study found that the number of revisions Darwin made was so great in his six editions that it is impossible to deal with the number without a variorum text (a text that contains variant readings of different editions of a text so they can be compared to determine changes). The study noted that of

> the 3,878 sentences in the first edition, nearly 3,000, about 75 percent, were rewritten from one to five times each. Over 1,500 sentences were added, and of the original sentences plus these, nearly 325 were dropped. Of the original and added sentences there are nearly 7,500 variants of all kinds. In terms of net added sentences, the sixth edition is nearly a third again as long as the first.[3]

When the *The Origin* manuscript was completed, it was sent to Dr. and Mrs. Hooker to proofread. Mrs. Hooker found parts of it so obscure that Darwin trembled, and "vowed to clarify his ideas in the proofs."[4] Darwin continued his clarification efforts through six more editions and for 12 more years.[5] When Darwin saw the first edition of *The Origin* in print, he lamented the style was "incredibly bad," and made so many corrections that he wrote to his publisher, John Murray, and offered to pay a major part of the cost of making the many corrections required. By "June 21st he had corrected only 130 pages, and by the next day only 20 more."[6]

The many corrections were a "long and dreary struggle. . . . The endless corrections, the despairing efforts to achieve clarity, the knowledge of what was involved . . . the last minute changes of fact and interpretation — all these had worn him out."[7]

The problem of errors was so great that the sixth edition of *The Origin* had to be completely re-typeset and, as a result, a "good many typographical errors were introduced which Darwin failed to catch." By 1878, six years after the sixth edition was completed, all the typographical errors were finally corrected and this edition is now considered Darwin's "final text."[8]

Darwin admitted that he had "much difficulty" in expressing himself "clearly and concisely," which caused him to lose much time, but forced him to "think long and intently about every sentence." Furthermore, Darwin admitted that his "power to follow a long and purely abstract train of thought is very limited," and that his memory was so poor that he has "never been able to remember for more than a few days a single date or a line of poetry."[9] These admissions in and of themselves show a spirit of honesty and humility on Darwin's part, but numerous errors may have been introduced into his writings as a result of these self-admitted shortcomings.

Most authors rewrite their materials to improve clarity, a task handled more effectively now with computers, but many of Darwin's changes involved actual errors. Barrett et al. listed 70 "errors"[10] in the text of Darwin's *The Descent of Man*, and Darwin himself listed 25 errors.[11] An example is that Darwin claimed on page 68 of *The Origin* that rhinoceroses are not killed by beasts of prey when, as Galton pointed out, "it is rare to find a Rhinoceros" that has *not* been attacked by "beasts of prey."[12]

Some of his other major conclusions also turned out to be wrong, such as his prediction that the "Negro races" would become extinct, and that men were more highly evolved than women.[13] Among the many other examples of Darwin's flawed research, probably the most serious was his acceptance of the inheritance of acquired characteristics theory (Lamarckian genetics) and his pangenesis idea — the view that evolution occurs by cells sending information to the gametes to alter the next generation. Darwin's many erroneous conclusions need to be studied further to determine how generalized the examples cited here are. Simonton adds that for

> many Darwinists, he appears to represent the model scientist, the bona fide perfectionist. . . . But if we delve carefully into his lifetime output, this idealized portrait begins to reveal many blemishes. He was capable of publishing erroneous interpretations and even silly conjectures. An early paper provided such a completely mistaken explanation for a

particular geological formation that it came to cause Darwin considerable embarrassment. Later, despite his extremely detailed work on the cirripedes, he was forced to admit that he had "blundered dreadfully about the cement glands."[14]

Other changes he made include excising "much theological language" from later editions of the *The Origin*.[15] Some historians allege that part of Darwin's concern was he was fully aware that his work would cause controversy because the direct intervention of God in creation was, "for most Victorians, even scientists, the only possible explanation for 'the origin of all animal forms.' This fantasy was precisely the last stronghold of British Natural Theology."[16] Darwin knew that his evolution theory would destroy the belief in God's intervention during creation, the last possible reason to believe in natural theology — and in God.

Darwin also evidently became less confident about his theory as he aged, and this was reflected in his books. Jones stated, "In his old age, faced with a wave of inconvenient discoveries, Darwin began to complicate his ideas" to deal with the many "inconvenient discoveries" that argued against his theory in the 1870s. Jones notes that "in 1859 Darwin was more confident" about his theory than in his later life. [17]

For example, Darwin wrote, "I can see no difficulty in a race of bears being rendered, by natural selection, more and more aquatic in their structure and habits, with larger and larger mouths, till a creature was produced as monstrous as a whale."[18] In the sixth edition, this claim was gone and, Darwin's "swimming bear . . . conceals itself with irony."[19] Hedtke even concludes from his study that Darwin indirectly acknowledged some of the fatal weaknesses of his theory in the sixth edition of *The Origin* published in 1872.[20] Some examples of his poor scholarship will now be reviewed.

Darwin's Questionable Claims about Fuegian Cannibalism

E. Lucas Bridges, an author and missionary to Tierra del Fuego, concluded from his firsthand experiences and interviews with the native peoples that Darwin naively and uncritically accepted verbal statements made by the Tierra del Fuego Indians (also called the Yagan Indians). For example, Darwin uncritically accepted the Fuegians' statements that they were cannibals without investigating, and Darwin said he was "certain" about his conclusion.[21] Darwin specifically concluded that the different Tierra del Fuego tribes "when at war are cannibals." Darwin also presumed, on the basis of concurrent "but quite independent evidence of the boy taken by Mr. Low, and of Jemmy Button . . . that when pressed in winter by hunger, they kill and devour their old women before they kill their dogs."[22]

Darwin related that his informants killed their victims by holding them over smoke to choke them. He wrote that his informant had mockingly imitated the screams of the victims and then

> described the parts of their bodies which are considered best to eat. Horrid as such a death by the hands of their friends and relatives must be, the fears of the old women, when hunger begins to press, are more painful to think of; we were told that they then often run away into the mountains, but that they are pursued by the men and brought back to the slaughter-house at their own fire-sides.[23]

Darwin concluded that the Fuegian way of life resulted in frequent famine, and "as a consequence, cannibalism accompanied by parricide" resulted.[24] He then used these conclusions in developing his views on race, which were in turn used to support the racism that developed later in areas such as Nazi Germany.[25] Darwin's conclusions about the Fuegians also supported the racism already common in Europe: "In their native habitat, the Fuegians seemed to epitomize the Europeans' image of the brutal and degraded savage."[26]

Many scholars have repeated Darwin's irresponsible account of Fuegian cannibalism, adding material from other sources, and some even concluding that "frequent and inevitable questions on cannibalism" arose about the Fuegians. An example of the "facts" used as support for the cannibalism claim includes the account of a

Mr. Low who visited the *Beagle* when it was in Tierra del Fuego. Low claimed:

> When hunger set in during the winter months, the Indians would kill the old women of their tribe and eat them. He had interviewed a Fuegian boy who had said that the women were suffocated in the smoke of a campfire. When asked why they did not eat their dogs, the boy had replied, "Doggies catch otters, old women good for nothing: man very hungry." As a joke the boy had imitated the sounds of a woman screaming. Jemmy had confirmed the truth of this story, and an appalled Darwin [recorded it in his notes].[27]

Hazlewood's investigation of the relevant historical documents led him to conclude that there were serious problems with Darwin's account. He notes that the three Fuegians Darwin interviewed were

> uncomfortable talking about the subject, and when they did there were inconsistencies in their stories: they would not eat vultures because the birds might have fed on a human; they would not dump their dead in the sea because they might be eaten by fish, which might in turn be eaten by them. When cannibalism was talked about, Jemmy would refer to his people with shame and deny that he had ever eaten a human. He would prefer, he claimed, to "eat his own hands."[28]

Hazlewood concluded that the Fuegians were actually very adverse to eating human flesh. Keynes noted that the practice of *tobacana*, a form of "kindly" euthanasia, could have produced a "misleading" conclusion that "gave rise to the mistaken notion that cannibalism was sometimes practiced in Tierra del Fuego."[29]

Darwin's Conclusions Were Wrong

Bridges was a missionary who lived among the Fuegian people for some time and knew them very well. He explained that when Darwin first arrived in Tierra del Fuego, the natives had a very limited knowledge of English. As a result, since they could not explain much in English, it was far easier for them to simply answer yes to many questions. Consequently, "The statements with which these young men . . . have been credited were, in fact, no more than agreement with suggestions made by their questioners."[30] While this fact alone does not disprove Darwin's claim that the Fuegians were cannibals, it casts serious doubt on the idea. Bridges continued by noting that it is not hard to

> imagine their reactions when asked what was, to them, a ridiculous question, such as: "Do you kill and eat men?" They would at first be puzzled, but when the inquiry was repeated and they grasped its meaning and realized the answer that was expected they would naturally agree. The interrogator would follow this with: "What people do you eat?" No answer. "Do you eat bad people?" "Yes." "When there are no bad people, what then?" No answer. "Do you eat your old women?" "Yes."

Bridges adds that, once this exchange began, the Fuegians, who acted like "irresponsible youngsters," were encouraged to tell wild stories

> by having their evidence so readily accepted and noted down as fact, would naturally start inventing on their own. We are told that they described, with much detail, how the Fuegians ate their enemies killed in battle and, when there were no such victims, devoured their old women. When asked if they ate dogs when hungry, they said they did not, as dogs were useful for catching otter, whereas the old women were of no use at all. The unfortunates, they said, were held in the thick smoke till they choked to death. The meat, they stated, was very good.

He concluded that once this "delectable fiction" was established, most subsequent attempt at denial would not have been believed, but would have been attributed to a growing unwillingness to confess the horrors in which they had formerly indulged. Accordingly, these young story-tellers allowed their imaginations full rein and vied with each other in the recounting of still more fantastic tales, emboldened by the admiration of the other two.[31]

Bridges' account casts considerable doubt on Darwin's conclusion that Fuegians practiced cannibalism. Nonetheless, the Fuegian cannibalism story is still promoted by Darwinists. An example is Steve Jones, professor of genetics at University College, London recently discussed Darwin's cannibalism statements as if they were valid.[32]

Darwin Was Wrong on His Assessment of the Fuegian Language

Darwin also concluded from his research that language evolved from animalistic emotional communication, such as grunts, into modern languages such as Chinese and English.[33] The evidence that Darwin used to back his theory of language evolution included fieldwork with the Fuegians, a people that lived in South America that he called "savages," "primitive beasts," and "cannibals."[34] Darwin concluded that these "savages" had an extremely primitive, animal-like language.

In contrast to Darwin, Thomas Bridges (born in 1886), a missionary who lived and worked intimately with the Fuegians for many years, concluded that the Fuegians, although they were "one of the poorest tribes of men, without any literature, without poetry, song, history or science . . . have a list of words and a style of structure surpassing that of other tribes [that were] far above them in the arts and comforts of life."[35] Darwin concluded that the Fuegians had only around 100 words in their language, called Yahgan, but Thomas Bridges identified over 32,000 words and inflections when researching the Yahgan language for his Yahgan-English dictionary.[36] To put this number in perspective, a speaker who knows basic grammar and 5,000 words is considered to have basic competence in that language.

Accusations of Forgery

In the 1870s, photographs were a "standard of truth in a wide variety of applications, from the popular to the scientific and documentary."[37] From the start, the camera "emerged as an authoritative source of information" to demonstrate a theory. Because photo illustrations were considered more objective than drawings and paintings, photographs were considered very convincing scientific support for a theory. In November of 1872, Darwin published his book *The Expression of the Emotions in Man and Animals* to prove that human emotions, and thus humans themselves, evolved from some lower animal type.[38] In this book, Darwin used photographs that have become famous for several reasons.

Besides the fact that Darwin's work was one of the first scientific books to use photographs, the main problem with his work was that "some of the photographs . . . were doctored."[39] The charge of doctoring photographs is often ignored in modern accounts of Darwin's work, likely because "strong is the compulsion to save the great men, to protect their reputation and [the reputation] of science herself."[40] Had such activity been discovered in the writings of Darwin's critics, however, they no doubt would not have been treated as gently.

The photographs were of people's faces expressing what Darwin considered were genetically based universal emotions existing in both man and beast, such as grief, joy, anger, disgust, surprise, contempt, fear, horror, and shame.[41] To prove humans had a lower animal past, Darwin wanted to demonstrate that the same emotional states were common, not only in human groups world wide, but also in animals. This view contradicted the beliefs of most Europeans at the time. Sir Charles Bell argued that there existed muscles in human faces that were without analogy in lower animals. Bell believed that these muscles were designed to display uniquely human emotions, and were evidence for both a Creator and against common descent.

Darwin was specifically trying to disprove the conclusions of Bell and others that human expressions reflect design by a divine being, believing instead that the origin of these expressions lies in evolution.[42] During the summer of 1840, Darwin read Bell's work on expression of emotions, which increased his interest on this subject, but he "could not at all agree with his belief that various muscles had been specially created for the sake of expression."[43] Darwin then determined to prove this idea wrong. Bell was a professor of surgery, and was both knighted and a medalist.

He further tried to prove that the key to understanding human emotions was to view these emotions as vestigial or residual habits inherited from our evolutionary ancestors. Darwin used his photographs of humans expressing emotions as proof of his theory:

> The photographs he selected for inclusion in *The Expression* were designed to interest and engage his readers, even at the expense of scientific objectivity. Consideration of the photographic illustrations in *The Expression* demonstrates that Darwin had the capacity to act as a shrewd strategist.[44]

Although Darwin admitted that some of the photographs he used were posed, and others were modified, Paul Ekman, a social psychologist and Darwinist at the University of California, San Francisco, "found from the Darwin archives and correspondence that the alterations were more extensive" than previously believed.[45] Furthermore, instead of photographing natural expressions elicited in normal human situations, many of the photographs which were implied or openly claimed to be typical humans responding to real situations, were actually posed! Thus, Darwin went far beyond simply retouching them, which would have been a problem even if Darwin had admitted that the photographs were doctored.

Judson related that Darwin used several photographs by London photographer Oscar Rejlander because Rejlander "proved especially skillful at securing the expressions Darwin wanted."[46] Rejlander also even occasionally posed for his own camera. Trodger determined that one picture of Rejlander's wife (see figure 1) was artificially produced for Darwin in order to illustrate "a most convincing sneer."[47] Rejlander is most often identified with the "composite printing"

Figure 1. Photograph purporting to be a "sneer" which was actually intentionally posed.

From *The Expression of the Emotions in Man and Animals* (London: J. Murray, 1872), p. 251.

technique (today called "trick photography") in which several negatives were

combined to create a photographic print with elements of several pictures. As a result, Rejlander was able to manipulate his images, and produce convincing photorealistic images that were actually artificially assembled in the darkroom.[48]

Rejlander put his trick photography skills to good use to help Darwin prove his thesis. The first and most celebrated photograph in Darwin's *The Expression* book is of a weeping baby that actually turned out to be a drawing Rejlander altered to make it look like a photograph.[49] Darwin titled this picture "mental distress."[50] It was a photographic copy of a drawing made from an original photograph.[51] This allowed Rejlander to "highlight elements of the image Darwin sought to express . . . the child's hair, cheeks, and brow . . . seem slightly more lively and energetic in the drawn version."[52] A major change was that the child was put into an unnaturally small chair by means of trick photography, making the child look "larger-than-life" as shown in figure 2. The goal was to create an "illustration that would have seemed persuasive to Darwin's readers."[53]

Darwin nowhere mentioned in his writings that this picture was actually an altered copy of a photograph that was "changed substantially from the photographic original."[54] Ironically, T. H. Huxley (called *Darwin's Bulldog* because of his major role as Darwin's apologist) was one of the main *critics* of Darwin's photographic manipulations.[55]

Figure 2. A "fake" photograph of an infant girl in a chair. The child was made to look much larger than life by using trick photography to put her in an unnaturally small chair for her size. See text for details.

From Charles Darwin, *The Expression of the Emotions in Man and Animals* (London: J. Murray, 1872) p. 148.

It was also discovered that Darwin used eight photographs by Professor Duchenne, a Paris physiologist who actually used electrodes to stimulate the facial muscles in patients.[56] Duchenne published a book that contained photographs of patients forced to endure such barbaric treatments (for example, see figure 3). The patients included those diagnosed as epileptic, spastic, and having palsy, paralysis, and multiple sclerosis. From another set of more than 40 photographs of mental patients, Darwin selected a woman diagnosed as insane to use as an example of a "normal" human expression![57] There is a considerable difference between using electrodes to force facial expressions and capturing the results of genuine emotions naturally expressed by a person. Likewise, substantial dissimilarity

Figure 3. This photograph reveals the use of electrodes on a mental patient to produce the "natural" expression of horror and agony. The picture printed in Darwin's book cut out the two men and the electrodes so that only a careful inspection would reveal evidence of electrodes.

The modified copy is in Charles Darwin, *The Expression of the Emotions in Man and Animals* (London: J. Murray, 1872) p. 300.

exists between artificial facial contortions touched up by an artist and capturing people on film in the natural act of expressing joy, disgust, or one of the many other human emotions. The *purpose* of using photography was to study facial expressions "without relying on the expertise of visual artists."[58]

To obtain scientifically meaningful photographs, it should first be determined that the person in the photograph actually manifested joy or the other emotions of concern and then, and only then, should photographs of his or her facial expression be used to represent that emotion. To artificially produce what an observer *thinks* is a sneer is quite different than evaluating the results of expressing this genuine emotion as confirmed by the subject. This is critical because "Darwin believed that the objectivity of photographic evidence could be used to challenge" existing ideas about the expression of emotion, thus proving his theory that human expressions were inherited from lower animals.[59]

In one engraved plate, Darwin[60] used extensive cropping that removed a "substantial portion of the original image."[61] In this case, Darwin instructed the engraver to remove the hands of the experimenter and the electrodes that were used to stimulate the facial muscles of the subject.[62] The altered picture is reproduced in figure 4.

Figure 4. A drawing from the photograph in Figure 3. The caption in Darwin's *The Expression of the Emotions in Man and Animals* says, "Fig. 21. Horror and Agony. Copied from a photograph by Dr. Duchenne." Note that the electrodes shown on the subject in Figure 3 are not shown on this etching. The etching is from the 1872 edition (London: J. Murray, 1872) p. 306.

Prodger concluded that Darwin's changes in the pictures were required because the original

> photographs were too honest, in that they recorded the actual situation of the sitter in his laboratory environment. To engage his readers, Darwin cultivated an appearance of objectivity that actually misrepresented experimental events.[63]

Darwinists have actually tried to justify what they call the compromises that Darwin made in preparing his illustrations. In an attempt to justify Darwin's behavior, some even argued that "rules about photographic objectivity did not exist then, partially because photographers frequently manipulated their work to enhance its visual appeal and clarity."[64] These arguments are an invalid defense because what Darwin was after was not visual appeal or clarity, such as is done for an art show, but photographic evidence that purported to accurately represent internal emotions in order to support evolutionism. As Prodger admitted, though, much of the criticism against Darwin is justified.

The fact is, "far from scientifically factual, these photographs formed part of a narrative strategy designed to advance his theoretical concerns."[65] In other words, Darwin used fraud to try to prove his evolution theory, as did Haeckel with his drawings. Although the photos are widely known and influential, the fact is, they were faked.[66] As is also true with Haeckel's drawings, Darwin's "photographic illustrations were carefully contrived to present evidence Darwin considered important to his work. . . . He knew that photography . . . [was] powerfully persuasive."[67]

Although the technology did not exist in the 1870s to produce the quality achieved today, Darwin was clearly amiss in not explaining in detail exactly how his photographs were done. It is inexcusable to pass off "contrived" photographs as accurate representations of research on emotions. Also of note is that Darwin claimed he arrived at his basic conclusions only at the close of his observations on facial expression around 1870, yet Ekman found that all of his basic conclusions were in his notebooks written in 1838–1839![68]

Current Research on Human Emotional Expression

Some of Darwin's obvious observations about the expression of emotions have proven correct. For example, he accurately showed that, although culture was influential, many basic emotional expressions were universal among humans. Much of the research on facial expressions, however, does not support Darwin's basic conclusion that virtually all human facial expressions are inherited in a Lamarckian fashion and are similar for many primates (for examples see Paul Ekman, *Darwin and Facial Expression*[69]). In addition, we now know that some of his other basic conclusions "are completely wrong."[70]

In support of the genetic role of expressive behavior, Darwin concluded that the major expressions in animals, including humans, "are not learned but are present from the earliest days and throughout life are quite beyond our control."[71] Current researchers have found that the empirical evidence does *not* support Darwin's general position, but rather that social factors have a critical influence on

> the non-verbal expression of emotional states both with and without purposeful or voluntary intent. There appear to be cultural conventions concerning stereotypic displays of pain that enable people to enact them with ease. Facial displays of many subjective states are subject to the influence of "display rules" that are internalized in the course of socialization.[72]

Craig also reported that his research on facial configurations elicited by the ingestion of sour, salty, and bitter solutions, found these solutions caused "negative facial expression components in all three regions of the face." In contrast to Darwin's conclusions, though, they did not result in the widely open, "squarish" mouth facial expression that Darwin claimed was characteristic of the "cry face."[73]

Darwin was also guilty of anthropomorphism, even claiming that monkeys expressed vexation, jealousy, grief, sadness, disgust, anger, pleasure, and other clear human emotions. Although some animals experience emotion, it is often difficult, if not impossible, for humans to scientifically determine many specific emotions that an animal is experiencing at any specific time.[74] Pet owners and farmers that keep animals know that dramatic differences in animal and human expressions exist. Except to frighten enemies or display submission, most animals, other than certain primates, are largely expressionless.

Furthermore, some of Darwin's examples appear open to other interpretations.[75] Darwin also relied heavily on anecdotal accounts by others rather than gathering empirical data himself. As a result, Ekman concluded, Darwin "often dealt with faulty data."[76] In conclusion, as stated in the introduction to the St. Martin's edition of Darwin's *Expression*, "Some of his conclusions are probably correct, others almost certainly incorrect."[77]

Julia Pastrana

One more example of Darwin's faulty research was the case of the so-called missing link, Julia Pastrana. In his discussion of her, Darwin includes incorrect claims about this so-called ape woman who was passed off by many Darwinists as evidence of a living ape-to-human transitional form. For example, Darwin incorrectly claimed she had four rows of teeth. What Darwin had written about Julia may have been correct about her character, however, he was wrong about her anatomy because "if anyone had bothered to ask her, she could have immediately responded that she certainly did not have any extra rows of teeth in her mouth (though she did have gum problems). . . . Real people don't have four rows of teeth."[78]

An English dentist examined the casts of Julia's jaws described by Darwin and concluded, in contrast to what Darwin had claimed, that she, in fact, had

> a few unusually large teeth projecting from greatly thickened and irregular alveolar processes . . . [but] she *did not* possess an excessive number of teeth in double rows . . . the overgrowth of her gum and alveolar process was responsible for her prognathism and what is described as simian appearance.[79]

Gylseth and Toverud also noted that "Darwin was likewise wrong in stating that Dr. Purland made the casts: it was actually a dentist by the name of Weiss" that made the casts.[80] This mistake and other errors about Julia are illustrative of many such minor and major mistakes Darwin made in his writings. If a Darwinism skeptic had made some of these same mistakes, evolutionists would have mercilessly condemned him or her.

Darwin, a Poor Scientist

Often, accounts of Darwin "have exaggerated his field skills and his ability to grasp fully the significance of many of his discoveries."[81] Many references "imply that Darwin made careful collections of specimens from around the world and that he understood their importance at the time of collection" but, in fact,

> Darwin remained in England after returning from his voyage of *HMS Beagle*, so most of his collecting was undertaken when he was very young. When the *Beagle* set sail he was aged just 22 . . . [and] when he began collecting specimens he was an inexperienced and rather disorganized graduate in divinity. He was appointed to the position of naturalist on *HMS Beagle* more because his social status made him a suitable companion for the captain, Robert FitzRoy, than for his abilities as a naturalist. Darwin was his *second* choice.[82]

Rees adds that a large problem was, when collecting specimens on the Galapagos Islands,

> Darwin rarely bothered to label any of the specimens he collected by island because he did not think it important. Although he was told during the final days of his visit that many trees and tortoises were unique to each island, by then it was too late and his collecting was finished. As the *Beagle* crossed the Pacific he ate the tortoises, and the carapaces — the most obvious clue to the adaptive radiation of the species — were thrown into the sea.[83]

Furthermore, when Darwin returned to England, he presented the Zoological Society with 80 mammals and 450 birds to be mounted and identified, but was forced to

> rely upon experts to identify and catalogue his collection because he lacked the expertise to do this work himself. During a visit to the Linnean Society, Darwin was forced to admit that "[he] knew no more about the plants, which [he] had collected, than the Man on the Moon."[84]

The fact is, "Darwin had great difficulty" telling the Galapagos Island finches apart and "mixed up the samples of birds collected from different islands," even admitting that he

> could not separate them into species and did not appreciate the significance of the shapes of their bills. . . . The specimens were badly labeled and not considered to be particularly important by Darwin. He had no sense that they were members of a closely related group with bills adapted to the exploitation of particular niches.[85]

In fact, it was Professor John Gould, then Zoological Society Superintendent of stuffed birds,

> who recognized that the specimens represented 12 species of closely related finches. It was only later that Darwin appreciated the evolutionary significance of this. The more detailed work on resource utilization by Galapagos finches was undertaken much later principally by David Lack.[86]

The Mysterious Mr. Collins

One error Darwin made in the first chapter of the *Origin* caused "intense research for nearly a century and a half."[87] The mystery, which was finally solved, turned out to be a spelling error of the name of a famous cattle breeder, a Mr. Collins who was actually Charles Colling. Colling was the most famous Shorthorn breeder, a man who became rich satisfying the British appetite for beef. Of note is the fact that the error persisted through all six editions of the *Origin*.[88] Darwin does discuss Colling's breeding program involving a famous bull named "Favorite," but Ogawa speculates that Darwin did not investigate Colling's work in much detail until after the publication of *The Origin*.[89] When Darwin discussed Colling later, he again misspelled his name, this time as "Collings."[90] Ogawa concludes that "Collins is a myth who has lived for 140 years on the strength of *On the Origin of Species* alone."[91]

Conclusions

Darwin is often regarded as one of the most highly esteemed scientists who ever lived.[92] A balanced view of his work requires an evaluation of his scholarly shortcomings. These few examples of the many Darwinian errors that exist illustrate the fact that his conclusions were based both on faulty analysis and data. His research was often very superficial and strongly biased toward his thesis. In the case of the Fuego Indians documented above, he was also very gullible in relying on informants who were not just inaccurate, but for several reasons were wrong.

Although much of what is presently known in the life sciences was unknown when Darwin wrote his major works, this does not excuse his adopting the many incorrect conclusions reviewed in this chapter. An excellent summation of Darwin's many errors by Simonton concluded that his mistakes have been forgotten or forgiven. An example is Darwin's erroneous

> geological paper on Glen Roy is politely ignored by geologists, and his work on the barnacles has been superseded by more accurate monographs. Darwin's theory of pangenesis has been reduced to a tiny footnote in the history of evolutionary theory. What remains in posterity's eyes is a sanitized Darwin whose career seems quite un-Darwinian — no variation and selection, no trial and error, no hits and misses. Yet I hope that this misperception will eventually enter the historical record as just another false idea that did not

survive cultural selection. This unjustified glorification of genius must be buried and fossilized along with the dinosaurs."[93]

Yet another example is Darwin's claim that the Ancon sheep was a new breed of sheep, proving that a new species can evolve in one generation. The sheep turned out to be a diseased sheep suffering from a lethal genetic deformity, not a new breed.[94] In view of the adulation given to Darwin, his many mistakes should neither be forgotten nor forgiven.

Endnotes

1. Charles Darwin, *The Origin of Species* (London: John Murray, 1859).

2. Daniel Dennett, *Darwin's Dangerous Idea: Evolution and the Meanings of Life* (New York: Simon and Schuster, 1996), p. 21.

3. Morse Peckham, editor, *The Origin of Species by Charles Darwin: A Variorum Text* (Philadelphia, PA: University of Pennsylvania Press, 1959), p. 9. A variorum contains variant readings of a text.

4. Ibid., p. 15.

5. Ibid., p. 15.

6. Ibid., p. 15.

7. Ibid., p. 15.

8. Ibid., p. 23–24.

9. Charles Darwin, edited by Nora Barlow, *The Autobiography of Charles Darwin* (New York: Norton, 1958), p. 136–137, 140

10. Paul H. Barrett et al., editors, *A Concordance to Darwin's The Descent of Man, and Selection in Relation to Sex* (Ithaca, NY: Cornell University Press, 1987).

11. Charles Darwin, edited by F. Burkhardt, *The Correspondence of Charles Darwin*, Volume 3 (New York: Cambridge University Press, 1987), p. 1135.

12. Charles Darwin, *The Correspondence of Charles Darwin*, Volume 7, 1858–1859, *Supplement to the Correspondence 1821–1857* (New York: Cambridge University Press, 1991), p. 417, 427.

13. Jerry Bergman, "The History of the Human Female Inferiority Ideas in Evolutionary Biology," *Biology Forum* 95 (2002):379–412.

14. D.K. Simonton, *Origins of Genius: Darwinian Perspectives on Creativity* (New York: Oxford University Press, 1999), p. 157.

15. Peckham, *The Origin of Species by Charles Darwin: A Variorum Text*, p. 10.

16. Ibid., p. 14.

17. Steve Jones, *Darwin's Ghost: The Origin of Species Updated* (New York: Random House, 2000), p. xxv.

18. Darwin, *The Origin of Species*, p. 184.

19. Jones, *Darwin's Ghost: The Origin of Species Updated*, p. xxv.

20. Randall Hedtke, *Secrets of the Sixth Edition* (Green Forest, AR: Master Books, 2010).

21. E.L. Bridges, *Uttermost Parts of the Earth* (London: Hodder and Stoughton, 1948), p. 33.

22. Charles Darwin, *The Expression of Emotions in Man and Animals: The Works of Charles Darwin*, Volume 10 (New York: AMS Press, 1896), p. 214.

23. Ibid., p. 214.

24. Charles Darwin, *Journal of Researches into the Natural History and Geology of the Counties Visited During the Voyage of the H.M.S. Beagle*, new edition (New York: D. Appleton, 1839), p. 236.

25. Jerry Bergman, "Darwinism and the Nazi Race Holocaust," *CenTech J.* 13(2) (1999):101–111; Richard Weikart, *From Darwin to Hitler: Evolutionary Ethics, Eugenics, and Racism in Germany* (New York: Palgrave Macmillan, 2004); Richard Weikart, *Hitler's Ethic: The Nazi Pursuit of Evolutionary Progress* (New York: Palgrave MacMillan, 2009).

26. Peter Bowler, *Charles Darwin; The Man and His Influence* (Cambridge, MA: Blackwell, 1990), p. 58.

27. Nick Hazlewood, *Savage — The Life and Times of Jemmy Button* (New York: Thomas Dunne Books/St. Martin's Press, 2001), p. 114.

28. Ibid., p. 114–115.

29. Richard Keynes, *Fossils, Finches and Fuegians — Charles Darwin's Adventures and Discoveries on the Beagle, 1832–1836* (London: HarperCollins, 2003), p. 214.

30. Bridges, *Uttermost Parts of the Earth*, p. 33.

31. Ibid., p. 33.

32. Jones, *Darwin's Ghost: The Origin of Species Updated*, p. 26.

33. T. Bever and M. Montalbetti, "Noam's Ark," *Science* 298 (2002): p. 1565.

34. Jerry Bergman, "Was Charles Darwin a Racist?" *CRSQ* 44(1) (Summer 2007):27–35.

35. Vera Barclay, *Darwinism Is Not for Children* (London, UK: Herbert Jenkins, 1950), p. 148.

36. Ibid., p. 147.

37. Phillip Prodger, *An Annotated Catalogue of the Illustrations of Human and Animal Expression from the Collection of Charles Darwin: An Early Case of the Use of Photography in Scientific Research* (Lewiston, NY: Edwin Mellen Press, 1998), p. 143.

38. Ibid., p. 149.

39. Horace Freeland Judson, *The Great Betrayal: Fraud in Science* (Orlando, FL: Harcourt, 2004), p. 49.

40. Ibid., p. 49.

41. Prodger, *An Annotated Catalogue of the Illustrations of Human and Animal Expression*, p. 62.

42. Ibid., p. 154.

43. Darwin, *The Autobiography of Charles Darwin*, p. 132.

44. Prodger, *An Annotated Catalogue of the Illustrations of Human and Animal Expression*, p. 146.

45. Judson, *The Great Betrayal: Fraud in Science*, p. 62.

46. Ibid., p. 63.

47. Ibid., p. 63.

48. Prodger, *An Annotated Catalogue of the Illustrations of Human and Animal Expression*, p. 170.

49. Judson, *The Great Betrayal: Fraud in Science*, p. 63.

50. Charles Darwin, *The Expression of Emotions in Man and Animals* (London: Julian Friedmann Publishers, 1979), p. 149.

51. Prodger, *An Annotated Catalogue of the Illustrations of Human and Animal Expression*, p. 173.

52. Ibid., p. 173.

53. Ibid., p. 174.

54. Ibid., p. 175.

55. Ibid., p. 177; Thomas Huxley, *Lay Sermons, Addresses, and Reviews* (New York: D. Appleton, 1915).

56. Laura Helmuth, "Boosting Brain Activity from the Outside In," *Science* 292 (2001):1284.

57. Prodger, *An Annotated Catalogue of the Illustrations of Human and Animal Expression*, p. 162.

58. Ibid., p. 141.

59. Ibid., p. 141.

60. Darwin, *The Expression of Emotions in Man and Animals*, p. 306.

61. Prodger, *An Annotated Catalogue of the Illustrations of Human and Animal Expression*, p. 166.

62. Ibid., p. 168–170.

63. Ibid., p. 179.

64. Ibid., p. 174.

65. Judson, *The Great Betrayal: Fraud in Science*, p. 141.

66. Ibid., p. 83.

67. Prodger, *An Annotated Catalogue of the Illustrations of Human and Animal Expression*, p. 144.

68. Charles Darwin, Paul Ekman, and Phillip Prodger, *Expression of the Emotions in Man and Animals* (New York: Oxford University Press, 1998), p. xxvii.

69. Paul Ekman, editor, *Darwin and Facial Expression: A Century of Research in Review* (New York: Academic Press, 1973).

70. Darwin, Ekman, and Prodger, *Expression of the Emotions in Man and Animals*, p. xv; Paul Ekman and Erika Rosenberg, *What the Face Reveals: Basic and Applied Studies of Spontaneous Expression Using the Facial Action Coding System (FACS)*, "Different Facial Responses to Four Basic Tests in Newborns," by Diana Rosenstein and Harriet Oster (New York: Oxford University Press, 1997), p. 302–319; Timothy Lenoir, editor, *Inscribing Science: Scientific Texts and the Materiality of Communication* (Stanford, CA: Stanford University Press, 1998).

71. Darwin, *The Expression of Emotions in Man and Animals*, p. 352.

72. Ekman and Rosenberg, *What the Face Reveals*, "Genuine, Suppressed, and Faked Facial Behavior during Exacerbation of Chronic Low Back Pain," by Kenneth D. Craig, Susan A. Hyde, and Christopher J. Patrick, p. 161–163.

73. Ibid., p. 323.

74. Darwin, Ekman, and Prodger, *Expression of the Emotions in Man and Animals*, p. xxix–xxx.

75. Paul Ekman, Joseph J. Campos, Richard J. Davidson, and Frans B.M. de Waal, *Emotions Inside Out: 130 Years after Darwin's the Expression of the Emotions in Man and Animals* (New York: The New York Academy of Sciences, 2003), p. 3.

76. Darwin, Ekman, Prodger, Expression of the Emotions in Man and Animals, p. xxxii.

77. Charles Darwin, *The Expression of Emotions in Man and Animals* (London: Julian Friedmann Publishers; New York: St. Martin's Press, 1979), introduction by S.J. Rachman, p. ii.

78. Christopher Hals Gylseth and Lars O. Toverud, *Julia Pastrana: The Tragic Story of the Victorian Ape Woman* (London: Sutton Publishing, 2003), p. 39.

79. Ibid., p. 40, emphasis added.

80. Ibid., p. 40.

81. Paul A. Rees, "The Evolution of Textbook Misconceptions about Darwin," *Journal of Biological Education* 41(2) (Spring 2007):53.

82. Ibid., p. 54.

83. Ibid., p. 54.

84. Ibid., p. 54.

85. Rees, "The Evolution of Textbook Misconceptions about Darwin," p. 57.

86. Ibid., p. 54.

87. Mariko Ogawa, "The Mysterious Mr. Collins: Living for 140 Years in *Origin of Species*," *Journal of the History of Biology* 34 (2001):461.

88. Ibid., p. 464.

89. Ibid., p. 468.

90. Ibid., p. 469.

91. Ibid., p. 476.

92. Simonton, *Origins of Genius: Darwinian Perspectives on Creativity*.

93. Ibid., p. 157.

94. Karlene Schwartz and Jane Vogel, "Unraveling the Yarn of the Ancon Sheep," *Bioscience* 44 (1994):764–768; Jerry Bergman, "The Ancon Sheep: Just another Loss Mutation," *Technical Journal* 17(1) (2003):18–19.

CHAPTER 10

Pangenesis: Darwin's Now Disproved Theory

Chapter Synopsis

Evolution is based on the natural selection of existing biological traits. Natural selection can only eliminate existing traits, it cannot create new ones. Evolution requires a theory to explain the origin of new genetic information. The theory of pangenesis was a major attempt to explain the source of new genetic information required to produce phenotypic variety. This theory, advocated by Darwin as the main source of new genetic variety, has now been empirically disproved. This is only one of many examples where Darwin was wrong.

Introduction

Given the existence of a cell as the supposed starting point for evolution, Darwinists today must document how a one-celled organism could have evolved into the enormous variety of life existing today.[1] Darwin noted that the struggle for existence was occurring all around him, and concluded that beneficial biological variations were more likely to survive, whereas the less useful ones often perished. While this *tends* to be true in some situations and with certain traits, it is a gross over-simplification and over-generalization that does not explain the arrival of the fittest.

Selection of characteristics produced by an existing animal genome is very different than evolving an entirely new trait or organ.

The most fundamental objection to the natural selection theory to explain the existence of all life is that selection, whether natural or artificial, does not have the power to create a new structure or organ. It can only change the *frequency* of a trait existing in the population. The famous French scientist Hugo De Vries long ago noted that although natural selection may explain the survival of the fittest, it cannot explain the *arrival* of the fittest.[2] Natural selection cannot create, as is often assumed, it can only sift.[3] Almost a century after De Vries, Charlesworth also observed that selection "merely acts as a sieve, preserving some variants and rejecting others; it does not create variation."[4]

A major problem with macroevolution theory, even before Charles Darwin (1809–1882) formally presented his ideas to the world in 1859, was the lack of a viable mechanism that could produce new genetic information. It is well documented that some animal types have lost the struggle for life and, as a result, became extinct. Although Darwin documented how "favored variations are preserved in the struggle for existence,"[5] in his *Origin of Species* book, the "problem of just how those variations were produced in the first place remained elusive as ever."[6] It is true that Darwin presented much evidence for natural selection (*survival* of the fittest) in his *Origin of Species*, but "ironically never explains where new species come from" in the first place — the problem of the *arrival* of the fittest.[7]

A coherent evolution theory requires a documented source of new biological variation on which natural selection can operate. Yet much disagreement still exists among Darwinists about the viability of various methods that could produce increased genetic information.

Darwin is often credited with formulating the modern theory of biological evolution. In his 1859 work, Darwin argued that what we now call genetic change was due to "random" changes in the genome, and these changes were then selected by natural selection.[8] Realizing that he had to explain how heritable variation arises in more detail than the "random" non-explanation claim, Darwin "increasingly retreated to Larmarck's view that different circumstances evoke different responses in organisms."[9]

Darwin's Pangenesis Theory

On May 27, 1865, Darwin sent a copy of a 30-page manuscript on pangenesis to T.H. Huxley to review.[10] Huxley was very impressed with the theory and suggested that Darwin publish his views. In 1868, Darwin's pangenesis theory was published as chapter 27 in Volume 2 of his *The Variation of Animals and Plants under Domestication*. Darwin said he was "forced" to develop his view from the facts of biology.[11] Darwin hoped this theory would solve the origin of variation problem and account "for all known genetic phenomena" and "all the observable facts and laws of inheritance."[12]

Pangenesis "was the next logical step in Darwin's theory of evolution, for he needed to explain how the variations arose upon which natural selection acted."[13] Nobel Laureate James D. Watson explained that Darwin, "desperate to support his theory of evolution by natural selection with a viable hypothesis of inheritance, put forth . . . pangenesis in the second half of the nineteenth century."[14]

Pangenesis was not a minor footnote to Darwin's theory; he believed that this mechanism was the *major* source of most all new genetic information that was required for evolution, thus was at the heart of his theory.[15] He first discussed this idea in 1836 and worked on it for 40 years until he published it in detail in 1875.[16] In the end, "Darwin spent a considerable part of his career attempting to launch a hypothesis that *On the Origin of Species* (1859) conspicuously lacks — a hypothesis to account for the facts of heredity."[17]

Significantly, "pangenesis was to remain the only general theory of inheritance until the end of the nineteenth century."[18] The main competing theory of inheritance involved trait blending, a view that Darwin knew would result in the *loss* of the variation that was required in order for natural selection to function. As Professor Gillham explained:

> The difficulty this "paint pot" view of heredity presented was that the variations on which natural selection was

supposed to act would be lost. If a variant is likened to a few drops of black paint and the predominant form to a bucket of white paint, the variant will vanish when mixed (crossed) into the bucket. So how could the small changes upon which natural selection acts accumulate? Darwin assumed the hereditary determinants were particulate.[19]

Darwin conceived the pangenesis theory to explain the *source* of these particulate hereditary determinants. He was convinced that the "constant supply of new variants" required by his theory could be produced by pangenesis.[20]

Pangenesis Forerunners

Although Darwin coined the word *pangenesis*, the idea itself was not new, but similar to theories discussed as far back as the early Greek philosophers.[21] Moore traces pangenesis back to c. 400 B.C.[22] For example, Hippocrates wrote that biological traits first acquired by "practice," such as increased muscle mass by weight lifting, in time

became an inherited characteristic and the practice was no longer necessary. The seed comes from all parts of the body, healthy from the healthy parts and sickly from the sickly. If therefore bald parents usually have bald children, gray-eyed parents gray-eyed children, if squinting parents have squinting children, why should not long-headed parents have long-headed children.[23]

Pangenesis is one theory of peripheral origin of variation, and contrasts with the germinal origin of variation theory.[24] Although Darwin was strongly influenced by his precursors who developed theories of peripheral origins of variation, especially Herbert Spencer and Charles Naudin, his views were in some respects fundamentally different from most other naturalists. Pangenesis was most similar to Buffon's theory that postulated organic molecules from all parts of the body were collected in the reproductive fluids.[25] Some scholars have concluded that Darwin evidently learned about pan-genesis theories similar to his own only after he developed his own idea.[26] Interestingly, Aristotle rejected pangenesis for many of the same reasons it is rejected today.[27]

Pangenesis Biology

Pangenesis is based on the belief that each and every part of an organism, including all organs (kidneys, bones, eyes, liver), tissues, somatic cells, and even parts of cells, produce "gemmules" during every stage of the organism's development, from embryo to adult. Thus, every developmental stage is subject to environmental modi-fication, not just the adult stage.[28] Darwin's pangenesis theory held that "environmental changes, acting on the reproductive organs or the body, were necessary to generate variation."[29] Darwin wrote that pangenesis implies every separate "unit" of heredity he called gem-mules came from the entire organization to reproduce itself.[30] These gemmules were "extremely minute, similar to the infectious agents found in small pox or rinderpest" and, for this reason, Darwin lik-ened them to granules or atoms.[31] Although produced throughout the lifetime of the organism, they can remain dormant for generations.

After the gemmules are modified by their environment, they are released from the cell and then travel from their source into the body's circulatory system to the sex cells called gametes.[32] In Darwin's words, cells "throw off minute granules or atoms, which circulate freely throughout the system, and when supplied with proper nutri-ents multiply by self-division subsequently becoming developed into cells like those from which they were derived . . . the granules must be thoroughly diffused [in] the steady circulation of fluids throughout the body."[33]

As these gemmules circulate throughout the body, they multiply by dividing several times when properly nourished, eventually col-lecting in the organism's gametes (both eggs and sperm) by a "mutual affinity."[34] In Darwin's view, the "sexual elements" (gametes) were "nothing but a collection of gemmules derived from somatic units."[35] The modified gemmules were eventually transmitted to the parent's offspring, causing an inherited difference in the offspring compared to the parents.

During the development of the offspring, the gemmules were believed to "unite with one another, or with partially formed cells, to produce new cells of the sort that had originally produced them."[36] Darwin believed that this system of gemmule inheritance was the mechanism that produced the variation on which natural selection acts. Darwin summarized his theory as follows:

> The hypothesis of Pangenesis, as applied to the several great classes of facts just discussed, no doubt is extremely complex, but so are the facts. The chief assumption is that all the units of the body, besides having the universally admitted power of growing by self-division, throw off minute gemmules which are dispersed through the system. . . . the gemmules grow, multiply, and aggregate themselves into buds and the sexual elements; their development depending on their union with other nascent cells or units.[37]

Darwin concluded that gemmules are also "capable of transmission in a dormant state, like seeds in the ground, to successive generations."

> The gemmules thrown off from each different unit throughout the body must be inconceivably numerous and minute. Each unit of each part, as it changes during development, and we know that some insects undergo at least twenty metamorphoses, must throw off its gemmules. But the same cells may long continue to increase by self-division, and even become modified by absorbing peculiar nutriment, without necessarily throwing off modified gemmules. All organic beings, moreover, include many dormant gemmules derived from their grandparents and more remote progenitors, but not from all their progenitors.[38]

He added that each cell of a plant has the potential of

reproducing the whole plant; but it has this power only in virtue of containing gemmules derived from every part. When a cell or unit is from some cause modified, the gemmules derived from it will be in like manner modified.[39]

Pangenesis was vital to Darwin's evolution theory because he concluded that it explained a wide variety of observational data.[40] Pangenesis is how the experiences of parents can be passed on to their offspring. Darwin argued that, once transmitted, the gemmules could show up in biological changes in the next generation, or could be passed on to future generations in the dormant state. If these gemmule stored traits showed up in latter generations they were called atavistic traits, an idea that introduced many harmful ideas into criminology.[41]

Darwin discussed his pangenesis idea in great detail and he felt confident that it would provide the mechanism necessary to produce the new genetic information required for macroevolution. Pangenesis, although a little known idea today, was dear to Darwin's heart. Sermonti concludes that the "pangenesis" theory teaches:

An egg is made from features of the parent organism that transmit their earthly past through the seminal fluid in the form of little particles. According to pangenesis, the entire organism generates the offspring. Only in this way could Darwin explain the evolution of the species — i.e., as a decanting of the vicissitudes of the parents' lives into the offspring. For Darwin, evolution was the cumulative experience of the world's organisms over time.[42]

Pangenesis theory was credited by some scientists as being superior to all previous attempts to explain the origin of new biological variations.[43]

Lethal Problems with Pangenesis

Darwin concluded that gemmules were somehow modified by the *direct action* of some body change, such as muscle development as a result of exercise.[44] How these "granules or atoms" were modified in the cell, or how they were "thrown off" and carried into what we now recognize as the genetic information in the gametes, was never explained by Darwin, even in theory.[45]

Nor could Darwin explain what gemmules were. This is why he used so many terms to describe them including granules, particles, atoms, and even cells, a term he waffled on because he believed that "the cell theory is not fully established."[46] The theory also produced little or no insight into determining which traits would be expressed, what could trigger their expression, and how they were expressed.

Darwin's argument that some gemmules were dormant for a time, and were somehow activated in later generations, was also problematic — what controlled this activation, and how they could be activated was never explained.[47] He argued that environmental modifications may require several generations to activate the gemmules and thus show up in the phenotype, allowing environmentally produced traits to appear in one's grandchildren!

Darwin had no experimental or empirical evidence for his theory, yet wrote about it in great detail as if he possessed solid empirical scientific evidence. Nonetheless, Darwin himself appeared to have some doubts about his pangenesis theory from the very beginning. In 1868, he wrote a letter to Hooker stating, "I fear Pangenesis is stillborn," adding that he was confident that it will "at some future time reappear, begotten by some other father and christened by some other name."[48] He later ignored his doubts and fought in support of his theory.

Pangenesis — a Lamarckian View

Pangenesis is actually a Lamarckian idea because it teaches that factors, such as exercise or learning, can cause changes in body cells that are passed on to one's progeny. In other words, in harmony with

Lamarck's teaching, Darwin taught that "acquired characteristics" *can* be inherited. The acquired characteristic theory was so central to Darwin's theory that he concluded any viable theory of inheritance *must* allow for its influence.[49] Darwin even believed that the gametes only contained "the characteristics of the living body brought to them from the somatic cells."[50] Zirkle concluded that Darwin's "famous chapter on pangenesis . . . showed that he had developed into a complete Lamarckian."[51] Darwin obtained the basic idea that use and disuse of body parts modified gemmules from Lamarck who "proposed the theory of the transmission of acquired characteristics. The transfer of worldly acquisitions from the environment to offspring was a sort of spontaneous generation of life from non-life, and this was evolution. Darwin never thought that evolution was anything else, and he would have disavowed the Theory of Evolution propounded in his name in the twentieth century."[52]

The changes in gemmules could be *quantitative* (the rearrangement and redistribution of unmodified gemmules) or *qualitative* (the gemmules themselves undergo alterations). It was the qualitative changes that Darwin believed were the heritable acquired characters.[53] Buss concluded that Darwin's pangenesis theory actually "bulwarked" the ideas of Lamarck.[54] Darwin adopted his pangenesis theory because he recognized that Lamarckianism explained a number of observations that could not be explained by his theory of evolution by natural selection.[55] Like Lamarckianism, pangenesis was soon shown to be erroneous by both laboratory and field research.[56]

Darwin's Lamarckian conversion is ironic. Just a few years earlier, in an 1844 letter to Hooker, Darwin called Lamarck's idea "nonsense" and his book "veritable rubbish."[57] Darwin recognized that surgical alterations, such as circumcision, were not heritable, but argued that gemmules were transmitted over many generations — a vague, *ad hoc* supposition that does not deal with the clear evidence against Lamarckianism. Darwin never could explain exactly what kind of environmental modifications were inherited, nor even under what conditions they were inherited.

Empirical Disproof of Pangenesis

In the late 1860s, Darwin's cousin, Francis Galton (1822–1911), "was immediately attracted to" the pangenesis theory as soon as he learned of it.[58] He was so enamored with the idea that he "scrambled to add a chapter on the subject in" his book on eugenics titled *Hereditary Genius.*[59]

To give the idea the proper mathematical foundation, Galton had undertaken a series of complex, well-designed experiments to scientifically attempt to prove Darwin's pangenesis theory. Specifically, Galton tried to test Darwin's idea that every "element" of the body produced its own individual gemmules. Galton hypothesized that not only gemmule combinations were passed on to the reproductive organs (thereby passing these characteristics to the next generation), but also that gemmules must be conveyed by the body's circulatory system to the gametes. He saw no other way that they could be physically transferred to the gametes.

Galton concluded that, if pangenesis were valid, the results of his experiments would be "of no small practical use; for it would become possible to modify varieties of animals by introducing slight dashes of new blood, in ways important to breeders."[60] As early as December 11, 1869, Galton began in earnest to experimentally test the pangenesis hypothesis.[61]

Galton's research involved transfusing blood between different rabbits in order to determine if the transfused blood could cause the appearance of new characteristics in the experimental animal's off-spring. He used various techniques of transfusion and eventually developed a cross-circulation system using the carotid arteries to exchange as much as half of a rabbit's blood supply.[62] If pangenesis was valid, the hypothetical gemmules in the rabbit's blood would become part of the heredity of the rabbit into which its blood was transfused.

Specifically, Galton transferred the blood of black rabbits into both silver-gray rabbits and a control group to determine if the off-spring of the two purebred silver-gray rabbits, one transfused and one not (the control), was gray, black, or in between. Darwin was anxious for the experiment to succeed.[63] By mid-winter, Galton had varied the experiment to the extent that he "tried everything" to get the experiment to work. He had bred a total of 124 offspring in 21 litters without producing a single "mongrel" rabbit.[64]

In the early 1870s, Galton concluded that no evidence of altera-tions existed as a result of the transfusions in successive generations of rabbits. On March 30, 1871, Galton reported his results to the London Royal Society. In Galton's words, the experiment produced "definite results," proving "beyond all doubt" that the pangenesis theory is false.[65] The rabbit experiments continued for another year and a half with consistent negative results.[66] Galton's words were unambiguous "The conclusion from this large series of experiments is . . . the doctrine of Pangenesis, pure and simple, as I have inter-preted it, is incorrect."[67]

Although all attempts by others to demonstrate pangenesis and other theories of peripheral origin of variations have likewise failed, some still held to the theory years after Darwin died. For example, Karl Pearson, in order to discredit the rabbit findings of Galton, wrote that pangenesis "is no more disproved by the statement that 'gemmules have not been found in the blood,' than the atomic the-ory is disproved by the fact that no atoms have been found in the air."[68] Castle et al. also included a discussion of pangenesis as a vari-able theory in his 1912 text, noting that all subsequent theories of peripheral origin of genetic modifications were based on Darwin's pangenesis theory.[69]

The pangenesis idea was included in Galton's book as late as the 1892 edition.[70] Gillham calls the 1892 edition the epitaph of pangen-esis.[71] Galton noted "serious objections" exist with the pangenesis theory and, if he were to revise his book, he would make major changes to this chapter.[72] Galton explains:

Marvelous as is the power of the theory of pangenesis in bringing large classes of apparently different phenomena under a single law, serious objections have since arisen to its validity, and prevented its general acceptance. It would, for example, almost compel us to believe that the hereditary transmission of accidental mutations of acquired aptitudes would be the rule and not the exception. But leaving out of the question all theoretical reasons against this belief, such as those which I put forward myself many years ago, as well as the more cogent ones adduced by Weissman in late years — putting these wholly aside, and appealing to experimental evidence, it is now certain that the tendency of acquired habits to be hereditarily transmitted is at the most extremely small.[73]

Darwin "was appalled" at Galton's experimental results, which shattered the keystone of his evolution theory.[74] Darwin was so disappointed in Galton's results that he was "uncharacteristically angry" at his cousin.[75] In spite of the devastating case against pangenesis, Darwin stubbornly held to it. Darwin even tried to defend his theory against Galton's experimental results by claiming in a *Nature* article that he had "not said one word about the blood."[76] The fact is, Darwin had mentioned the "circulation of fluids," which could only mean blood, or its accessory systems such as the lymph system. Moore notes that Darwin's reaction

> was, indeed, a strange rejoinder: if gemmules were present throughout the body, surely they would be present in blood. Possibly Darwin was having troubles with the Idols of the Cave. Galton replied with mock contrition, saying how sorry he was to have misinterpreted what his uncle had said.[77]

The "sharp riposte" Galton "received from Darwin must have been totally unexpected in view of the fact that during the course of Galton's experiments the two men had frequently corresponded."[78] Darwin knew exactly how Galton was researching pangenesis, yet did not object to his methodology until the negative results were in!

Darwin also tried to discredit Galton's work by claiming that other means existed for transferring the gemmules from the somatic cells to the gametes, yet could not come up with a single plausible method. Darwin even argued that "blood can form no necessary part of my hypothesis" because the "lowest animals," such as protozoa, do not possess iron or copper oxygen-carrying blood, nor do plants.[79] The problem with Darwin's argument is not that all life does not have blood, but that blood in animals must be involved in gemmule transport if pangenesis were true.

Protozoa use the cell cytoplasm to circulate nutrients throughout their cell. Plants could use their nutrient transport system, such as xylem (which conducts water and dissolved substances) or phloem (which conducts dissolved food substances) to transport the gemmules to the germ-plasm in the seeds. As Galton noted, gemmule movement in the circulatory system is the *only way* it could work because no other physical route exists to connect body cells to the gametes. Galton used for his research an animal circulatory system that uses blood, but any circulatory system would work. Darwin even tried to argue that two classes of gemmules existed. One class was the type that Galton researched in rabbits, which was subject to environmental modification and widely disseminated throughout the organism.

For most people, August Weisman's "doctrine of continuity of the germ line . . . dealt a final blow" to both Lamarckianism and pangenesis.[80] But for some adherents, pangenesis was "so *ad hoc* as to withstand any criticism which sought to point up any fact inconsistent with it."[81]

Darwin may have irrationally clung to pangenesis because he realized that there was no other known alternative for creating new information from which nature could select. Nor did he ever conceive of an alternative. As Margulis and Sagan concluded:

> When all was said and done about "grandeur in this view of life" (one of Darwin's last phrases in the great book), it was abundantly clear that in 500 pages of closely spaced type the

title question — on the origin of species — had been entirely circumvented — abandoned, ignored, or coyly forgotten.[82]

Margulis and Sagan then quoted Australian biologist George Miklos who stated the " 'struggle for existence' has been accepted uncritically for generations by evolutionary biologists with the *Origin of Species* quoted like so much Holy Writ, yet the origin of species was precisely what Darwin's book was about."[83] Moore concluded that the pangenesis hypothesis was

> not very useful because it was so formulated that it could explain anything, and hence could not be tested. Darwin listed many diverse aspects of inheritance and said all were determined by gemmules. The hypothesis was not well regarded, even though there was not a better one to take its place. . . . But surely Galton's experiments transfusing blood should have been accepted as fatal to the hypothesis.[84]

Many biologists at the turn of the 20th century recognized this major shortcoming of Darwinism and switched their support to other theories, such as orthogenesis. Stanford even concluded that Darwin's pangenesis theory impeded scientific thought and, as a result, Darwin failed "to conceive of scientifically serious alternative theoretical possibilities" even though by 1867 he had been working on his pangenesis idea for about 27 years.[85] Several of the new theories that opposed orthodox Darwinism were variants of vitalism, the belief that an immaterial force is required for evolution and life. Nonetheless, pangenesis was considered by a number of evolutionists as a viable theory for decades.[86]

Summary

Darwin was aware that his idea was merely "a provisional hypothesis or speculation," but believed it was the best extant theory to explain the origin of the species, and, until a better one was advanced, it will "serve to bring together a multitude of facts which are at present left disconnected by any efficient cause."[87] Darwin's theory turned out to be an "*ad hoc* hypothesis, with some physiological pretensions borrowed mainly from Herbert Spencer's recent *Principles of Biology*."[88]

After pangenesis was effectively falsified around 1900, a number of Neo-Darwinian theories were developed to explain the origin of new biological information, all of which have now been rejected.[89] In the past century, Neo-Darwinists continued to debate the source of new genetic information required to propel macroevolution.[90]

This state of affairs has not been due to any lack of theories. The "hopeful monster" idea developed by Richard Goldschmidt was another proposed theory that was also soon discredited.[91] Ideas such as "creative evolution" by Henri Bergson received wide support for a time, but, when carefully examined, were soon abandoned as untenable. The most common source of the new genetic information required for Neo-Darwinism is currently believed to be natural selection acting on beneficial mutations (those that confer an advantage to an organism compared to its competitors).

Even the beneficial mutation solution to the origin of new genetic information problem is now viewed by some biologists as inadequate.[92] Neo-Darwinists often argue that they agree on the fact of evolution, but disagree about the method. This problem is widely recognized, and some researchers are even proposing a new theory called "post-Darwinism." Bagemihl argues for this new theory as follows:

> Survival of the fittest, natural selection, random genetic mutations, competition for resources — we all know how evolution works, right? Not quite. Over the past two decades, a quiet revolution has been taking place in biology. Some of the most fundamental concepts and principles in evolutionary theory are being questioned, challenged, reexamined, and (in some cases) abandoned altogether. A new paradigm is emerging: post-Darwinian evolution. "Heretical" ideas are being proposed by post-Darwinian evolutionists, such as the self-organization of life, the notion that the environment

can beneficially alter the genetic code, and suite of evolutionary processes to accompany the once hegemonic principle of natural selection. Moreover, many of the developments in this theorizing reflect surprising convergences with another "new" science, chaos theory.[93]

Another proposal, called "The Theory of Sudden Origins," is a variation of Goldschmidt's hopeful monster position.[94] This theory postulates that stress induces major mutational events that provide the source of genetic variation from which natural selection can then select.[95]

Kirschner and Gerhart conclude that the origin of new variation is still a major weakness in Darwin's theory.[96] They propose a new theory, which they call "facilitated variation," that involves slight changes in the regulation of conserved core processes, which can produce major changes in organisms. This new idea is now being peer reviewed and refined. These "new ideas" are all, in part, a resurrection of older discarded ideas, and no post-Darwinian theory has yet been able to widely challenge Neo-Darwinism. There are even attempts to resurrect a modified form of Lamarckianism or pangenesis.[97]

The attempt to resurrect pangenesis is based partly on the evidence that genes can be repressed, that RNA can function as genes (such as in retroviruses or even in cells), or as a template for modifying DNA. Another example, which uses two genomes to produce new combinations, is graft hybridization.[98] These examples, though, all involve very different mechanisms than Darwin proposed. Clearly, as stated by one Harvard biochemist, "evolutionary theory is a tumultuous field where many differing views are now competing for dominance."[99]

Endnotes

1. Armand Delsemme, *Our Cosmic Origins; From the Big Bang to the Emergence of Life and Intelligence* (Cambridge, MA: Cambridge University Press, 1998).

2. Hugo De Vries, *The Mutation Theory*, Volume 2 (Chicago, IL: Open Court Publishing Co., 1910), p. 185.

3. Hugo De Vries, *The Mutation Theory*, Volume 1 (Chicago, IL: Open Court Publishing Co., 1909), p. 99–123.

4. Brian Charlesworth, "On the Origins of Novelty and Variation," *Science* 310:1619 (December 9, 2005): p. 1619.

5. Charles Darwin, *The Origin of Species* (London: John Murray, 1859).

6. Gerald Geison, "Darwin and Heredity: The Evolution of His Hypothesis of Pangenesis," *Journal of the History of Medicine* 24(4) (October 1969): p. 375.

7. Lynn Margulis and Dorion Sagan, *Acquiring Genomes: A Theory of the Origins of Species* (New York: Basic Books, 2002), p. 3.

8. Marc W. Kirschner and John C. Gerhart, *The Plausibility of Life: Resolving Darwin's Dilemma* (New Haven, CT: Yale University Press, 2005).

9. Ibid., p. 17.

10. Geison, "Darwin and Heredity: The Evolution of His Hypothesis of Pangenesis."

11. Charles Darwin. *The Variation of Animals and Plants Under Domestication* (London: John Murray, 1868), p. 357.

12. Peter J. Vorzimmer, *Charles Darwin: The Years of Controversy* (Philadelphia, PA: Temple University Press, 1970), p. 41, 120.

13. Nicholas Wright Gillham, *A Life of Sir Francis Galton* (New York: Oxford University Press, 2001), p. 173–174.

14. James D. Watson, *DNA: The Secret of Life* (New York: Alfred A. Knopf, 2003), p. 6.

15. Charles Darwin, *The Variation of Animals and Plants Under Domestication*, Volume 2 (New York: D. Appleton, 1896), p. 349–399; De Vries, *The Mutation Theory*, p. 631–650; John Dewey, *The Influence of Darwin on Philosophy and Other Essays in Contemporary Thought* (Bloomington: IN: University Press, 1910), reprint 1965.

16. Rasmus G. Winther, "Darwin on Variation and Heredity," *Journal of History of Biology* 33 (2000):425–455.

17. Yongsheng Liu, "Further Evidence for Darwin's Pangenesis," *Rivista di Biologia-Biology Forum* 97(1) (2004): p. 53.

18. John Alexander Moore, *Science as a Way of Knowing: The Foundations of Modern Biology*, "Pangenesis" (Cambridge, MA: Harvard University Press, 1993), chapter 11, p. 235.

19. Gillham, *A Life of Sir Francis Galton*, p. 174.

20. Moore, *Science as a Way of Knowing: The Foundations of Modern Biology*, p. 238.

21. Ernest L. Abel, *Ancient Views on the Origins of Life* (Cranbury, NJ: Associated University Presses, Inc., 1973); Geison, "Darwin and Heredity: The Evolution of His Hypothesis of Pangenesis," p. 394.

22. Moore, *Science as a Way of Knowing: The Foundations of Modern Biology*, p. 235.

23. Hippocrates, *Medical Works: A New Translation from the Original Greek Made Especially for English Readers by the Collaboration of John Chadwick and W.N. Mann* (Oxford: Blackwell, 1950), p. 103.

24. William Ernest Castle, John Merle Coulter, Charles Benedict Davenport, Edward Murray East, and William Lawrence Tower, *Heredity and Eugenics: A Course of Lectures Summarizing Recent Advances in Knowledge in Variation, Heredity, and Evolution and Its Relation to Plant, Animal, and Human Improvement and Welfare* (Chicago, IL: University of Chicago Press, 1912).

25. Bentley Glass, review of "The Early History of the Idea or the Inheritance of Acquired Characters and of Pangenesis," *The Quarterly Review of Biology* 21 (1946): p. 379.

26. Geison, "Darwin and Heredity: The Evolution of His Hypothesis of Pangenesis," p. 394.

27. Moore, *Science as a Way of Knowing: The Foundations of Modern Biology*, p. 236–237.

28. Watson, *DNA: The Secret of Life*, p. 6.

29. Winther, "Darwin on Variation and Heredity," p. 425.

30. Darwin, *The Variation of Animals and Plants Under Domestication*, p. 357–358.

31. Elof Axel Carlson, *The Unfit: A History of a Bad Idea* (Cold Spring Harbor, NY: Cold Spring Harbor Press, 2001), p. 143.

32. Philip Callahan, *The Evolution of Insects* (New York: Holiday House, 1972), p 44.

33. Darwin, *The Variation of Animals and Plants Under Domestication*, p. 374, 379.

34. Conway Zirkle, "The Early History of the Idea of the Inheritance of Acquired Characters and of Pangenesis," *Transactions of the American Philosophical Society* 35 (1946): p. 119.

35. Geison, "Darwin and Heredity: The Evolution of His Hypothesis of Pangenesis," p. 376.

36. Moore, *Science as a Way of Knowing: The Foundations of Modern Biology*, p. 248.

37. Darwin, *The Variation of Animals and Plants Under Domestication*, p. 396–397.

38. Ibid., p. 397.

39. Ibid., p. 398.

40. Moore, *Science as a Way of Knowing: The Foundations of Modern Biology*, p. 248.

41. Jerry Bergman, "Darwinian Criminality Theory: A Tragic Chapter in History," *Rivista di Biologia/ Biology Forum* 98(1) (2005):47–70.

42. Giuseppe Sermonti, *Why Is a Fly Not a Horse?* (Seattle, WA: Discovery Institute Press, 2005), p. 34.

43. Gillham, *A Life of Sir Francis Galton*, p. 175.

44. Ibid., p. 174.

45. Zirkle, "The Early History of the Idea of the Inheritance of Acquired Characters and of Pangenesis," p. 119.

46. Carlson, *The Unfit: A History of a Bad Idea*, p. 143.

47. Gillham, *A Life of Sir Francis Galton*, p. 179.

48. Charles Darwin, edited by Francis Darwin, *The Life and Letters of Charles Darwin* (New York: D. Appleton, 1896), p. 260–261.

49. Vorzimmer, *Charles Darwin: The Years of Controversy*, p. 258.

50. Callahan, *The Evolution of Insects*, p. 4.

51. Zirkle, "The Early History of the Idea of the Inheritance of Acquired Characters and of Pangenesis," p. 119.

52. Sermonti, *Why Is a Fly Not a Horse?* p. 34.

53. Geison, "Darwin and Heredity: The Evolution of His Hypothesis of Pangenesis," p. 377.

54. Leo W. Buss, "Evolution, Development, and the Units of Selection," *Proceedings of the National. Academy of Science* 80 (1983): p. 1387.

55. Zirkle, "The Early History of the Idea of the Inheritance of Acquired Characters and of Pangenesis," p. 119.

56. Margulis and Sagan, *Acquiring Genomes: A Theory of the Origins of Species*, p. 28.

57. Zirkle, "The Early History of the Idea of the Inheritance of Acquired Characters and of Pangenesis," p. 119.

58. Gillham, *A Life of Sir Francis Galton*, p. 174.

59. Ibid., p. 174.

60. Francis Galton, "Experiments in Pangenesis," *Proceedings of the Royal Society* 19 (1871):393–410.

61. Gillham, *A Life of Sir Francis Galton*, p. 175.

62. D.W. Forrest, *Francis Galton: The Life and Work of a Victorian Genius* (New York, NY: Taplinger, 1974), p. 102.

63. Gillham, *A Life of Sir Francis Galton*, p. 177.

64. Ibid., p. 177.

65. Galton, "Experiments in Pangenesis," p. 395.

66. Gillham, *A Life of Sir Francis Galton*, p. 178–179.

67. Galton, "Experiments in Pangenesis," p. 404.

68. Karl Pearson, *The Grammar of Science* (London: Adam and Charles Black, 1900), p. 335.

69. Castle et al., *Heredity and Eugenics*, p. 142–143.

70. Francis Galton, *Hereditary Genius* (New York: Macmillan and Co., 1892), p. 349–358.

71. Gillham, *A Life of Sir Francis Galton*, p. 185.

72. Galton, *Hereditary Genius*, p. xiv–xv.

73. Ibid., p. xiv–xv.

74. Carlson, *The Unfit: A History of a Bad Idea*, p. 148.

75. Gillham, *A Life of Sir Francis Galton*, p. 177.

76. Charles Darwin, "Pangenesis," *Nature* 3:502-503 (April 27, 1871): p. 502.

77. Moore, *Science as a Way of Knowing: The Foundations of Modern Biology*, p. 250.

78. Forrest, *Francis Galton: The Life and Work of a Victorian Genius*, p. 103.

79. Darwin, "Pangenesis," p. 502.

80. Buss, "Evolution, Development, and the Units of Selection," p. 1387.

81. Vorzimmer, *Charles Darwin: The Years of Controversy*, p. 257.

82. Margulis and Sagan, *Acquiring Genomes: A Theory of the Origins of Species*, p. 26.

83. Ibid., p. 26.

84. Moore, *Science as a Way of Knowing: The Foundations of Modern Biology*, p. 250–251.

85. P. Kyle Stanford, "Darwin's Pangenesis and the Problem of Unconceived Alternatives," *British Journal of Philosophy of Science* (2006): p. 3, 5.

86. Castle et al., *Heredity and Eugenics; De Vries, The Mutation Theory.*

87. Darwin, *The Life and Letters of Charles Darwin*, p. 350.

88. Vorzimmer, *Charles Darwin: The Years of Controversy*, p. 120.

89. P.J. Bowler, *The Eclipse of Darwinism: Anti-Darwinian Theories in the Decades around 1900* (Baltimore, MD: Johns Hopkins University Press, 1983).

90. Richard Morris, *The Evolutionists: The Struggle for Darwin's Soul* (San Francisco, CA: W.H. Freeman, 2001; Kim Sterelny, *Dawkins vs. Gould: Survival of the Fittest* (Oxford, Cambridge: Icon Books, 2007).

91. Richard Goldschmidt, *The Material Basis of Evolution* (New Haven, CT: Yale University Press, 1982), introduction by Stephen J. Gould.

92. Margulis and Sagan, *Acquiring Genomes: A Theory of the Origins of Species.*

93. Bruce Bagemihl, *Biological Exuberance: Animal Homosexuality and Natural Diversity* (New York: St. Martin's Press, 1999), p. 245–246.

94. Goldschmidt, *The Material Basis of Evolution*, introduction by Stephen J. Gould.

95. Bruno Maresca and Jeffrey H. Schwartz, "Sudden Origins: A General Mechanism of Evolution Based on Stress Protein Concentration and Rapid Environmental Change," *The Anatomical Record (Part B: New Anatomy)* 289B (2006): p. 42.

96. Kirschner and Gerhart, *The Plausibility of Life: Resolving Darwin's Dilemma.*

97. Edward Steele, Robyn Lindley, and Robert Blanden, *Lamarck's Signature: How Retrogenes are Changing Darwin's Natural Selection Paradigm* (Reading, MA: Perseus, 1998); Liu, "Further Evidence for Darwin's Pangenesis"; Yongsheng Liu, "Darwin and Mendel: Who Was the Pioneer of Genetics?" *Rivista di Biologia Biology Forum* 98 (2005):305–322; Yongsheng Liu, "Historical and Modern Genetics of Plant Graft Hybridization," *Advances in Genetics* 56 (2006):101–129.

98. Liu, "Further Evidence for Darwin's Pangenesis"; Yongsheng Liu, "Reversion: Going Back to Darwin's Works," *Trends in Plant Science* 10(10) (2005):459–460.

99. Jonathan Esenster, "Death to Intelligent Design," *Harvard Crimson* (March, 31, 2003): p. 2.

PART FOUR

Darwin, Racism, and Sexism

CHAPTER 11

Was Darwin a Racist?

Chapter Synopsis

It is widely acknowledged that Darwinism contributed to the problem of 19th- and 20th-century racism. It is sometimes claimed, however, that Darwin himself was not a racist but, rather, others misused and even misquoted his writings. In this chapter, Darwin's own views as recorded in his writings are explored. Darwin clearly held beliefs that today would be considered blatantly racist. Furthermore, his writings made a major contribution to the problem of racism and were widely used to support racism. Darwin's conclusions were in stark contrast to the historical Christian biblical view that all humans are brothers and sisters, all descendants of the first humans, Adam and Eve, who were created about six thousand years ago.

Introduction

Darwinism has made a major contribution to many social problems including racism, sexism, Laissez-faire capitalism, communism, and even Nazism.[1] Racism is the belief that biological differences in humans create a hierarchy that ranks some races as superior, and others as inferior. This view of humanity has been used to exclude certain groups, such as African Americans, from their equal rights in American society. The topic of racism is very important to understanding Darwinism because Darwin's theory of biological origins appears to have reflected his personal attitudes toward non-Caucasian races.

Darwin's attitude toward non-Caucasians was hinted at very early in his life. In the early 1800s, for example, Darwin was concerned that his brother, Erasmus, might marry author and reformer Harriet Martineau (1802–1876). [2] Charles Darwin wrote to his sister Caroline about his concerns, stating that if Erasmus married her, he would not be "much better than her 'nigger.' — Imagine poor Erasmus a nigger to so philosophical & energetic a lady." Darwin concluded that "perfect equality of rights is part of her doctrine. I much doubt whether it will be equality in practice. We must pray for our poor 'nigger.'"[3]

In Darwin's defense, it should be noted that Africans were commonly called "niggers" in his day and the words "colored" or "black" are 20th-century terms. A major argument supporting the view that Darwin was not a racist is that he opposed slavery, as did most people in his social class. His opposition to slavery, however, must be put into the context of his other statements about human races, which will now be briefly reviewed.

Racism Common in Darwin's Writings

The concept of race was critical to Darwinian theory because Darwinism required the conclusion that some races were *superior* to others, and therefore would eventually win out in the struggle for existence. Darwin based his conclusion on the fact that there exist observable biological differences not only between animal kinds, but also within *any one* animal kind. The theory went beyond this, however, and argued that such differences can aid an organism in the struggle for life against other creatures, both those of its own kind and those of other kinds.

Some of these differences in animal populations confer an evolutionary advantage that allows an animal to prevail in competition against other animals in the evolutionary struggle for life. Darwinists reason that a rabbit that can run slightly faster, or that has slightly better hearing than other rabbits, is more likely to escape its enemies and is thus more likely to survive to pass on this advantage to its offspring. The same is true of other races or breeds of animals. The complete title of Darwin's most famous work, *The Origin of Species*, was *The Origin of Species by Means of Natural Selection or the Preservation of Favored Races in the Struggle for Life.*

The "favored races" expression is obviously racist and was central to Darwin's ideas, as elaborated in Darwin's later writings. Even though Charles Darwin did not discuss human evolution in *The Origin of Species*, he did draw clear racist conclusions in his 1871 book *The Descent of Man.* It was also obvious in *The Descent of Man* that Darwin's remarks about animal races, which he discussed in 1859, applied to humans. This is especially obvious in chapter 7, which is titled "On the Races of Man." This almost 40-page long chapter covers in detail his clear racist conclusions about humans.

Darwin's Racism and the Tierra del Fuego Natives

Although Darwin first discussed human evolution in the book *The Descent of Man and Selection in Relation to Sex* (1871), he wrote much about the various human races in earlier books, beginning with the very first book he published, his 1839 *Journal of Researches.* In this early work, Darwin discussed in detail his perceptions of different races. When the exploratory ship *Beagle*, on which Darwin was a naturalist, first visited Tierra del Fuego, a territory located at the southern tip of South America, in

Figure 1. A Fuegian Indian in native dress with a typical family dwelling in the background. Drawn by a *Beagle* crewmember.

Reproduced from Robert FitzRoy, *Narrative of the Surveying Voyages of His Majesty's Ships Adventure and* Beagle *between the years 1826 and 1836* (London: H. Colburn, 1839).

1833, Darwin's original reaction to the natives was shock. He described them as "savages" who were "without exception the most curious and interesting spectacle I had ever beheld."[4]

Darwin then superimposed animal traits and imagery on Tierra del Fuego natives. He concluded from his interactions with them that it was hard to believe "how wide was the difference, between savage and civilized man," which Darwin concluded was "greater than between a wild and domesticated animal."[5] He added that the Fuegians were a "very different race from the stunted miserable wretches further to the Westward." Darwin concluded that the del Fuego natives resembled the devils in such plays as *Der Freischutz.*[6]

This is the first indication in his writings that he saw non-Europeans in terms of what in his writings became an increasingly dominant bestialized image of certain races as "savages." This view foreshadowed the evolutionary connections that he later, in vivid terms, wrote existed between humans and animals. After meeting the Fuegians, Darwin concluded they were "the most abject and miserable creatures" he had ever seen and that these

> poor wretches were stunted in their growth, their hideous faces bedaubed with white paint, their skins filthy and greasy, their hair entangled, their voices discordant, their gestures violent and without dignity. *Viewing such men, one can hardly make oneself believe they are fellow-creatures, and inhabitants of the same world.* It is a common subject of conjecture what pleasure in life some of the less gifted animals can enjoy: how much more reasonably the same question may be asked with respect to these barbarians. At night, five or six human beings, naked and scarcely protected from the wind and rain of this tempestuous climate, sleep on the wet ground coiled up like animals.[7]

The language that Darwin used to describe these people was "overwhelmingly negative in tone, alternating between uninhibited outbursts of aesthetic revulsion and the recurrent images of bestiality."[8] For example, Darwin said that, in order to obtain food, they "unceasingly" wandered, and did not have "a home, and still less that of domestic affection; unless indeed the treatment of a master to a laborious slave can be considered as such. How little can the higher powers of the mind be brought into play!"[9]

He added:

> To knock a limpet from the rock does not even require cunning, that lowest power of the mind. Their skill in some respects may be compared to the instinct of animals; for it is not improved by experience: the canoe, their most ingenious work, poor as it is, has remained the same, for the last two hundred and fifty years.[10]

Figure 2. Fuegian Indians. Top left: Fuegia Basket in 1833. Top middle: Jimmy Button's wife in 1834. Lieutenant Sulivan called her the most attractive female in the group. Top right: Jimmy Button in native dress, 1833. Bottom left: Jimmy Button in European dress. Bottom middle: York Minister in 1832. Bottom right: Jimmy Button in 1834. Drawn by a *Beagle* crew member.

Reproduced from Robert FitzRoy, *Narrative of the Surveying Voyages of His Majesty's Ships Adventure and* Beagle *between the years 1826 and 1836* (London: H. Colburn, 1839).

Comparisons of "primitive" humans with animals in an attempt to bestialize them continued throughout Darwin's later writings. For example, Darwin claimed that when a European man would display his bare arms to a Fuegian, "they expressed the liveliest surprise and admiration at its whiteness, just in the same way in which I have seen the ourang-outang do at the Zoological Gardens."[11] Another example of Darwin's negative attitude toward the "primitive" Fuegians is that when Fuegians met after a time of separation, the

> meeting was less interesting than that between a horse, turned out into a field, when he joins an old companion. There was no demonstration of affection; they simply stared for a short time at each other; and the mother immediately went to look after her canoe.[12]

Darwin's reactions to "civilized" Fuegians were not as negative as that to other "primitive races" such as the Hottentots. He even reviewed in some detail their positive qualities, such as their intelligence.[13] Although Darwin wrote that the Fuegians "rank among the lowest barbarians," he was "continually struck with surprise" that the three Fuegians who had lived a few years in England learned some English, and "resembled us in disposition and in most of our mental faculties."[14] Darwin also concluded that the lowly nature of Fuegians could be changed.

Darwin's Use of the Term "Savages"

Darwin consistently called those humans he judged as members of an inferior race, including both the native South Americans and the native Australians, "savages" and "barbarians."[15] Most telling is Darwin's suggestion that the inferior "savage races" eventually would be eliminated by natural selection. In Darwin's words: "At some future period, not very distant as measured by centuries, the civilized races of man will almost certainly exterminate and replace throughout the world the savage races" as part of the process of evolution by natural selection.[16] Darwin also wrote in 1881 that in the future, "an endless number of the lower races will have been eliminated by the higher civilized races throughout the world."[17]

Darwin likewise concluded that the anthropomorphous apes will also "no doubt be exterminated" by natural selection.[18] After they became extinct, Darwin believed that the gap between humans and apes "will then be rendered wider, for it will intervene between man in a more civilized state, as we may hope, than the Caucasian, and some ape as low as a baboon, instead of as at present between the Negro or Australian and the gorilla."[19]

In chapter 7 on human races in volume 1 of Darwin's *The Descent of Man*, he admitted that "even the most distinct races of man, with the exception of certain negro tribes, are much more like each other in form than would at first be supposed."[20] Nonetheless, he added that there is

> no doubt that the various races, when carefully compared and measured, differ much from each other — as in . . . the form and capacity of the skull, and even in the convolutions of the brain. . . . The races differ also in constitution, in acclimatization, and. . . . Their mental characteristics are likewise very distinct; chiefly as it would appear in their emotional, but partly in their intellectual, faculties. Every one who has had the opportunity of comparison, must have been struck with the contrast between the taciturn, even morose, aborigines of S. America and the lighthearted, talkative negroes.[21]

These quotes document that racism was central to Darwin's beliefs. Evidence for this conclusion includes the fact that Darwin did not attribute his racist thoughts to others even though he used thousands of references and quotes in his writings. In his study of Darwin, Ellingson concluded that Darwin's writings included the "constant play of bestial similes, metaphors, and comparisons" that represents "Darwin's protoevolutionary thinking." Ellingson adds that Darwin's "rhetoric is very difficult to distinguish from other bestializers of the 'savage,' such as Volney or the American racist anthropologists."[22] It also is clear that Darwin's latter works reflected the beliefs of many 19th-century Europeans that they were superior to other races. Darwin's discussions in the *Descent of Man* (1871) were

> written after, and partially in response to, the ascent of scientific racism to a position of dominance in British anthropology. Darwin's later discussions of race do show an unfortunate degree of accommodation with some of the ideas of the racist anthropologists; and his negative representation of the Fuegians would be used by those with overtly racist agendas as "scientific evidence" in support of their position.[23]

Darwin's Attitude Toward Those He Called Savages

Darwin interviewed many Fuegians, but quickly grew frustrated with, in his words, "their apparent difficulty in understanding the simplest alternative."[24] Darwin argued that the communication problem existed because the Fuegian adults possessed the mental maturity of young children.

> Every one accustomed to very young children, knows how seldom one can get an answer even to so simple a question as whether a thing is black *or* white; the idea of black or white seems alternately to fill their minds. So it was with these Fuegians, and hence it was generally impossible to find out, by cross-questioning, whether one had rightly understood anything which they had asserted.[25]

Darwin's attitude toward those persons he called "savages" was very obvious in his writings. He wrote that after he spent some time with "these savages" he came "to hate the very sound of their voices, so much trouble did they give us. . . . On leaving some place we have said to each other, Thank Heaven, we have at last fairly left these wretches!"[26]

Darwin did not expect much of such inferior races, and he generalized about what he called their undeveloped intellects compared to westerners. He concluded that Europeans are under a great disadvantage when interacting

> with savages like these, who have not the least idea of the power of fire-arms. . . . Nor is it easy to teach them our superiority except by striking a fatal blow. Like wild beasts they do not appear in all cases to compare numbers; for each individual if attacked, instead of retiring, will endeavor to dash your brains out with a stone, as certainly as a tiger under similar circumstances would tear you [to pieces].[27]

He concluded we cannot easily "put ourselves in the position of these savages," or even understand their behavior because the "savages of the lowest grade, such as these of Tierra del Fuego, have seen objects struck, and even small animals killed by the musket, without being in the least aware how deadly an instrument it was."[28]

Darwin concluded that the Fuegians were like wild beasts because, he erroneously assumed, they did not respond normally to physical threats. His only evidence consisted of observations such as they did not run away when a pistol was fired in the air as he expected.[29] This response is not surprising because when Darwin visited them, the Fuegians had been in contact with Europeans and their weapons for over three hundred years. [30] They were by then, no doubt, used to hearing weapons fired. Smith concluded that "the only evidence Darwin was looking for was the minimum needed to justify the placement of the Fuegians in a predetermined taxonomic niche, the 'savage slot' . . . in the evolutionary hierarchy of cultures."[31]

Human Differences Reflected Evolutionary Development Differences

For Darwin, perceived differences in evolutionary development from savagery to civilization energized his racist views. As Ellingson noted, Darwin for this reason saw evolutionary differences even between human groups that were physically very similar, such as the Tahitians.[32] He then suggested that although New Zealanders belong to the same human racial group as the Tahitians, in comparison, the New Zealanders were clearly inferior. Darwin concluded that the New Zealander

> may, perhaps, be superior in energy, but in every other respect his character is of a much lower order. One glance at their respective expressions, brings conviction to the mind, that one is a savage, the other a civilized man.[33]

Darwin also noted that he thought the Hottentots were one of the lowest human races in existence, even lower than the Negro, and, "If it could be proved that the Hottentot had descended from the Negro, I think he would be classed under the Negro group, however much he might differ in colour and other important characters from Negroes."[34]

Darwin's List of Inferior Humans

Brantlinger concluded that natural historians and "race scientists" from

> Darwin down to World War II hierarchized the races, with the white, European, Germanic, or Anglo-Saxon race at the pinnacle of progress and civilization, and the "dark races" ranged beneath it in various degrees of inferiority. . . . Johannes Fabian writes of the "denial of coevalness" to those identified as primitive or savage. The term "Stone Age" applied to modern Australians or Bushmen is an obvious example: the illusion that certain people, races, or cultures are unable to speak the present and future tenses of history is implicit in the words *primitive* and *savage*.[35]

The humans that Darwin concluded were clearly "inferior" included Hottentots, Negroes, New Zealanders, Australians, Tahitians, Fuegians, and several other ethnic groups. The "superior" peoples included the Europeans and these superior individuals that evolved by natural selection "from barbarians."[36] The barbarians to whom Darwin referred included the Fuegians, because "such were our ancestors."[37] Darwin also concluded that he would rather be descended from a "little monkey" or an "old baboon" than "a savage who delights to torture his enemies, offers up blood sacrifices, practices infanticide without remorse, treats his wives like slaves, knows no decency, and is haunted by the grossest superstitions."[38] The importance of Darwin's ideas to the development of racism has been well documented.[39] In one of the most detailed studies of Darwin's views on human race, Green concluded:

> What we call "social Darwinism" — the belief that competition between individuals, tribes, nations, and races has been an important, if not the chief, engine of progress in human history — was endemic in much of British thought in the mid-nineteenth century . . . [and] Darwin's *Origin of Species* gave a powerful boost to this kind of thinking, and that Darwin himself was deeply influenced by this current of thought.[40]

Darwin Believed Inferior Races Supported Evolution

A major conclusion Darwin drew from his encounters with the Fuegians was that they were very low in the hierarchy of human evolution. Darwin's evidence for evolution in this "extreme part of South America" was that humans living there exist

> in a lower state of improvement than in any other part of the world. . . . The Australian, in the simplicity of the arts of life, comes nearest the Fuegian: he can, however, boast of his boomerang, his spear and throwing-stick, his method of climbing trees, of tracking animals, and of hunting. Although the Australian may be superior in acquirements, it by no means follows that he is likewise superior in mental capacity: indeed, from what I saw of the Fuegians when on board, and from what I have read of the Australians, I should think the case was exactly the reverse.[41]

By saying "the case was exactly the reverse," Darwin meant that the Australian was the "leading contender" for "the world's ultimate savage, the lowest of the low."[42] He saw the existence of "savages," and the range of human races — from the lowest to the highest — as clear evidence that our higher mental faculties "have been gradually developed" by evolution.[43] Darwin even argued that "there is no fundamental difference between man and the higher mammals in their mental faculties."[44] Another conclusion Darwin drew from his ethnographic foray also reflected his attitude that the evolutionary inferiority of the Fuegian race would "retard their civilization." He then wrote:

> In Tierra del Fuego, until some chief shall arise with power sufficient to secure any acquired advantages . . . it seems scarcely possible that the political state of the country can be improved. At present . . . no one individual becomes richer than another.[45]

Darwin concluded that the Fuegian natives were in the lowest state of savagery, and actually argued that their low state is too egalitarian to permit the improvements required to allow some Fuegians to accumulate the property, wealth, and power necessary to produce a more developed society. Ellingson concluded:

> The most problematic feature of Darwin's ethnography is not its racism but its ethnographic shallowness. Of course, the *Beagle's* sailing schedule, and Darwin's primary interest in and commitment to other scientific research subjects, did not allow for extended residence with a people or for participant-observation ethnography, if such an idea had even occurred to him. Nor did the company of his companions on the ship, with their military preoccupations and defensive hostility to the natives, encourage sympathy or even closer contact with the Fuegians.[46]

Fuegians Incapable of Being Evangelized

One of the most telling indicators of Darwin's attitude toward the Fuegians that revealed "the true depth of his racism . . . was his belief that the Fuegians were incapable of being evangelized."[47] Darwin knew enough about the Scriptures to realize that all humans, and only humans, could be evangelized. As Lubenow noted, "Darwin often compared the Indians of Tierra del Fuego to animals" and probably the

> best evidence of how lowly he viewed the Fuegians is seen in how he viewed them spiritually. . . . The holy Scriptures make a clear and qualitative distinction between all humans and all animals. In Genesis 9, God gives the humans the right to use any and all animals for food. Yet human life is protected as sacred because we are made in God's image. Anyone who kills a human being in what we call "Murder 1" must forfeit his own life. [Darwin] . . . having studied for the ministry at Cambridge . . . had to be aware of the distinction that Scripture makes between humans and animals. . . . Although Darwin later denied human uniqueness, he was aware that the Bible taught that only humans were created in God's image and that Christ commanded his disciples to evangelize all humans.[48]

Lubenow then quoted Admiral Sir James Sulivan, who as a lieutenant was a shipmate with Darwin on the *Beagle*, wrote:

> Mr. Darwin had often expressed to me his conviction that it was utterly useless to send Missionaries to such a set of savages as the Fuegians, probably the very lowest of the human race. I had always replied that I did not believe any human beings existed [that were] too low to comprehend the simple message of the Gospel.[49]

Darwin eventually realized that missionary activity *was* possible, and could be successful, even among the Fuegians. To Darwin's credit, he admitted he was wrong. In a letter to Sulivan, dated 30 June 1870, Darwin wrote, "... the success of the T. del Fuego mission ... is most wonderful, and shames me, as I always prophesied utter failure." In another letter to Sulivan, dated 20 March 1881, Darwin wrote, "I ... predicted that not all the Missionaries in the world could have done what has been done."[50]

Lubenow concluded by noting that, although Darwin lived in a racist society, "the fact that Darwin would have denied the Indians of Tierra del Fuego the gospel, whereas other Englishmen at great sacrifice did give those same Indians the gospel, suggests that his incipient ideas on evolution, even at that early date, caused Darwin to be even more racist than some of his peers. And the theory of evolution he developed is equally racist."[51]

Accounts of Fuegians by Others

Descriptions of the Fuegians by other people who visited them during the same period in which Darwin wrote helps us to appreciate the extent of Darwin's unjustified negative view of them. Charles Wilkes, commander of the United States Exploring Expedition, visited Tierra del Fuego only a few years after Darwin. His reviewers described Wilkes as a very perceptive and sensitive observer who had devoted considerable effort to develop a code of conduct for his crew to avoid harming the indigenous peoples that they encountered on their voyages. Wilkes described his encounter with the Fuegians as follows:

The expression of the younger ones was extremely prepossessing, evincing much intelligence and good humor. They ate ham and bread voraciously, distending their large mouths, and showing a strong and beautiful set of teeth. A few strips of red flannel distributed among them produced great pleasure; they tied it around their heads as a sort of turban. Knowing they were fond of music, I had the fife played, the only instrument we could muster. They seemed much struck with the sound. The tune of "Yankee Doodle" they did not understand; but when "Bonnets of Blue" was played, they were all in motion keeping time to it. The vessel at this time was under way, and no presents could persuade them to continue any longer with us.[52]

Darwin wrote that they were

extremely imitative, repeating over our words and mimicking our motions. They were all quite naked. I have seldom seen so happy a group. They were extremely lively and cheerful, and anything but miserable, if we could have avoided contrasting their condition with our own.[53]

Wilkes painted a very different picture of the Fuegians than did Darwin. Darwin's racial negativism was partly a reflection of the white superiority and the "darker races" inferiority belief that pervaded European society and discourse (scientific as well as non-scientific) in the 19th century.[54] In Darwin's case, he carried his prejudices with him on his journey to Tierra del Fuego so that what appeared in his writings to be an objective, rational assessment of non-European peoples and customs based on firsthand, ostensibly scientific "observation" was to a significant extent an artifact that resulted from his racist framework.

Because Darwin's writings were critical in the development of evolutionary theory, his thoughts on the application of his own racism to evolution are crucial to understanding the history of racism. Although Darwin was far less racist than many of his disciples (such as Spencer, Haeckel, Hooton, Pearson, and Huxley), his theory provided the *basis* for their extreme racism such as expressed in the eugenics movement. Darwin's works also supported the polygenist view of human origins in the major 19th century debate between monogenism and polygenism (the view that all humans had one ancestor versus the view that we had several ancestors) and this one ancestor is the origin of all the races.

Darwin's Support of Eugenics

Although known as a kind and gentle man, Darwin openly supported the racism that his theory permitted. Darwin also generally supported eugenics, even though he opposed some of the extreme forms of eugenics espoused by many in his day. A major source of the racism inspired by Darwinism came not from Darwin himself, but from the pen of Darwin's cousin, Francis Galton. Darwin was fully convinced that eugenic theory was valid, and he "canonized Galton with the words; 'we now know, through the admirable labours of Mr. Galton, that genius . . . tends to be inherited.'"[55]

After reading *Hereditary Genius*, one of Galton's major works supporting eugenics, Darwin wrote to Galton on December 3, 1869, "I do not think that I ever in my life read anything more interesting and original . . . you have made a convert of an opponent . . . a memorable work."[56] Darwin ended his book on human evolution by noting the "advancement of the welfare of mankind is a most intricate problem."

> As Mr. Galton has remarked, if the prudent avoid marriage, whilst the reckless marry, the inferior members tend to supplant the better members of society. Man, like every other animal, has no doubt advanced to his present high condition through a struggle for existence consequent on his rapid multiplication; and if he is to advance still higher he must remain subject to a severe struggle. Otherwise he would soon sink into indolence, and the more highly-gifted men would not be more successful in the battle of life than the less gifted. . . . There should be open competition for all men; and the most able should not be prevented by laws or customs from succeeding best and rearing the largest number of offspring.[57]

Because Darwin agreed with Galton does not in itself prove that Darwin fully supported government enforced eugenics that many of Galton's followers advocated. Darwin was favorable to the fundamental presuppositions of eugenics, but insisted that eugenic programs should be voluntary, and not mandated by the state. Darwin and many others agreed with Galton on the issue of biological determinism of both intellectual and moral traits.

The coercive ideology was primarily what later created the controversy over eugenics. Although Darwin's support for Galton and eugenics did not directly extend to overt racism, Darwin's works have inspired many coercive eugenic advocates, including the most prominent racist today, David Duke, as well as others.[58]

As Darwin grew older, he took a stronger stand in support of eugenics. When his son George, an active supporter of eugenics and a leader in the movement, published an article that advocated "better breeding" of humans, it was strongly criticized by anatomist George Mivart PhD MD FRS because he felt it could lead to moral anarchy. As a result of Mivart's valid criticisms, Darwin ruthlessly attacked him in writing. Although Mivart may have overreacted, Darwin's defense of his son's work in eugenics was so strong that he formally cut off all communication with Mivart.[59]

The Biblical View of Mankind

The Scriptures and all three "religions of the book" — Jews, Muslims, and Christians — teach that all humans descended from one man and woman, Adam and Eve, thus all are brothers and sisters and all races are equal before God. For example, Paul, in his message on Mars Hill, taught that God made every race of men out of one man (Acts 17:26). Although some Christians, such as Weisman, have used the Scriptures to justify their own racism, such as the belief that the curse of Ham produced the black race,[60] these ideas have been extensively refuted and were never widely accepted.[61] Weikart concluded that racism

predated Darwinism, but during the nineteenth century — in part through the influence of Darwinism — it would undergo significant transformations. Before the nineteenth century, the intellectual dominance of Christianity militated against some of the worst excesses of racism. Christian theology taught the universal brotherhood of all races, who descended from common ancestors — Adam and Eve. Most Christians believed that all humans, regardless of race, were created in the image of God and possessed eternal souls.[62]

This doctrine implied that all people were equally valuable, and this teaching

> motivated Europeans to send missionaries to convert natives of other regions to Christianity. As contact with other races increased during the nineteenth century, the Protestant missionary movement blossomed, sending out multitudes of missionaries to convert non-European peoples to Christianity. . . . Even though some Christian groups, especially in lands with race-based slavery, developed theological justifications for racial inequality, most Christian churches believed that people of other races were valuable and capable of adopting European religion and culture.[63]

Even as an old man Darwin believed in the intellectual inequality of the races. When reading a book written by Alfred Wallace, the man credited as being the co-discoverer of evolution by natural selection, Darwin strongly objected to his statement of Wallace that "the savage . . . possesses [a brain] . . . but very little inferior to that of the average members of our learned societies."[64] Darwin marked this passage in his copy of Wallace's book with "a triply underlined 'No' and with a shower" of exclamation marks.[65] Darwin made it very clear here that he agreed with the conclusion that the brain of "the prehistoric races . . . such as the Australians or the Andaman Islanders, are very little above those of many animals."[66]

Conclusions

Anthropologist Marvin Harris and others, based on evidence such as outlined above, have "not hesitated to call Darwin a 'racist.'"[67] Supporters for this view "have no difficulty in finding passages [in Darwin's writings] that seem to out-Spencer Spencer," the extreme social Darwinist and racist.[68] The fact that Darwin was not consistent, indicating he held mixed views at different times in his life, does not negate his important contribution to racism.

Darwin's racist ideas were exploited by his followers, especially those who already had developed racist ideas and prejudices, to support their own racist beliefs. For example, Darwin described the Fuegians and other non-Caucasians as "savages of the lowest grade" and "miserable, degraded savages" who are living in a "savage land" and in "a savage state" with a "wild cry" as they roam around like "wild beasts."[69] It also is clear from the writings of racists that many of them used Darwin as support for their racism.[70] From this review, it is easy to understand why they used Darwin's words to support racism.

In an attempt to obscure the charge that Darwin held racist ideas, his defenders often point to the fact that Darwin opposed slavery and approved of missionaries going to Africa. This behavior, although inconsistent with racism, strongly reflected the views of his social class. Even though he held racist views, Darwin did not approve of brutality and did support humanitarian efforts to help other races. He also supported limited animal "rights." For example, he opposed mistreatment of dogs. Many racists today, such as the former head of the Klu Klux Klan, David Duke, also claim that they oppose mistreatment of minorities and dogs, but this does not negate either their racism or Darwin's.

Endnotes

1. Jerry Bergman, "Evolution and the Origins of the Biological Race Theory," *CEN Technical Journal* 7(2) (1993):155–168; Jerry Bergman, "Darwinism and the Nazi Race Holocaust," *CEN Technical Journal* 13(2) (1999):101–111; Jerry Bergman, "The Darwinian Foundation of Communism," *CEN Technical Journal* 15(1) (2001):89–95; Jerry Bergman, "Darwin's Critical Influence on the Ruthless Extremes of Capitalism," *CEN Technical Journal* 16(2) (2002):105–109; Jerry Bergman, "The History of the Human Female Inferiority Ideas in Evolutionary Biology," *Rivista di Biologia/ Biology Forum* 95(2) (2002):379–412; Jerry Bergman, "Darwin's Cousin Sir Francis Galton (1822–1911) and the Eugenics Movement," *CRSQ* 39(3) (2002):169–176; Jerry Bergman, "Darwinism and the Teaching of Racism in Biology Textbooks," *CEN Technical Journal* 18(1) (2004):65–70.

2. Harriet, Martineau, edited by Maria Weston Chapman, *Harriet Martineau's Autobiography* (Boston, MA: J.R. Osgood and Co., 1877, reprinted in 1983; New York: Virago).

3. Charles Darwin, edited by Frederick Burkhardt and Sydney Smith, *The Correspondence of Charles Darwin*, Volume 1: 1821–1836 (New York: Cambridge University Press, 1985), p. 518–519.

4. Charles Darwin, *Journal of Researches into the Geology and Natural History of the Various Countries Visited by H.M.S. Beagle under the Command of Captain FitzRoy, R.N. from 1832 to 1836* (London: Henry Colburn, 1839), facsimile reprint (New York: Hafner, 1952), p. 228.

5. Ibid., p. 228.

6. Ibid., p. 228.

7. Ibid., p. 235–236, emphasis mine.

8. Ter Ellingson, *The Myth of the Noble Savage* (Berkeley and Los Angeles, CA: University of California Press, 2001), p. 141.

9. Darwin, *Journal of Researches into the Geology and Natural History of the Various Countries Visited by H.M.S. Beagle*, p. 236.

10. Ibid., p. 236.

11. Ibid., p. 189.

12. Charles Darwin, *Journal of Researches into the Natural History and Geology of the Countries Visited during the Voyage of H.M.S. Beagle Round the World: Under the Command of Capt. FitzRoy, R.N.*, second edition (New York: D. Appleton, 1896), p. 222.

13. Ibid., p. 206–207.

14. Charles Darwin, *The Descent of Man, and Selection in Relation to Sex* (London: John Murray, 1871); facsimile reprint (Princeton, NJ: Princeton University Press, 1981), 1:34.

15. Charles Darwin, *The Origin of Species* (1859), facsimile reprint of first edition (Cambridge, MA: Harvard University Press, 1964), p. 18, 34, 36, 198, 215.

16. Darwin, *The Descent of Man, and Selection in Relation to Sex*, p. 201.

17. Charles Darwin, edited by Francis Darwin, *Charles Darwin: His Life Told in an Autobiographical Chapter, and in a Selected Series of his Published Letters* (New York: D. Appleton, 1893), p. 69.

18. Darwin, *The Descent of Man, and Selection in Relation to Sex*, p. 201.

19. Ibid., p. 201.

20. Ibid., p. 215–216.

21. Ibid., p. 216.

22. Ellingson, *The Myth of the Noble Savage*, p. 141–142.

23. Ibid., p. 141–142.

24. Darwin, *Journal of Researches into the Natural History and Geology of the Countries Visited during the Voyage of H.M.S. Beagle Round the World*, p. 208.

25. Ibid., p. 208.

26. Darwin, *Journal of Researches into the Geology and Natural History of the Various Countries Visited by H.M.S. Beagle*, p. 241.

27. Ibid., p. 239–240.

28. Ibid., p. 239–240.

29. Ibid., p. 239.

30. Eric Smith, "So Much for the Noble Savage," *New York Times Book Review* (Aug. 19, 1990): 31.

31. Richard G. Fox, editor, *Recapturing Anthropology: Working in the Present*, "Anthropology and the Savage Slot : The Poetics and Politics of Otherness," by Michel-Rolph Trouillot (Santa Fe, NM: School of American Research Press, 1991), p. 17.

32. Ellingson, *The Myth of the Noble Savage*, p. 143; Darwin, *Journal of Researches into the Geology and Natural History of the Various Countries Visited by H.M.S. Beagle*, p. 486.

33. Darwin, *Journal of Researches into the Geology and Natural History of the Various Countries Visited by H.M.S. Beagle*, p. 501.

34. Ibid., p. 424.

35. Patrick Brantlinger, *Dark Vanishing: Discourse on the Extinction of Primitive Races, 1800–1930* (Ithaca, NY: Cornell University, 2003), p. 2.

36. Darwin, *The Descent of Man, and Selection in Relation to Sex*, p. 404.

37. Ibid., p. 404.

38. Ibid., p. 405.

39. Michael Bradley, *The Iceman Inheritance: Prehistoric Sources of Western Man's Racism, Sexism and Aggression* (New York: Kayode Publications Limited, 1991), p. 39–40.

40. John C. Green, *Science, Ideology, and World View* (Berkeley, CA: University of California Press, 1981), p. 123.

41. Darwin, *Journal of Researches into the Natural History and Geology of the Countries Visited during the Voyage of H.M.S. Beagle Round the World*, p. 230.

42. Ellingson, *The Myth of the Noble Savage*, p. 147.

43. Darwin, *The Descent of Man, and Selection in Relation to Sex*, p. 35.

44. Ibid., p. 35.

45. Darwin, *Journal of Researches into the Geology and Natural History of the Various Countries Visited by H.M.S. Beagle*, p. 242.

46. Ellingson, *The Myth of the Noble Savage*, p. 144.

47. Marvin Lubenow, *Bones of Contention* (Grand Rapids, MI: Baker Books, 2004), p. 145.

48. Ibid., p. 145.

49. Ibid., p. 145.

50. Ibid., p. 145–146.

51. Ibid., p. 146.

52. Ellingson, *The Myth of the Noble Savage*, p. 145–146.

53. Ibid., p. 145–146.

54. Ibid.

55. Daniel J. Kevles, *In the Name of Eugenics; Genetics and the Uses of Human Heredity* (New York, NY: Alfred A. Knopf, 1985), p. 20.

56. Nicholas Wright Gillham, *A Life of Sir Francis Galton: From African Exploration to the Birth of Eugenics* (New York: Oxford University Press, 2001), p. 169.

57. Darwin, *The Descent of Man, and Selection in Relation to Sex*, p. 403.

58. Jerry Bergman, "Darwinism's Influence on Modern Racists and White Supremacist Groups: The Case of David Duke," *Journal of Creation* 19(3) (December 2005):103–107.

59. Adrian Desmond and James Moore, *Darwin: The Life of a Tormented Evolutionist* (New York: Time Warner Books, 1991), p. 613.

60. Charles Weisman, *The Origin of Race and Civilization as Studied and Verified from the Holy Scriptures* (Burnsville, MN: Weisman Publications, 1996).

61. Ken Ham and A. Charles Ware, *One Race, One Blood* (Green Forest, AR: Master Books, Inc., 2010).

62. Richard Weikart, *From Darwin to Hitler: Evolutionary Ethics, Eugenics, and Racism in Germany* (New York: Palgrave Macmillan, 2004), p. 103.

63. Ibid., p. 103.

64. Charles Darwin, edited by Francis Darwin, *More Letters of Charles Darwin. A Record of His Work in a Series of Hitherto Unpublished Letters*, Volume 2 (London: John Murray, 1903), p. 40.

65. Ibid., p. 40.

66. Ibid., p. 40.

67. Green, *Science, Ideology, and World View*, p. 95.

68. Ibid., p. 96.

69. Lubenow, *Bones of Contention*, p. 143.

70. Bergman, "Darwinism's Influence on Modern Racists and White Supremacist Groups."

CHAPTER 12

Darwin Inspires Eugenics

Chapter Synopsis

The role that Darwin played in the eugenics movement — and ultimately in the Nazi Holocaust — was reviewed, concluding that it is well documented that the ideas of Darwin as published in his books played a critical role. Darwin's writings or those of his disciples were often cited in eugenic literature as support for their ideas.

Introduction

One of the major criticisms of the movie *Expelled* is that Ben Stein and the movie's producers linked Darwinism with eugenics and Nazism. Eugenics is a nightmare of the recent past that has resulted in the death of tens of millions of innocent people in Nazi Germany and elsewhere. Millions more were also forcibly sterilized, including by the German and American governments, as a result of this teaching.

It is often claimed by modern Darwinists that Darwin himself did not teach eugenics, but rather it is a perversion of his teachings, a pseudoscience that Darwin never even implied in his writings. For example, Fischer wrote the following about the last quarter of the 19th century:

> A new form of Judeophobia emerged that not only stirred up
> a wave of hatred throughout Europe but also produced the

soil on which the Nazi mentality would be nourished. This was the emergence of biological racism based on the pseudo-scientific theories spun out by the followers of Darwin, who extended and misinterpreted his biological findings to fit their ideological agendas.[1]

In fact, the eugenic implications of Darwin's ideas were crystal clear in his writings. One of many examples is when Darwin wrote that the "advancement of man from a former semi-human condition to his present state" was due to survival of the fittest — natural selection eliminating the weak and inferior humans and leaving the superior humans to continue populating the earth.[2]

Darwin's writings on humans reek with overgeneralizations and inaccurate claims that contributed to prejudice and racial hatred of others. One of many examples is that he claimed, "Most savages are utterly indifferent to the sufferings of strangers, or even delight in witnessing them. . . . Some savages take a horrid pleasure in cruelty to animals, and humanity with them is an unknown virtue."[3] Darwin then quoted approvingly a putative Spanish maxim: "Never, never trust an Indian."[4]

Darwin then noted that, in the case of "savages, the weak in body or mind are soon eliminated; and those that survive commonly exhibit a vigorous state of health."[5] Darwin next detailed how natural selection of the weak could not work in modern society as it did with savages because natural selection was impeded by civilization. Darwin made the implications of this idea to eugenics crystal clear, noting that civilization does its

> utmost to check the process of elimination; we build asylums for the imbecile, the maimed, and the sick; we institute poor-laws; and our medical men exert their utmost skill to save the life of every one to the last moment. There is reason to believe that vaccination has preserved thousands, who from a weak constitution would formerly have succumbed to small-pox. Thus the weak members of civilized societies

propagate their kind. No one who has attended to the breeding of domestic animals will doubt that this must be highly
injurious to the race of man. It is surprising how soon a
want of care, or care wrongly directed, leads to the degeneration of a domestic race; but excepting in the case of man
himself, hardly any one is so ignorant as to allow his worst
animals to breed.[6]

The reason why we aid the helpless, Darwin opined, was not
because humans were made in the image of God, but rather because
it was an incidental result of the survival instincts that we acquired
by evolution. Nonetheless, Darwin realized it is unlikely that civilized British society would intentionally cause the weak and helpless
to die and, therefore, he concluded, "we must bear without complaining the undoubtedly bad effects of the weak surviving and
propagating their kind" adding in support of eugenics:

> There appears to be at least one check in steady action,
> namely the weaker and inferior members of society not
> marrying so freely as the sound; and this check might be
> indefinitely increased, though this is more to be hoped for
> than expected, by the weak in body or mind refraining from
> marriage.[7]

Darwin did not support the view that humans should be treated
like domestic animals, but that we should continue to care for the
"imbecile, the maimed, and the sick." He explained why, negating
humanitarian reasons:

> The aid which we feel impelled to give to the helpless is
> mainly an incidental result of the instinct of sympathy,
> which was originally acquired [by evolution] as part of the
> social instincts, but subsequently rendered . . . more tender
> and more widely diffused. Nor could we check our sympa-
> thy, if so urged by hard reason, without deterioration in the
> noblest part of our nature. The surgeon may harden himself

whilst performing an operation, for he knows that he is acting for the good of his patient; but if we were intentionally to neglect the weak and helpless, it could only be for a contingent benefit, with a certain and great present evil.[8]

Although Darwin appears hesitant to apply the logic of selection to humans, his "disclaimer" here is questionable for several reasons. First of all, Darwin's own writings on morality argue that sympathy is ultimately good only insofar as it promotes survival of the fittest. If in civilized societies sympathy leads to a situation where it threatens the survival of the human race, he argues that we should logically follow the dictates of "hard reason" rather than sympathy. Darwin may have advocated sympathy here, but his writings undermined the rational basis for doing so.

Second, Darwin's disclaimer is part of a rhetorical strategy that he often used whereby he states some shocking implication of his work, then appears to backtrack and, last, attempts to justify the original claim. For example, Darwinists who cite Darwin's comment about his sympathy often fail to note that after this comment Darwin spent the rest of this section arguing that civilized societies should allow natural selection to kill off people in various ways, and argues that this is required for evolution. In Darwin's final word on the subject at the end of *The Descent of Man*, he makes his view very clear: human societies must allow natural selection to operate to kill off the less fit or else they are doomed:

> Man, like every other animal, has no doubt advanced to his present high condition through a struggle for existence consequent on his rapid multiplication; and if he is to advance still higher he must remain subject to a severe struggle. Otherwise he would soon sink into indolence.[9]

Even if Darwin's disclaimer about sympathy was the view that he accepted, he is here only arguing against allowing people to die without any support. He is not arguing against trying to prevent those that he considers evolutionarily unfit from freely reproducing.

Most eugenists in America and Britain believed that their policies were perfectly consistent with Darwin's concern about compassion because they were not advocating leaving people to the mercy of nature but merely curtailing the reproduction by the unfit and encouraging reproduction by the fit.[10] Thus, their proposal followed the "kinder, gentler" approach Darwin wrote about. Thus, in spite of Darwin's words about sympathy, strong grounds exist for Darwin's culpability in supplying the logical justification for eugenics.

Darwin's sons clearly saw a connection between their father's theory and eugenics and for this reason several became leaders in the eugenics movement. Sewell documents that there is "no doubt about the lineage of eugenics itself," noting that in the "years leading up to the First World War, the eugenics movement looked like a Darwin family business." Specifically:

> Darwin's son Leonard replaced his cousin Galton as chairman of the national Eugenics Society in 1911. In the same year an offshoot of the society was formed in Cambridge. Among its leading members were three more of Charles Darwin's sons, Horace, Francis and George. The group's treasurer was a young economics lecturer at the university, John Maynard Keynes, whose younger brother Geoffrey would later marry Darwin's granddaughter Margaret. Meanwhile, Keynes's mother, Florence, and Horace Darwin's daughter Ruth, sat together on the committee of the Cambridge Association for the Care of the Feeble-Minded ... a front organization for eugenics.[11]

Some readers, such as Adolf Hitler, took the eugenic implications of Darwinism very seriously and decided that we should not bear "the undoubtedly bad effects of the weak surviving and propagating their kind."[12] Darwin added that there was, fortunately, at least one check that did operate in modern society, "namely the weaker and inferior members of society" did not marry as often as others, and it "is more to be hoped for than expected," that the "weak in body or mind" would refrain from marriage.[13]

This approach by Darwin is called *passive eugenics*, and Darwin's hope as expressed in his writings was rapidly translated into governmental policy throughout the world, including Canada and even South America.[14] Darwin wrote that eugenics has solved many social problems for another reason: namely, through force "the civilised races have extended, and are now everywhere extending, their range, *so as to take the place of the lower races*," which he believed would eventually lose in the survival of the fittest struggle.[15] This approach is called *active eugenics*, and it is the method that Hitler and others used in their attempt to produce a superior race by Darwinian methods. Yale University Professor Nancy Stepan concluded that to

> Darwin, man was no longer a created being, but arose by the natural process of evolution from an animal ancestor. Man was fully part of nature, shaped by the same evolutionary laws shaping animal life. Man differed from animals only in degree, not kind.[16]

This fact was critical in the development of racism in not only German science, but also in German government policy. As to why Darwinism caused a holocaust in Germany but not in the United States, Caplan opines a major reason was because the "innocuous rise of eugenics in Weimar Germany" was

> an adjunct to efforts at public-health reform. Germans eager for a rebirth after the disaster of the First World War eagerly seized on the hope extended by physicians, geneticists, psychiatrists, and anthropologists that using social Darwinism to guide public health was the vehicle for German regeneration.[17]

Darwin scholar Harvard Professor Janet Browne wrote that Darwin's belief in "God had virtually disappeared" after he developed his theory of evolution, which he called the theory of

transmutation. After Darwin's belief in God had "virtually disappeared," man became "nothing to him now except a more developed
animal."[18] The Darwinian view of man as "nothing more" than an
animal was critical in allowing eugenic policy to thrive. And this
view was widely accepted in Europe and America, especially in
Germany.[19]

It is clear from these few quotes that Darwin's own writings
could be and often were used widely to not only condone but to
actively encourage both passive and active eugenics.

Darwin's cousin Francis Galton — the man who coined the
term "eugenics" — was much more open and direct about advocating eugenics. Galton's views were an important foundation of the
eugenics movement, and Darwin openly admired and supported his
eugenic ideas. Darwin was not naïve about eugenics as some argue,
but studied in detail — and even carefully annotated — Galton's
eugenic writings.[20] Darwin was so impressed with eugenics that he
wrote that Galton's eugenic bible "*Hereditary Genius* was a 'great
work.'"[21]

It did not take much of a leap of thought to go from Darwin's
and Galton's ideas to the Nazi views as taught by Richard Wagner,
Ernst Haeckel, Houston Chamberlain, and others. From them Hitler
gleaned the ideas that ended up producing the Holocaust.[22] As I
have documented elsewhere, Joseph Stalin and Chairman Mao were
also openly influenced by Darwin's ideas.[23] To confirm this, one
needs only to read the works of Hitler, Stalin, Lenin, and Mao. The
fact is:

> So-called "social Darwinism" is not, as is typically assumed
> today, a misapplication of Darwinism, it *is* Darwinism, and
> it provides an open rationale for eugenics and racism. This
> had abhorrent consequences in the twentieth century; and
> unless we understand Darwinism's flaws, there is no reason
> to believe it will not have equally abhorrent consequences in
> our own.[24]

The association of the Holocaust with Darwinism has been well documented by scholars. One of the most authoritative histories of the Holocaust, *The Complete History of the Holocaust* edited by Mitchell Geoffrey Bard, concluded, "The Nazis combined their racial theories with the evolutionary theories of Charles Darwin to justify their treatment of the Jews."[25] Reading *Mein Kampf* (especially in German) makes this both obvious and very clear.

Hitler was also called "one of the most honest politicians of our time, doing in most instances precisely what he said he would do. This is particularly evident in his treatment of the Jews."[26] And Hitler made it very clear what he was going to do to "evolutionarily inferior people," obviously reflecting Darwin's ideas, and why. Poliakov observed that Darwinism was directly used to support militarists such as Hitler:

> While scientists were trying to unravel the future of the human race, in the light of natural selection . . . a number of politicians were looking to Darwinism to support their political philosophy. It is true that the "survival of the fittest" looked much the same as the rule that "might is right" . . . but nevertheless the theory of natural selection, as popularly understood, did seem to endow aggressive instincts and imperialistic ambitions with all the dignity of scientific truth. As early as 1889 Max Nordua observed that Darwin was well on the way to becoming the supreme authority for militarists in all European countries. "Since the theory of evolution has been promulgated, they can cover their natural barbarism with the name of Darwin and proclaim the sanguinary instincts of their inmost hearts as the last word of science."[27]

It is also true that racism, even racial science, existed before Darwin, but Darwin "carried out the task of accommodating the new evolutionary science to the old racial science. As a result, many aspects of the old racial science passed more or less intact into the post-Darwinian decades."[28]

Although Darwin was not alone in developing the new biological racism that flourished in the last century, those persons who influenced Hitler and other leading Nazis such as Earnst Haeckel were influenced by Darwin. Stepan wrote:

> Darwin read widely in the biological literature on man — Prichard, Lawrence, Latham, Chambers, Nott and Gliddon, Hamilton Smith. Darwin's annotations of these works indicate that he took to his readings a commitment to the idea of human races as discrete, biological units with distinct moral and mental traits. He searched the available literature on man for evidence that all the elements of his evolutionary scheme — variation, struggle, migration and extinction — were found at the human, racial level.[29]

No evidence exists that Hitler ever read any of Darwin's writings and probably a far more important influence on Hitler was the many Darwinists in Germany. The level of support in Nazi Germany was so strong that "there were so many doctors and scientists involved in the Nazi crimes that to weed them all out would have left post war Germany with hardly any at all, an intolerable situation in a nation reeling from starvation and decimation."[30]

A stimulus to Darwin's own ideas on race were his colleagues' writings on evolution and its contribution to racism. Stepan notes that "in the first rush of evolutionary speculation in the 1860s" a particularly important influence on Darwin was the work of evolutionist

> Alfred Russel Wallace, who first appeared in print on the subject of evolution, man and race in 1864. Lyell's book on the antiquity of man in 1863 contained considerable material on the cranial capacities of ancient and modern races, while Huxley's provocative *Man's Place in Nature*, which also appeared in 1863, emphasized the smallness of the distance separating man from his nearest animal neighbours, the primates. Between 1866 and 1868 Darwin also corresponded

frequently with Wallace on the subject of sexual selection, which Darwin believed played a role in differentiating the races of mankind.[31]

Conclusions

It is well documented that Darwin's ideas had a major influence on 19th-century biological racism as well as on Nazism. The end result was the Holocaust, in which 11 million perished — and the loss of over 200 million lives in World War II and the communist holocaust. Darwin, though, did more than all of his mentors to establish evolutionism in science and society. For this reason his work, and that of Darwin's cousin Francis Galton, were among the most important influences causing the appropriation of eugenics into the Nazi movement in collusion with Darwin's disciples in Germany. Well-known eugenists also influenced Darwin. Besides his cousin Francis Galton, Darwin admitted that he "profited" from infamous eugenists Herbert Spencer's writings, and generally felt "enthusiastic admiration for his transcendent talents."[32] In his autobiography, Darwin stated that he believed that "selection was the keystone of man's success in making useful races of animals and plants" and, after Thomas Malthus, he concluded that "favorable variations would tend to be preserved, and unfavorable ones to be destroyed."[33]

Endnotes

1. Klaus P. Fischer, *The History of an Obsession: German Judeophobia and the Holocaust* (New York: Continuum, 1998), p. 47.
2. Charles Darwin, *The Descent of Man, and Selection in Relation to Sex* (London: John Murray, 1871), p. 167.
3. Ibid., p. 94.
4. Ibid., p. 95.
5. Ibid., p. 168.
6. Ibid., p. 168.
7. Ibid., p. 169.
8. Ibid., p. 168–169.
9. Ibid., p. 403.

10. Edwin Black, *War Against the Weak: Eugenics and America's Campaign to Create a Master Race* (New York: Four Walls Eight Windows, 2003).

11. Denis Sewell, *The Political Gene: How Darwin's Ideas Changed Politics* (London: Picador, 2010), p. 54.

12. Darwin, *The Descent of Man, and Selection in Relation to Sex*, p. 169.

13. Ibid., p. 169.

14. Richard Graham, editor, *The Idea of Race in Latin America, 1870–1940* (Austin, TX: The University of Texas Press, 1990).

15. Darwin, *The Descent of Man, and Selection in Relation to Sex*, p. 169, emphasis mine.

16. Nancy Stepan, *The Idea of Race in Science: Great Britain 1800–1960* (Dawson, England: Archon Books, 1982), p. 50.

17. Arthur Caplan, "Deadly Medicine: Creating the Master Race," *The Lancet* 363 (May 22, 2004):1742.

18. Janet Browne, *Charles Darwin: Voyaging* (Princeton, NJ: Princeton University Press, 1995), p. 513.

19. Paul Lombardo, *Three Generations, No Imbeciles: Eugenics, the Supreme Court and Buck v. Bell* (Baltimore, MD: Johns Hopkins University Press, 2008); Stepan, *The Idea of Race in Science: Great Britain 1800–1960*.

20. Stepan, *The Idea of Race in Science: Great Britain 1800–1960*, p. 51.

21. Darwin, *The Descent of Man, and Selection in Relation to Sex*, p. 168.

22. Richard Weikart, *From Darwin to Hitler: Evolutionary Ethics, Eugenics, and Racism in Germany* (New York, Palgrave Macmillan, 2004).

23. Jerry Bergman, "The Darwinian Foundation of Communism," *CEN Technical Journal* 15(1) (2001):89–95.

24. Benjamin Wiker, *The Darwin Myth: The Life and Lies of Charles Darwin* (Washington, DC: Regnery Publishing, Inc., 2009), p. xii.

25. Mitchell Geoffrey Bard, editor, *The Complete History of the Holocaust* (San Diego, CA: Greenhaven Press, 2001), p. 34.

26. Ibid., p. 37.

27. Léon Poliakov, *The Aryan Myth* (New York: Barns & Noble Books, 1996), p. 298.

28. Stepan, *The Idea of Race in Science: Great Britain 1800–1960*, p. 52.

29. Ibid., p. 51.

30. Caplan, "Deadly Medicine: Creating the Master Race," p. 1742.

31. Stepan, *The Idea of Race in Science: Great Britain 1800–1960*, p. 51.

32. Charles Darwin, edited by Nora Barlow, *The Autobiography of Charles Darwin 1809–1882* (New York: Norton, 1958), p. 108–109.

33. Ibid., p. 119–120.

CHAPTER 13

Darwin's View of Women

Chapter Synopsis

Darwinists once widely taught that women were at a "lower level of development" than men due to an "earlier arrest of individual evolution" in human females.[1] Because they had smaller brains, women were also believed to be "eternally primitive" and childlike, less spiritual, more materialistic, and "a real danger to contemporary civilization."[2] These views were not those of a small minority of intellectuals, but were "a majority view in the formative sociology of the late Victorian period."[3] Charles Darwin's writings played a major role in the development of this attitude.

Introduction

The central mechanism of Darwinism is survival of the fittest, requiring biological differences from which nature can select. As a result of natural selection, inferior animals were more likely to become extinct and, conversely, superior ones were more likely to thrive and leave a greater number of offspring.[4] The biological racism of late 19th-century Darwinism has now been both well documented and widely publicized. Especially influential in the development of biological racism was the eugenics theory developed by Charles Darwin's cousin, Sir Francis Galton.[5]

Less widely known is that many leading evolutionists, including Darwin, taught that women were both biologically and intellectually inferior to men. As Siegel explained, "Darwin not only explains the ways in which women are inferior to men; he also explains the origin of their inferiority."[6] Although selection struggles existed between groups, they were "more intense among members of the same species" because they "have similar needs and rely upon the same territory to provide them with food and mates."[7] Until recently, Darwinists taught that the intense struggle for mates within the same species was a major factor in producing male superiority for all sexual species.

The intelligence gap that many leading Darwinists believed existed between males and females due to selection was so great that some evolutionists classified the sexes as two distinct species — males as *Homo frontalis* and females as *Homo parietalis*.[8] Darwin himself concluded that the differences between human males and females were so large that it was surprising "such different beings belong to the same species" and that "even greater differences" had not evolved.[9] Natural and sexual selection were at the core of Darwinism, and human female inferiority was both a major proof and a chief witness of this theory.[10]

Darwin concluded that men shaped women's evolution to the male's liking by sexual selection, just as animal breeders shaped animals to the needs of humans.[11] Conversely, war tended to prune the weaker men, allowing only the more fit to return home and reproduce. Men were also the hunters, another activity that pruned weaker men. Women, in contrast, were not subject to these selection pressures because they "specialized in the 'gathering' part of the primitive economy" that did not require the strength or stamina of war or hunting.[12]

The reasons for belief in the biological inferiority of women are complex, but Darwin's natural and sexual selection ideas were believed to be major factors. Male superiority was so critical for evolution that the "male rivalry component of sexual selection was *the key*, Darwin believed, to the evolution of man: of all the causes which have led to the differences . . . between the races of man . . . sexual selection has been the most efficient."[13]

Richards concluded that Darwin's views about women logically followed from evolutionary theory, "thereby nourishing several generations of scientific sexism."[14] Importantly, Darwin's ideas, as elucidated in his writings, had a major impact on both science and society. As a result, scientists were inspired to use biology, ethnology, and primatology to build support for the conclusion that women had a "manifestly inferior and irreversibly subordinate" status to men.[15]

The extent of the doctrine's adverse effects can be gauged from the fact that the "biological inferiority of women" concept heavily influenced many theorists that have had a major role in shaping past generations — from Sigmund Freud to Havelock Ellis.[16] As eloquently argued by Durant, both racism and sexism were central to Darwinism:

> Darwin introduced his discussion of psychology in the *Descent* by reasserting his commitment to the principle of continuity . . . [and] . . . Darwin rested his case upon a judicious blend of zoomorphic and anthropomorphic arguments. Savages, who were said to possess smaller brains and more prehensile limbs than the higher races, and whose lives were said to be dominated more by instinct and less by reason . . . were placed in an intermediate position between nature and man; and Darwin extended this placement by analogy to include not only children and congenital idiots but also women, some of whose powers of intuition, of rapid perception, and perhaps of imitation were "characteristic of the lower races, and therefore of a past and lower state of civilization."[17]

Darwin's Personal Beliefs

Darwin's theory of origins may have been reflected in his personal attitudes about women. Among the more telling indications of Darwin's attitude toward women are statements he penned as a young man that listed what he viewed as advantages of marriage, including children and a constant companion "who will feel interested in one, object to be beloved and played with — *better than a dog anyhow &mdash*; Home, and someone to take care of house — Charms of music and female chit-chat. These things are good for one's health."[18]

Darwin's arguments against marriage included his conclusion that if he remained single, he would have had more freedom to travel, more time and money, and less anxiety and responsibility. He adds that having many children would force him to earn a living, adding that if his wife does want to live in London, "then the sentence is banishment and degradation."[19]

Darwin also wrote that, as a married man, he would be a "poor slave . . . worse than a negro," but then reminisced, "One cannot live this solitary life, with groggy old age, friendless & cold & childless staring one in one's face." Darwin concluded his evaluation on the philosophical note, "There is many a happy slave" and shortly thereafter, in 1839, married his cousin, Emma Wedgewood.[20]

On the basis of such statements, many Darwin biographers concluded that he had a very low opinion of women. Brent wrote, "It would be hard to conceive of a more self-indulgent, almost contemptuous, view of the subservience of women to men."[21] Richards concluded that Darwin had

> clearly defined opinions on woman's intellectual inferiority and her subservient status. A wife did not aspire to be her husband's intellectual companion, but rather to amuse his leisure hours . . . and look after his person and his house, freeing and refreshing him for more important things. These views are encapsulated in the notes the then young and ambitious naturalist jotted not long before he found his "nice soft wife on a sofa" . . . (although throughout their life together it was Charles who monopolized the sofa, not Emma).[22]

Darwin supporters often claimed that the "reason Darwin's theory was so . . . sexist, and racist is that Darwin's society exhibited these same characteristics." Obviously, his society and social class were influential in developing his views but, as Hull notes, Darwin was not "so callow that he simply read the characteristics of his society into nature."[23]

Women's Inferiority Doctrine Central to Evolution

A reading of Darwin's writings and those of his disciples reveals that the women's inferiority doctrine was *central* to early evolution theory. The major justifications Darwin gave for his female inferiority conclusions are summarized in his classic work, *The Descent of Man*. In this book, Darwin argued that *adult females* of most species resembled the *young* of both sexes and that "males are more evolutionarily advanced than females."[24] He concluded that since female evolution progressed at a slower rate than male evolution, a woman was "in essence, a stunted man."[25] This degrading view of women rapidly spread to Darwin's scientific and academic contemporaries.

For example, Darwin's contemporary and disciple, anthropologist McGrigor Allan, concluded that women were less evolved than men and "physically, mentally and morally, woman is a kind of adult child . . . it is doubtful if women have contributed one profound original idea of the slightest permanent value to the world."[26] Carl Vogt, professor of natural history at the University of Geneva, also accepted many of "the conclusions of England's great modern naturalist, Charles Darwin."[27]

One conclusion accepted very early was that because women's brains were smaller than man's, they were less intelligent and less evolved, an idea that has been refuted based on numerous studies.[28] Women are, on average, not as tall as men, weigh less, and most all their organs are smaller.

Vogt argued "the child, the female, and the senile White" all had both the intellectual features and personality of a "grown up Negro," and that in the female, intellect and personality are similar to both infants and members of the "lower" races.[29] Vogt concluded from his study that human females are closer to the lower animals than human males and, likewise, have a greater resemblance to human apes than males.[30]

Vogt even concluded that the gap between males and females becomes greater as civilizations progress and is greatest in the advanced European societies.[31] Darwin was "impressed by Vogt's work and proud to number him among his advocates."[32] The many other Darwinists who accepted the conclusion that sexual selection had enormous creative power included eminent physiologist George John Romanes. Romanes "shared Darwin's view that females were less highly evolved than males — ideas which he articulated in several books and many articles that influenced a generation of biologists."[33]

Females and Sexual Selection

Darwin concluded that many of the differences between males and females were due partly, or even largely, to sexual selection.[34] This included even the male and female genitalum.[35] He argued that in order to pass on his genes, a male must prove himself *both* physically and intellectually superior to other males in the competition for females. Conversely, a woman must be superior *only* in sexual attraction. Darwin also concluded that "sexual selection depended on two different intraspecific activities: the male struggle with males for possession of females; and female choice of a mate."[36] In his words, evolution resulted from a "struggle of individuals of one sex, generally males, for the possession of the other sex."[37] For this reason men were more sexually aggressive than women.[38]

In support of his conclusion, Darwin cited Australian "savage" women, who he claimed were constantly at "war both between members of the same tribe and distant tribes," resulting in sexual selection from sexual competition.[39] To support his view that "the strongest party always carries off the prize," Darwin also cited the North American Indian custom that required males to fight male competitors to gain wives.[40] The result was that a weaker man seldom could "keep a wife that a stronger man thinks worth his notice."[41]

Darwin used many similar examples to illustrate the evolutionary forces that he concluded produced men of superior physical and intellectual strength and women who were docile. He reasoned that this is true since humans evolved from lower animals, and "no one disputes that the bull differs in disposition from the cow, the wild-boar from the sow, the stallion from the mare, and, as is well known to the keepers of menageries, the males of the larger apes from the females."[42] Darwin argued that similar differences also existed among human males and females. The result of this selection was that men are "more courageous, pugnacious and energetic" than women and have a more inventive genius.[43]

A major problem in applying these observations from the animal kingdom to humans is that scientists now debated the "most complex problems of economic reforms not in terms of the will of God," as was once common, "but in terms of the sexual behavioral patterns of the cichlid fish."[44] Darwin and his disciples convinced a generation of evolutionists that science has proved what was widely assumed then; namely, that women differed considerably from men in both mental disposition and intelligence. The differences resulted in white women that were so inferior to white men that many of their traits were seen as "characteristic of the lower races, and therefore of a past and lower state of civilization."[45] In summary, Darwin concluded that the intellectual superiority of males is proved by the fact that men attain

> a higher eminence, in whatever he takes up, than can women — whether requiring deep thought, reason, or imagination, or merely the use of the senses and hands. . . . We may also infer . . . that if men are capable of a decided preeminence over women in many subjects, the average of mental power in man must be above that of women.[46]

Males were also believed by many Darwinists to be the superior sex because they varied to a greater degree than females in most *all* traits.[47] This was important because variations from the norm were accepted by most Darwinists to be a result of evolutionary mechanisms. Proponents of this women's inferiority argument used evidence such as the fact that a higher percent of *both* the mentally deficient *and* the mentally gifted were males. They reasoned that since selection operates to a greater degree on men, the weaker males would be more rigorously eliminated than the weaker females, raising the evolutionary level of males as a whole.

Furthermore, although Darwin attributed most female traits to male sexual selection, he concluded that only a few male traits were caused by female selection. One reason was because he believed that most females were not as choosy about their mate's physical or mental traits as were males.[48] Consequently, men not only were "more powerful in body and mind" than women, but even had "gained the power of selection" — evolution was in the males' hands, and females were largely passive in this area.[49] This is why many Darwinists believed instinct and emotions dominated women's behavior, a trait that was their "greatest weakness."[50]

Darwin held these "male supremacy" views, which he believed were a central prediction of evolution, for his entire life.[51] Shortly before his death, Darwin stated that he agreed with Galton's conclusion that "education and environment produce only a small effect" on the mind of most women because "most of our qualities are innate and not learned."[52] In short, Darwin believed, as do many sociobiologists today, that biology rather than the environment was the primary source of most all mental qualities, including both behavior and morals.[53] Obviously, Darwin almost totally ignored the influence of many more critical factors, including culture, family environment, social conditioning, and the fact that relatively few occupational and intellectual opportunities existed in Darwin's day for women.[54]

Problems with the Inferior Female Claims

Major problems with the sexual selection hypothesis included the fact that marriages in many societies are arranged by relatives mostly for pragmatic considerations, such as to unite certain families, to obtain a dowry, or to release the parents from the need to support female offspring. Darwin also argued that the

> intellectual superiority of the human male was innate but how had it come about? By sexual selection, said Darwin, not by female choice . . . considering the condition of women in barbarous tribes — where men kept women "in a far more abject state of bondage than does the male of any animal" — it was probably the male that chose. Different standards of beauty selected by the male might, thus, account for some of the differentiation of tribes.[55]

Traits that Darwin concluded were due to sexual selection include the numerous secondary sexual characteristics that differentiate humans from all other animals, including the human torso shape and limb hairlessness. What remains unanswered is why females would select certain traits in a male such as lack of hair when they had been successfully mating with hair-covered mates for eons, and no non-human primate preferred these "human" traits.

Darwin's conclusion that a single cause explains a wide variety of sexual differences is problematic.[56] If sexual selection caused the development of the male beard and its lack in females, why do women often prefer clean-shaven males? Obviously, cultural norms are critical in determining what is considered sexually attractive, and these standards change, precluding the long-term sexual selection required to biologically evolve them.[57] Another factor is that sexual selection would select females who found hairy men attractive rather than evolve the desire for men with traits that few men had then, such as hairless.

Conclusions and Implications

The Darwinian conclusion that women are inferior has had many major unfortunate historical social consequences. Sexual selection is believed to be critical in evolution, and among the data Darwin and his followers gathered to support the inferiority of women view, natural and sexual selection were critical.[58] Disproof of women's inferiority means that a major mechanism originally hypothesized to account for evolutionary advancement turned out to be erroneous. The data, although much more complete today, are similar to those that Darwin utilized to develop his theory, yet support radically different conclusions. This vividly demonstrates how important both preconceived ideas and theory are in interpreting data. The idea of women's evolutionary inferiority developed partly because

> measurement was glorified as the essential basis of science: both anatomists and psychologists wanted above everything else to be 'scientific.' . . . Earlier psychological theory had been concerned with those mental operations common to the human race: the men of the nineteenth century were more concerned to describe human differences.[59]

These human differences were not researched to understand and help society overcome them, but rather to justify a theory postulated to support a specific set of social beliefs. The implications of Darwinism cannot be ignored today, because the results of this belief have been tragic, especially in the area of racism. Richards concluded that it is irresponsible

> to ignore the role of such baggage in Darwin's science. The time-worn image of the detached and objective observer and theoretician of Down House, remote from the social and political concerns of his fellow Victorians who misappropriated his scientific concepts to rationalize *their* imperialism, *laissez-faire* economics, racism and sexism, must now give way before the emerging historical man, whose writings were in many ways so congruent with his social and cultural milieu.[60]

Hubbard et al. go even further and call Darwinism "blatant sexism" and placed major responsibility for scientific sexism and its mate, social Darwinism, squarely at Darwin's door.[61] Advancing knowledge has shown that social Darwinism is not only wrong, but tragically harmful and still adversely affects society today, such as in the modern form of Darwinism called sociobiology. Hubbard concluded that Darwin "provided the theoretical framework within which anthropologists and biologists have ever since been able to endorse the social inequality of the sexes." Consequently, "it is important to expose Darwin's androcentrocism," not only for historical reasons, but also because it "remains an integral and unquestioned part of contemporary biological theories."[62]

The modern equality of the sexes policy in both the United States and Europe and the lack of support for the position of female biological inferiority is a goal in considerable contrast to the conclusions derived from evolutionary biology in the middle and late 1800s.[63] The women's movement early on recognized the deleterious effect of Darwin's teaching and, for this reason, have produced considerable literature attacking Darwin's ideas related to women.[64] The history of these teachings is a clear illustration of the excesses to which Darwinism can lead.

Endnotes

1. David D. Gilmore, *Misogyny: The Male Malady* (Philadelphia, PA: University of Pennsylvania Press, 2001), p. 124.

2. Ibid., p. 125.

3. Ibid., p. 124.

4. Charles Darwin, *The Descent of Man and Selection in Relation to Sex* (New York: D. Appleton and Company, 1871), 1896 edition; Elizabeth Mann Borgese, *Ascent of Women* (New York: Braziller, 1963); John A. Phillips, *Eve; The History of an Idea* (San Francisco, CA: Harper & Row Publishers, 1984).

5. Jerry Bergman, "Eugenics and the Development of Nazi Race Policy," *Perspectives on Science and Christian Faith* 44(2) (June 1992):109–123; George Stein, "Biological Science and the Roots of Nazism," *American Scientist* 76 (1) (Jan.–Feb. 1988):50–58.

6. Charles Darwin, edited by Frederick Burkhardt and Sydney Smith, *The Correspondence of Charles Darwin*, Volume 1, 1821–1836 (New York: Cambridge University Press, 1985), p. 204.

7. Evelyn Reed, *Woman's Evolution; From Matriarchal Clan to Patriarchal Family* (New York: Pathfinder Press, 1975), p. 45.

8. David Oldroyd and Ian Langham, editors, *The Wider Domain of Evolutionary Thought*, "Darwinism and Feminism: The 'Women Question' in the Life and Work of Olive Schreinr and Charlotte Perkins Gilman," by Rosaleen Love (Holland: D. Reidel, 1983), p. 113–131.

9. Sue V. Rosser, *Biology and Feminism; A Dynamic Interaction* (New York: Twayne, 1992), p. 59.

10. Michael T. Ghiselin, *The Economy of Nature and the Evolution of Sex* (Berkeley, CA: University of California Press, 1974).

11. Oldroyd and Langham, *The Wider Domain of Evolutionary Thought*, "Darwin and the Descent of Women," by Evelleen Richards, p. 78.

12. Gwynne Dyer, *War* (New York: Crown Publishers, Inc., 1985), p. 122.

13. Wilma George, *Darwin* (London: Fantana Paperbacks, 1982), p. 136, emphasis added.

14. Evelleen Richards, "Will the Real Charles Darwin Please Stand Up?" *New Scientist* 100 (Dec. 22/29, 1983):887.

15. Elaine Morgan, *The Descent of Woman* (New York: Stein and Day, 1972), p.1.

16. Stephanie A. Shields, "Functionalism, Darwinism, and the Psychology of Women; A Study in Social Myth," *American Psychologist* 30(1) (1975):739–754.

17. Charles Darwin, *The Descent of Man, and Selection in Relation to Sex*, Volume 1 (London: John Murray, 1871), p. 326–327; David Kohn, editor, *The Darwinian Heritage*, "The Ascent of Nature in Darwin's *Descent of Man*," by John R. Durant (Princeton, NJ: Princeton University Press, 1985), p. 295.

18. Charles Darwin, edited by Nora Barlow, *The Autobiography of Charles Darwin 1809–1882* (New York: W.W. Norton & Company, Inc., 1958), p. 232–233.

19. Ibid., p. 232–233.

20. Ibid., p. 234.

21. Peter Brent, *Charles Darwin: A Man of Enlarged Curiosity* (New York: Harper and Row, 1981), p. 247.

22. Richards, "Will the Real Charles Darwin Please Stand Up?" p. 886.

23. David Hull, "Uncle Sam Wants You," a review of the book *Mystery of Mysteries: Is Evolution a Social Construction?* by Michael Ruse, *Science* 284 (1999):1131–1132.

24. Bettyann Kevles, *Females of the Species: Sex and Survival in the Animal Kingdom* (Cambridge, MA: Harvard University Press, 1986), p. 8.

25. Shields, "Functionalism, Darwinism, and the Psychology of Women; A Study in Social Myth," p. 749.

26. Allan, J. McGrigor, "On the Real Differences in the Minds of Men and Women," *Journal of the Anthropological Society* 7 (1869): 210.

27. Carl Vogt, edited by James Hunt, *Lectures on Man: His Place in Creation, and the History of Earth* (London: Longman, Green, Longman, and Roberts, 1864).

28. Dolph Schluter, "Brain Size Differences," *Nature* 359 (Sept. 17, 1992):181; Carol Tavris, *The Mismeasure of Women: Why Women Are Not the Better Sex, the Inferior Sex, or the Opposite Sex* (New York: Simon and Schuster, 1976); Leigh Van Valen, "Brain Size and Intelligence in Man," *American Journal of Physical Anthropology* 40 (1974):417–423; M. Morbek, A. Gallaway, and A. Zihlman, editors, *The Evolving Female: A Life-History Perspective*, "Women's Bodies, Women's Lives: An Evolutionary Perspective," by A. Zihlman (Princeton, NJ: Princeton University Press, 1997); J.P. Rushton and C.O. Ankney, "Brain Size and Cognitive Ability; Correlations with Age, Sex, Social Class, and Race," *Psychonomic Bulletin Review* 3(1) (1996):21–36.

29. Vogt, *Lectures on Man: His Place in Creation, and the History of Earth*, p. 192.

30. Roger Lewin, *Bones of Contention* (New York: Simon and Schuster, 1987), p. 305.

31. Oldroyd and Langham, *The Wider Domain of Evolutionary Thought*, "Darwin and the Descent of Women," by Evelleen Richards, p. 75.

32. Ibid., p. 74.

33. Kevles, *Females of the Species: Sex and Survival in the Animal Kingdom*, p. 8–9.

34. Bernard Campbell, editor, *Sexual Selection and the Descent of Man 1871–1971*, "Sexual Selection, Dimorphism, and Social Organization in the Primates," by John Hurrell Crook (Chicago, IL: Aldine Publishing Company, 1972).

35. William G. Eberhard, *Sexual Selection and Animal Genitalia* (Cambridge, MA: Harvard University Press, 1985).

36. George, *Darwin*, p. 69.

37. Charles Darwin, *The Origin of Species by Means of Natural Selection* (New York: D. Appleton, 1959), 1897 edition, p. 108.

38. R. Thornhill and N.W. Thornhill, "The Evolutionary Psychology of Men's Coercive Sexuality," *Behavioral & Brain Sciences* 15(2) (1991):363.

39. Darwin, *The Descent of Man, and Selection in Relation to Sex*, p. 561.

40. Ibid., p. 562.

41. Ibid., p. 562.

42. Ibid., p. 563.

43. Ibid., p. 557.

44. Morgan, *The Descent of Woman*, p. 1.

45. Darwin, *The Descent of Man and Selection in Relation to Sex*, p. 563–564.

46. Ibid., p. 564.

47. Ibid.

48. Oldroyd and Langham, *The Wider Domain of Evolutionary Thought*, "Darwin and the Descent of Women," by Evelleen Richards, p. 65.

49. Darwin, *The Descent of Man and Selection in Relation to Sex*, p. 597.

50. Shields, "Functionalism, Darwinism, and the Psychology of Women; A Study in Social Myth," p. 742.

51. Richards, "Will the Real Charles Darwin Please Stand Up?" p. 885.

52. Darwin, *The Autobiography of Charles Darwin 1809–1882*, p. 43.

53. Richards, "Will the Real Charles Darwin Please Stand Up?" p. 67–68.

54. George C. Williams, *Sex and Evolution* (Princeton, NJ: Princeton University Press, 1977).

55. George, *Darwin*, p. 74.

56. Ibid., p. 71.

57. Marcia Millman, *Such a Pretty Face; Being Fat in America* (New York: W.W. Norton and Company, 1980); Anne Scott Beller, *Fat & Thin: A Natural History of Obesity* (New York: McGraw Hill, 1977).

58. S. Sleeth Mosedale, "Corrupted — Victorian Biologists Consider "The Women Question," *Journal of the History of Biology* 9 (1978):1–55.

59. Elizabeth Fee, "Nineteenth-Century Craniology: The Study of the Female Skull," *Bulletin of the History of Medicine* 53 (1979):419.

60. Richards, "Will the Real Charles Darwin Please Stand Up?" p. 887, emphasis added.

61. Ruth Hubbard, Mary Sue Henifin, and Barbara Fried, *Women Look at Biology Looking At Women; A Collection of Feminist Critiques* (Cambridge, MA: Schenkman Publishing Co, 1979).

62. Ibid., p. 16.

63. Ashley Montagu, *The Natural Superiority of Women*, fifth edition (Walnut Creek, CA: Rowman and Littlefield, 1999).

64. Gloria Steinem, *Revolution from Within: A Book of Self-Esteem* (Boston, MA: Little, Brown and Company, 1992); Lester D. Stephens, "Evolution and Women's Rights in the 1890s: The Views of Joseph LeConte," *The Historian* 38(2) (1976):239–252; Linda Jean Shepherd, *Lifting the Veil: The Feminine Force in Science* (Boston: Shambhala, 1993); Rosser, *Biology and Feminism; A Dynamic Interaction*; Patricia Adair Gowaty, *Feminism and Evolutionary Biology*, "Possible Implications of Feminists Theories for the Study of Evolution," by Sue V. Rosser (New York: Springer-Verlag, 1997), chapter 2; L.S. Hollingworth, "Variability As Related to Sex Differences in Achievement," *American Journal of Sociology* 19 (1914):510–530; Hubbard, Henifin, and Fried, *Women Look at Biology Looking At Women; A Collection of Feminist Critiques*; Flavia Alaya, "Victorian Science and the 'Genius' of Women," *Journal of the History of Ideas* 38 (1977):261–280.

CHAPTER 14

Darwin Was Wrong: Natural Selection Cannot Explain Macro-Evolution

Chapter Synopsis

Darwin's theory of natural selection was reviewed, concluding that it is limited to producing a conserving effect and cannot account for macro-evolution. Natural selection may help to explain the survival of the fittest but cannot explain the arrival of the fittest. It cannot create, it can only eliminate. Several new scientific studies were summarized that support this conclusion.

Introduction

Evolution is defined here as the progression from molecules to humans purely by natural forces, or progression from the goo to you by way of the zoo as a result of time, accidents, and the outworking of natural law. If Darwin was correct, the harm his evolution theory has caused society would be unfortunate, but an inevitable consequence of the progress of knowledge in biology.

The tragedy is, as has been well documented by both creationists and evolutionists, evolution never occurred and could never have occurred, and this conclusion is the result of science, not theology or religion. Most of Darwin's major conclusions in his *Origin* book have turned out to be wrong, including even his rudimentary organ idea.[1]

Natural selection is widely acknowledged as Darwin's main contribution to evolution. In fact, as documented in chapter 8, natural selection is an ancient idea that was popularized by Charles Darwin in his 1859 book titled *The Origin of Species*. Harrow wrote:

> As many historians of biology have noted, it's not that no one had ever thought of undirected evolution as a way to account for the diversity of life on earth; before Darwin came along, the idea had been brewing in the minds of many scholars. The revolution occurred because, in 1859, Darwin was able to outline a detailed mechanism for such changes — namely, natural selection and "survival of the fittest," along with other details, such as how isolating a population on an island can give rise to such changes.[2]

Although hailed as a revolutionary idea by many, including scientists, Darwin simply applied the well-known fact of artificial selection called breeding that has been practiced for centuries by farmers to the natural world. Darwin knew that breeders interbreed animals and plants that have the traits they desire in order to produce a new strain that has a greater level of the desirable traits. Examples include cows that produce large amounts of milk, horses that can break racing speed records, or dogs that have some desired trait.

By repeating this process for many generations, often by extensive inbreeding, a life form with an extreme level of the desired trait can often be produced. For example, if a breeder wants seedless fruit he breeds those plants that have produced fruit with the fewest number of seeds with each other. By inbreeding in this way breeders were eventually able to create a tree that produced fruit with few or no seeds.

Darwin concluded that the same selective force breeders use must also occur in the wild except that humans select *for* certain traits, but nature selects *against* many traits. This process, called *survival of the fittest*, was at the heart of his evolution theory. Darwin knew that certain traits, such as the ability to outrun enemies or attract mates, helped an animal to survive in the wild. Thus, animals with these traits had an advantage in the wild and, consequently, were better able to compete in the struggle to survive. The result was that they were more likely to survive and to produce a larger number of offspring than those lacking the traits that helped them to compete for mates, food, and other life-giving resources in nature.[3]

This process resulted in those traits that were an advantage in the wild to become more common. Instead of intelligent selection by humans, selection in nature occurred as a result of the struggle for life by eliminating those life forms that were less fit to survive. In the words of Dr. Ernst Mayr, Professor Emeritus at Harvard University, "What Darwin called natural selection is actually a process of elimination."[4]

The enormous "power" claimed for natural selection to achieve most anything in nature was described by Fodor, who listed some examples that he described as "typical of the laudatory epithets" that

> abound in the literature: "The universal acid" (philosopher Daniel Dennett in *Darwin's Dangerous Idea*, 1995); "a mechanism of staggering simplicity and beauty . . . [it] has been called the greatest idea that anyone ever had . . . it also happens to be true (biologist Jerry Coyne in *Why Evolution is True*, 2009); "the only workable theory ever proposed that is capable of explaining life we have" (biologist and ethnologist Richard Dawkins, variously). And as Dennett continues in *Darwin's Dangerous Idea*: "In a single stroke, the idea of evolution by natural selection unifies the realm of life, meaning, and purpose with the realm of space and time, cause and effect, mechanism and physical law."[5]

Darwin viewed this mechanism not only as a means of pruning less fit life forms, a fact that was historically widely accepted, but as the basis for forming whole new species in the wild. Natural selection was Darwin's answer to both how and why species originated.[6] Darwin's book was titled

> *On the Origin of Species.* . . . But there is an irony in Darwin's choice of [his] title: his book did not explore what actually triggers the formation of new species. Others have since

grappled with the problem of how one species becomes two, and with the benefit of genetic insight, which Darwin lacked, you might think they would have cracked it. Not so. Speciation still remains one of the biggest mysteries in evolutionary biology.[7]

More than 1,000 years of breeding, combined with current research, has documented that clear limits exist in the ability of breeders to modify life. This fact has forced the conclusion that natural selection cannot account for macro-evolution level changes.[8]

Clear Limits Exist in Both Artificial Breeding and Natural Selection

A major problem for the molecules-to-humans evolution theory is the fact that clear limits exist in what can be produced by artificial selection and, likewise, what natural selection is able to achieve is also severely limited. Breeders have been able to breed larger apples but have not been able to produce apples that are larger than a mature watermelon. Nor have they been able to breed a horse-sized animal from a dog.

The reason breeding and natural selection are able to produce new varieties in existing life forms is because a great deal of genetic variation exists in all life forms. This fact is obvious to all dog fanciers — modern dogs came from the wolf kind, an achievement due to 4,000 years or so of breeding efforts by humans. Darwin believed that an almost unlimited amount of variation is possible in life, a conclusion that we know today is false.

Darwin also accepted the Larmakian idea of pangenesis, an idea that has also now been disproved.[9] As documented in chapter 10, pangenesis theory argued that the environment can change the genetic information in the sex cells called gametes that allow animals to pass on new traits to their offspring, such as the muscle bulk that weight lifters have acquired during their lifetime of working out.

Natural Selection Cannot Create New Life Forms

Natural selection does not provide evidence for evolution as defined in this chapter because it can select only for what already exists. The problem for evolution is not the *survival* of the fittest, but the *arrival* of the fittest. The only explanation still on the table today for the creation of new genetic information is mutations. Mutations are mistakes that occur when the genetic machinery copies genes, such as during cell division or reproduction, or by damage that occurs to genes caused by mutagens. Examples of mutagens include the radiation given off by radioactive substances such as plutonium or by x-rays. In other words, evolution from molecules to man has resulted from the accumulation of damage to the blueprint of life, the genes.

Survival of the fittest does have an important function in nature, primarily in a conserving role. If a mutation occurs that results in a life form being *less* fit, natural selection tends to cause that life form to be stillborn or to die earlier than other similar animals. Consequently, it does not allow the less fit animal to pass on its genes to the next generation or, at the least, causes it to have fewer offspring. In theory, this effect both reduces the mutation load in all life forms and prunes out inferior animals, reducing the level of degeneration in the living world. In spite of the many grandiose claims for natural selection quoted above, the fact is that natural selection cannot create, it can only function to help weed out the less fit and reduce the genetic degeneration problem.

As Salisbury explained in 1969, until a functional structure exists, there is "nothing for natural selection to act on."[10] He added that the mechanism proposed to produce functional life, mutations, falls short by "hundreds of orders of magnitude of producing, in a mere four billion years, even a single required gene."[11]

Since the only viable possibility left to create new genetic variety is mutations, a conclusion that was disproved, no known means exists of producing new significant variations that molecule-to-human evolution demands.[12] Mutations can produce only minor changes, such as blue eyes in humans and, as documented by Behe,[13] clear limits exist in their ability to produce new variety.

The fact that a great deal of inborn variety exists in all life has actually been a major evidence proving that the basic animal kinds are stable within clear limits, as is illustrated by the following observation:

> If the various breeds of dogs did not exist and a paleontologist found fossils of animals similar to dachshunds, greyhounds, mastiffs, and Chihuahuas, there is no question that they would be considered different species. Indeed, the differences in size and shape exhibited by these breeds are greater than those between members of different genera in the family Canidae.[14]

Neo-Darwinists often incorrectly assume that this inborn variety, which natural selection and breeders select from, is due to mutations instead of the natural variety typical of the living world, as is clearly the case with dogs.

New Evidence Against Natural Selection

The many problems with natural selection as a major mechanism of evolution has been increasingly documented in the scientific literature. As Fodor and Piattelli-Palmarini write, the "evidence against natural selection is mounting up."[15] The problem has been so serious historically that

> in his last years, Darwin himself veered away from classical Darwinism. When a Scottish engineer named Fleeming Jenkin confronted him with objections that he could not answer, Darwin quietly altered the sixth edition of *The Origin of Species* in such a way as to show that he was reverting to the despised doctrines of Lamarck. Hardin describes this tersely: "Jenkin had put his finger on a critically weak point in Darwinian theory — its dependence on a mistaken theory of heredity. The unanswerableness of the criticisms led Darwin to make one of the strangest about-faces in the progress of

science. Darwin, a long-time anti-Lamarckian, became an unwilling and unavowed convert" to Lamarckism.[16]

The situation today is far worse.[17] New research has argued that "Natural selection may have little role to play in one of the key steps of evolution — the origin of new species. Instead it would appear that speciation is merely an accident of fate."[18]

The Accidental Origins Theory

Professor Mark Pagel, an evolutionary biologist at the University of Reading, United Kingdom, came up with a potential solution to this problem. He reasoned that if "new species are the sum of a large number of small changes . . . then this should leave a telltale statistical footprint in their evolutionary lineage."[19] Pagel knew that, thanks to the recent advanced DNA sequencing technology, reliable genetic trees were now abundant and cheap. From this data Pagel obtained what he regarded as reliable phylogenetic trees to test his hypothesis. Pagel's lab obtained over

130 DNA-based evolutionary trees from the published literature, ranging widely across plants, animals and fungi. After winnowing the list to exclude those of questionable accuracy, they ended up with a list of 101 trees, including various cats, bumblebees, hawks, roses and the like.[20]

The lab scientists then "measured the length between each successive speciation event, essentially chopping the tree into its component twigs at every fork." They next counted the number of twigs of each length, evaluated the pattern produced, and concluded that if speciation results by natural selection causing many small changes, the branch lengths would fit a bell-shaped normal curve because the incremental changes would add up to "push the new species over some threshold of incompatibility," or a lognormal curve would result if the changes multiplied together.[21] The results, to the researchers great surprise, found:

Neither of these curves fitted the data. The lognormal was best in only 8 per cent of cases, and the normal distribution failed resoundingly, providing the best explanation for not a single evolutionary tree. Instead, Pagel's team found that in 78 percent of the trees, the best fit for the branch length distribution was another familiar curve, known as the exponential distribution ... the exponential has a straightforward explanation — but it is a disquieting one for evolutionary biologists. The exponential is the pattern you get when you are waiting for some single, infrequent event to happen ... [such as] a radioactive atom to decay.[22]

In other words, they found clear gaps just like we find in the fossil record, and not a continuum as gradualist Darwinism predicts. Professor Odum wrote that according to the latest theory of evolution:

Species remain unchanged in a sort of evolutionary equilibrium for long periods; then, once in a while, the equilibrium is "punctuated" when a small population splits off and rapidly evolves into an entirely different species without transitional forms being deposited into the fossil record. So far, no one has come up with a good explanation of what might cause such "macroevolutionary leaps."[23]

The findings of both genetics and the fossil record support the separate creation conclusion, but evolutionists were forced to propose a new naturalistic idea to explain it called the "happy accidents" theory, or what some call the "hopeful monster" hypothesis. The implications of the results for evolutionary speciation were very clear: "It isn't the accumulation of events that causes a speciation, it's single, rare events falling out of the sky, so to speak. Speciation becomes an arbitrary, happy accident when one of these events happens."[24]

Holmes concluded that the major finding "emerging from the statistical evidence ... is that the trigger for speciation must be some single, sharp kick of fate that is, in an evolutionary sense unpredictable."[25] The conclusion of the study was that "the utter arbitrariness of speciation" clearly "removes speciation from the gradual tug of natural selection . . . accidental nature or speciation means that the grand sweep of evolutionary change is unpredictable."[26]

This fits with the famous metaphor by the late Harvard Professor Stephen Jay Gould, who argued that, if history could be rewound backward and the evolution of life on earth replayed again, "it would turn out differently every time."[27] The finding also has independent support in the work of other researchers. For example:

> Luke Harmon at the University of Idaho in Moscow and his colleagues have examined 49 evolutionary trees to see whether there are bursts of evolutionary change early in a group's history, when unfilled niches might be expected to be most common. There is little evidence for such a pattern, they report in a paper . . . accepted for publication in the journal *Evolution*.[28]

These findings are devastating to Darwin's theory of natural selection. At the least they force natural selection to a minor role of fine-tuning life and reducing de-evolution. In fact, they support the expectations of the creation worldview because they document gaps in the genetic record that support the gaps in the fossil record as predicted by creationism.

Conclusions

Natural selection means only that fitter animals are better able to survive in a natural environment, a redundant statement like saying millionaires have a lot of money. By definition, the more fit animals have a survival advantage, an idea that does not help to explain the *arrival* of the fittest, and thus fails to explain the origin of species as Darwin claimed.[29] Ernst Mayr, who John Maynard Smith calls "one of the great shining figures in biology," concluded that when Darwin published his epic work *The Origin of Species* in 1859, "He actually did not have a single clear-cut piece of evidence for the existence of [natural] selection" as the creator of all plant and animal types.[30]

Darwin actually only helped to explain the survival of existing species, and neither he nor anyone else has been able to explain the arrival of new animal kinds. As documented above, the fact that natural selection cannot create, only eliminate, is an obvious fact, but scrupulously avoided in the evolution literature. The reason for this is because much

> of the vast neo-Darwinian literature is distressingly uncritical. The possibility that anything is seriously amiss with Darwin's account of evolution is hardly considered. . . . So onlookers are left with the impression that there is little or nothing about Darwin's theory to which a scientific naturalist could reasonably object. The methodological skepticism that characterizes most areas of scientific discourse seems strikingly absent when Darwinism is the topic.[31]

In their new book, Fodor and Piattelli-Palmarini document numerous examples of why natural selection is often only a porthole explanation of phenotypic variations. The fact is, explanations are not proof, nor are they even a scientific prediction that can be proved, but are only ideas that have the potential of being converted into a hypothesis that can be tested by the scientific method.[32] Fodor and Piattelli-Palmarini concluded from their study, that the internal evidence for natural selection as an explanation for most of nature is "very thin."[33] What then is the source of variety?

Pagel concluded that the "broad canvas of life — the profusion of beetles and rodents, the death of primates, and so on — may have less to do with the guiding hand of natural selection and more to do with evolutionary accident-proneness" that results from these drastic changes.[34] In other words, this theory explains the enormous variety of life, and life itself is primarily the result of accidents, time, and chance. The theory that only drastic random changes, such as by micro-mutations, can explain evolution is reminiscent of Goldschmit's hopeful monster idea, which concluded that for a single species to become two separate species some subset of the original species must become unable to reproduce with its fellows. How this happens is the real point of contention. By the middle of the 20th century, biologists had worked out that reproductive isolation sometimes occurs after a few organisms are carried to newly formed lakes or far-off islands. Other speciation events seem to result from major changes in chromosomes, which suddenly leave some individuals unable to mate successfully with their neighbours. It seems unlikely, though, that such drastic changes alone can account for all or even most new species.[35]

These conclusions, as well as all of the findings reviewed in this book, eloquently disprove Darwin's basic theory and support the separate creation hypothesis. This explains the genetic gaps that Pagel's lab documented, as well as the finding that natural selection has a very limited role in nature. It cannot explain the arrival of the fittest, but can only fine tune what already exists by eliminating the less fit organisms. The science clearly documents that Darwin's attempt to murder God has in fact failed and it is only a matter of time that this research becomes more widely known.

Endnotes

1. Jerry Bergman and George Howe, *"Vestigial Organs" Are Fully Functional: A History and Evaluation of the Vestigial Organ Origins Concept* (Terre Haute, IN; Creation Research Society Books, 1990).

2. Jason Harrow, "The Philosophy of Intelligent Design," Princeton University Thesis, 3006, p. 22.

3. John Maynard Smith, "Natural Selection and the Concept of a Protein Space," *Nature* 225 (February 7, 1970):563–564.

4. Ernst Mayr, *What Evolution Is* (New York: Basic Books, 2001), p. 117.

5. Jerry Fodor and Massimo Piattelli-Palmarini, "Survival of the Fittest Theory: Darwinism's Limits," *New Scientist* (February 6, 2010): p. 28.

6. Norman MacBeth, "The Question: Darwinism Revisited," *The Yale Review* 56(4) (1967): 616–617.

7. Bob Holmes, "Accidental Origins," *New Scientist* (March 13, 2010): p. 31.

8. Michael Behe, *The Edge of Evolution* (New York: The Free Press, 2007).

9. Jerry Bergman, "Pangenesis as a Source of New Genetic Information: The History of a Now Disproven Theory," *Rivista di Biologia/ Biology Forum* 99(3) (2006):425–444.

10. Frank B. Salisbury, "Natural Selection and the Complexity of the Gene," *Nature* 224 (October 25, 1969):342.

11. Ibid., p. 342–343.

12. Jerry Bergman, "The Elimination of Mutations by the Cell's Elaborate Protein Quality Control System: A Major Problem for Neo-Darwinism," *CRSQ* 43(2) (2006):68–74.

13. Behe, *The Edge of Evolution.*

14. P. Raven, G. Johnson, J. Losos, and S. Singer, *Biology* (New York: McGraw Hill, 2005), p. 459.

15. Fodor and Piattelli-Palmarini, "Survival of the Fittest Theory: Darwinism's Limits," p. 28.

16. MacBeth, "The Question: Darwinism Revisited," p. 329.

17. Steven Meyers, *The Signature in the Cell* (New York: Harper Collins, 2007).

18. Holmes, "Accidental Origins," p. 31.

19. Ibid., p. 32.

20. Ibid., p. 32.

21. Ibid., p. 32.

22. Ibid., p. 32.

23. Eugene Odum, *Ecology: A Bridge Between Science and Society* (Sunderland, MA: Sinauer, 1997), p. 235.

24. Holmes, "Accidental Origins," p. 32.

25. Ibid., p. 32.

26. Ibid., p. 32.

27. Ibid., p. 32.

28. Ibid., p. 33.

29. Jerry Bergman, "Darwinism and the Deterioration of the Genome," *CRSQ* 42(2) (September 2005):104–114.

30. Mayr, *What Evolution Is*, p. 121.

31. Fodor and Piattelli-Palmarini, "Survival of the Fittest Theory: Darwinism's Limits," p. 28.

32. Ibid.

33. Jerry Fodor and Massimo Piattelli-Palmarini, *What Darwin Got Wrong* (New York: Farrar, Straus and Giroux, 2010), p. 31.

34. Holmes, "Accidental Origins," p. 31.

35. Ibid., p. 31.

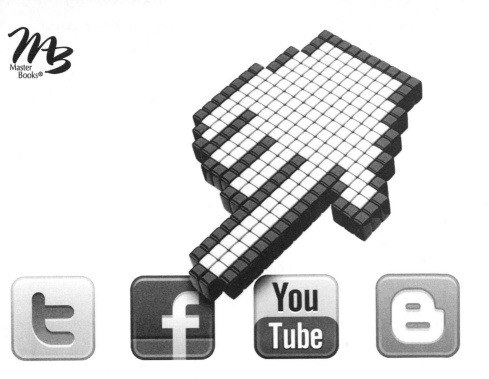

Connect with Master Books®

masterbooks.net   An imprint of New Leaf Publishing Group

facebook.com/**masterbooks**

twitter.com/**masterbooks4u**

youtube.com/**nlpgvideo**

nlpgblogs.com

nlpgvideos.com

join us at **Creation**Conversations.com

Persuaded by the Evidence
True Stories of Faith, Science, and the Power of a Creator
Edited by Doug Sharp and Jerry Bergman

A unique and interesting collection of true stories from Christians — each sharing a personal journey to find the biblical truth of a six-day creation! From scientists in the midst of complex research to youth ministers and more, see how each began at a different point and place in life to question the supposed truth of evolution, and how faith and actual evidence led to embracing a creation-based, biblical worldview.

ISBN: 978-0-89051-545-7 • $13.99 • trade paper • 288 pages

Secrets of the Sixth Edition
Darwin Discredits His Own Theory
by Randall Hedtke

Touted as fact, and presented as infallible, Darwin's *On the Origin of the Species* is the basis for modern science. Amazingly, Darwin himself abandoned some of the core mechanisms of his own theory later in life, but they remain unchallenged pillars of science today.

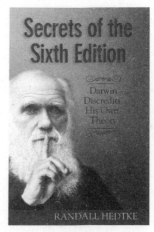

Includes a look at Darwin's research and the faulty basis of his theories, extensive documentation of the weakness of his logic, and indisputable evidence that he acknowledged these fatal flaws.

ISBN: 978-0-89051-597-6 • $11.99 • trade paper • 160 pages

Available at Christian bookstores nationwide and at www.nlpg.com